THE BIBLE DOCTRINE
OF SALVATION

A Study of the Atonement

THE BIBLE DOCTRINE
OF SALVATION

A Study of the Atonement

By
C. RYDER SMITH, B.A., D.D.

formerly Professor of Theology
in the University of London

LONDON:
THE EPWORTH PRESS

THE EPWORTH PRESS
(FRANK H. CUMBERS)
25-35 City Road, London, E.C.1

MELBOURNE   CAPE TOWN
NEW YORK   TORONTO

SET IN MONOTYPE BASKERVILLE AND PRINTED IN
GREAT BRITAIN BY THE CAMELOT PRESS LTD.,
LONDON AND SOUTHAMPTON

CONTENTS

TO MY STUDENTS, 1920–1940

INTRODUCTION

Two remarks have often been made about the doctrine of the Atonement—first, that no one account of it has ever been officially and finally adopted by the Church, and, second, that the account of it current in any given period has reflected the general ideas of the time. For instance, it is agreed that Anselm's account has some relation to the concepts of feudalism, though the nature of that relation may be debated. Yet the exponents of all historical theories in all periods have all claimed to find their theories in the Bible, and, in spite of the many modern discussions of every kind of Biblical subject, the appeal to the Bible is still the final appeal. After many years of the study of its teaching, it seems to me that the New Testament has a consistent account of the Work of Christ, and that this account is the climax and completion of certain truths that gradually worked themselves clear in Old Testament thought. The full bearing of some of the chapters below that deal with the Old Testament will only be clear when the chapters on the New are read. No apology is made for the number and length of the chapters on the Old Testament. They include some discussions that would otherwise fall under the New Testament. In addition, it is usually more difficult to trace the slow emergence of incomplete ideas than to describe them when they are full-grown. On the other hand, the complete meaning of a fully-grown idea is often only discernible when its history is known. The New Testament writers assume that their readers will take their words in their contemporary sense, and only the study of the Old Testament reveals this. None the less, the Old Testament chapters below only prepare the way for the discussion of New Testament teaching. For Christians this is final.

Yet, since no generation can escape from itself, the doctrine of the Work of Christ for to-day must use the thought-forms of to-day. These are predominantly psychological. Every one is a psychologist—or thinks he is. Modern theories of the Atonement, therefore, in one way or another, use psychological analogies. All theists will admit at once that this kind of thought-form, like all others, must be inadequate, for man cannot 'by searching find out God'. This doctrine, like every other doctrine that involves God, must run up into mystery. Yet, to admit that we cannot know all is not to admit that we cannot know anything. The word 'analogy' is intentionally used above. It is suggested that psychology may furnish some materials for the understanding of the Bible doctrine of salvation. It is further suggested that psychology is more likely to give guidance than any other study, for psychology is the science of human nature, and, since God's purpose in salvation is to save *men*, it may reverently be supposed that the 'way of salvation' will suit the nature of the being whom God seeks to save. This means, for instance, that psychology is likely to lead us nearer to the truth than the study of feudalism brought Anselm. The method here pursued, therefore, is both Biblical and psychological. It will be necessary, first, to describe briefly certain psychological presuppositions. After this the teaching of the Old Testament about salvation is examined. Finally, a more detailed exposition of the teaching of the various New Testament writers is attempted. It will be found that it is claimed that both in the Old Testament and in the New the place taken by ideas derived from the sacrificial system of the Jews is secondary.

A further remark ought to be made about the use of the Old Testament here. For the present subject, it is chiefly important as preparing the way for Jesus and for New Testament thought about Him. Its principal value, therefore, is its evidence for the *beliefs* of Israel. In recent times much study has been devoted to the discovery of the historical facts that lie behind the Hebrew records. Sometimes the result has been that scholars have doubted the accuracy of the records. For the present purpose, however, the prime question is not 'What were the *facts* of history?' but 'What were the *ideas* of the Hebrew people?' and to answer the latter question the records themselves are our authorities. Such problems, therefore, as the historicity of Abraham, or the reliability of this or that part of the so-called 'historical' books, or the authenticity of particular Prophetic oracles, do not much concern this study. The books of a people—and in particular, a collection of books gradually accepted by a people as authoritative for it—are the key to *its mind*.

None the less it seems best to try to trace the historical *growth* of the pertinent ideas, and to do this the documents must be dated. It is convenient to treat the Old Testament under three periods—the period from Moses to Elisha, the period of the Written Prophets, and the post-Exilic period (or, more exactly, the period from about 450 B.C. onwards). It will be found that the line between the last two cannot be exactly drawn, but this is a characteristic of all attempts to divide living history into sections. The documents used for the different periods are dated according to the findings of the great majority of Hebrew scholars. The chief instances for the present study are the assignment of the work of the Deuteronomic school to the seventh and sixth pre-Christian centuries, and the dating of the 'Priestly' legislation of Exodus, Leviticus and Numbers, in its present form, in the centuries after the Exile.

All writers about the New Testament have to decide the difficult question of the right way to quote the first three Gospels. It would be out of place to discuss this vexed question here, but it seems to me that the scholars are probably right who claim that there are four documents behind our Gospels—the Gospel of Mark, a document usually named 'Q' that was used along with Mark by the authors of Luke and Matthew, and two 'special sources' used respectively by Luke and Matthew. It also seems to me that Mark and Q are of more value than the 'special sources'. In the few quotations that belong to the 'special sources', I have drawn attention to this fact. Under 'Paul' I have used all the Epistles ascribed to the Apostle except the Pastorals and, of course, Hebrews. The Gospel and Epistles of John seem to me to be so closely connected that, whether they are by the same author or not, they may be used together.

It will be found that there are no references to other books on the Atonement in the following pages. This is because the author's method has been to study the Bible for himself, and because to discuss the findings of other writers point by point would have doubled the length of the book. No doubt he owes much of which he is unaware to writers of the days of his youth. In recent years a large number of books on the subject of the Atonement have appeared. They do not raise any major issue on which any serious student of the subject will not himself have pondered. To say this, of course, is not to deny their great value. On this subject, after two millenniums of Christian thought, any violent originality is almost sure to be spurious. The discussion of the meaning of the phrases 'the Kingdom of God' and 'the Son of Man' comes nearest to furnishing an exception. Even here, however, the writer has had to be content to make his own position clear. Readers of other books will note that sometimes he has silently agreed with their authors and sometimes silently differed from them. He is greatly obliged to Rev. Professor Eric S. Waterhouse, Rev. Professor F. Bertram Clogg, and Rev. George W. Anderson, M.A., for reading the typescript in its several parts and making a number of valuable suggestions. The contraction *E.R.E.* is sometimes used for the *Encyclopædia of Religion and Ethics*, and *H.D.B.* for *Hastings' Dictionary of the Bible* (5 vols.).

C. R. S.

N.B.—In the revised edition I have altered a number of sentences and added others in order to make the meaning clearer. There are also a few other alterations.

CHAPTER I

PSYCHOLOGICAL PRESUPPOSITIONS

One of the chief services of the modern study of psychology is its full exhibition of a phenomenon that has always dominated human life, though at different times it has been recognized with varying degress of clearness—the phenomenon that man is ineradicably both 'corporate' and 'individual'. Every man is a separate 'self' and yet no man is altogether such a 'self'. Again, every true society has its own organic unity, yet it is at the same time a collection of individuals. While it is often convenient for purposes of study to isolate one of these two aspects of human life, or rather to make one or the other the primary object of investigation, yet neither can ever be altogether isolated, for they involve each other. It is sometimes said, for instance, that when Luther faced the Emperor and the Papal Legate at Worms, and cried—whether literally or in effect—'Here stand I; I can no other; so help me God', an individual defied the two great Mediaeval societies, State and Church, and modern individualism was born. Yet Luther claimed to derive his teaching from Augustine and Paul, and he was only able to do this because he himself was 'part and parcel' of the society called the Church, for without it he would never have heard of either. Again, when Luther spoke at Worms, he spoke for many others beside himself, as the sequel showed. If he had been merely 'individual', he could neither have derived from the past nor influenced the future. The 'corporate' factor in human life was inevitably there. On the other hand, to turn to a very different illustration, a victorious cricket eleven practises the 'corporate'. Unless the team 'play together', it is likely to lose the game. It must be more than a collection of players, however individually good; it must be an organic unity. Yet it must also be more than this. The individual bowler decides how to bowl each ball, the individual batsman what to do with it. There is an act of will, and it is in 'will' that the individual side of human nature is most prominent. But there is no need to elaborate a commonplace. Psychologists are unanimous here.

The phrase 'corporate personality' is often used to denote the organic unity of various societies, but objection may be taken to both words. While every true society has a living unity that may rightly be called organic, it is doubtful whether this unity ought to be called 'personality', both because no one yet knows what the nature of the unity is, and because 'personality' is best known in individuals. The word, therefore, may suggest that a society is more nearly like an individual person than it really is. Again, the term 'corporate' is, of course, metaphorical. It compares a society to a body. The comparison has a great example in the writings of Paul (e.g. 1 Corinthians xii), and it describes the organic with vividness, yet it is also true that a society is in some ways unlike a body—for instance, its 'members' have each a will of his own. In some discussions this seems to be forgotten, with lamentable results. The word 'societary' is not common, but it has the *imprimatur* of the *Oxford English Dictionary*, and, as it 'begs no questions', it will generally be used instead of 'corporate' in this book.

Two unsolved mysteries here emerge. The word 'organic' has already been used several times, and it is agreed that it describes a fact, but no one yet knows fully how to define it. We can only say that it describes the kind of unity that is proper to life. For instance, an animal has a kind of unity that a machine lacks, for an animal is alive. A machine is 'organized', but not 'organic'. But when we pass beyond this statement and begin to try to say what the distinctive unity of organic or living things is, we are at once at a loss. We cannot define 'life', even in a tree; all we can do is to give examples of it. Another mystery attends this one. While we are well aware that the individual and societary factors always go together in human life, no one can accurately and fully explain this connexion. Indeed, to describe this is a well-known 'bone of contention' among psychologists. Yet none of the disputants denies that there is an intimate connexion. In many studies this vital connexion is taken for granted without explanation, and there seems to be no good reason why this should not be confidently done in theology. It is unreasonable to require that in this one study, and in this only, the fact must not be accepted without explanation. It will appear later that this is an important point.

The two words 'sin' and 'punishment' require some definition. Historically, there have been two chief definitions of the former, and, though there may not seem at first to be much difference between them, it is in fact so great as almost to demand two different theologies. One school of theologians has defined sin as 'anything contrary to the will of God', while another has preferred to say 'anything contrary to the *known* will of God'. The second school has gone on to emphasize the element of choice or will. In other words, it has defined sin in terms of the individual. Probably this is the commoner meaning to-day. For instance, under the first definition it was a sin for Abraham to marry more than one wife or for Philemon to own a slave, for we believe that polygamy and slavery are both contrary to God's will, yet few would call either of the two a sinner on this ground, for neither knew that he was doing wrong. If the second account of sin be adopted, however, it is plain that the phrase 'original sin' is a misnomer, for it refers to something that comes to every man willy-nilly. It is a societary concept. Yet, while the phrase may be rejected, there is no getting away from the phenomenon meant. Just as people were concluding that 'original sin' is a theological figment, such writers as Freud and Jung brought the idea back, though under a different terminology. We don't now trace the phenomenon to the first sin of a man called Adam, but we admit that, whenever any man sins, there are societary results, for 'no man sinneth' only 'unto himself'. In consequence, through the manifold individual sins of the past, mankind, at any given stage, is much worse than it ought to be at that stage. This phenomenon may be called by some such name as 'racial degradation'. This is morally evil, though it is not 'sin' under the second of our definitions. It is not 'original' in the sense that it derives from our common 'origin' in Adam, but it is racial—and so societary—for it permeates the largest society of all, mankind. What is denied to theologians may be allowed to psychotherapists.

In thinking of 'heaven' and 'hell', Christians have been almost incurably hedonist. Happiness has bulked more largely in accounts of 'heaven' than holiness, and pain more largely than sin in accounts of 'hell'. In harmony with this, accounts of 'punishment' have stressed misery more than evil. Curiously enough, the right emphasis has been given in the concept of the Devil, for both the imp of the Mediaeval plays and the Satan of Milton are uniformly bad, but not uniformly miserable. The core of the punishment of sin is that it makes the sinner a worse man, not that it makes him a more unhappy man. In true Christian thinking, as in true psychology, pleasure and pain are epiphenomena —that is, they are never to be sought direct, or for their own sakes, or, rather, they are never to be sought at all. Here it is eminently clear that 'he that seeketh his life shall lose it'. Pleasure and pain are only accompaniments of greater things. Whatever secondary elements there may be in the punishment of sin, the core of punishment is degradation of character, or, to speak religiously, it is to lose the Holy Spirit and so to be separate from God. It follows that punishment is primarily individual. The bearing of this on our subject will appear later.

To return to the societary, it needs to be noted that the bond of a true society is neither always local nor always physical. The members of a cricket eleven, for instance, must sometimes be all in the same place, but they need not all be 'of one blood'. The Jewish race, on the other hand, may be 'of one blood', but it is never altogether in one place. Indeed, it is notoriously difficult to say what exactly it is that makes a true society. We cannot say much more than that it is a distinctive kind of life, and that the nearest word to explain this kind of life is 'spiritual'. Yet both 'life' and 'spirit' defy analysis. They fall among the elementary things that every one knows, but no one can define. Sometimes, indeed, we turn to the French term for 'spirit' and speak of *esprit de corps*, but this carries us no further. Can any one describe the bond that binds the British Empire together better than by saying that it has 'a common spirit'? The 'golden link of the Crown' is its great emblem, but is it more than an emblem? To be 'of one blood' means much to many societies, as does to live in one place to many peoples, but neither is essential to every society.

Yet the societary covers much larger ground than the term 'spirit' does in common speech. The idea occurs whenever there is some degree of fellowship between human beings. For instance, when any one gives a beggar twopence, it is because, even though he has never seen the man before and will never see him again, he has some slight degree of sympathy with him—or, to use an Anglo-Saxon word, of fellow-feeling. Sympathy or fellow-feeling is a societary concept. Of course, in the major examples of the societary the degree of fellowship is much greater—in the home, for instance. The measure of a mother's sympathy with her child is not twopence, but her life. Here the paradox of the societary appears. Is a home one or several? It is both. Is a Church one or several? Here Paul asserts the paradox in set terms—'They are many members, but one body' (1 Corinthians xii. 20). Is a cricket team one or eleven? Again, it is both. This, of course, is only to say again that man is always both individual and societary. Men are always separate and yet always 'one with' others. Once more, though no one can fully resolve this paradox—even, indeed, if the word 'antinomy' is used instead of 'paradox', in order to bring out the fact that the logical contradiction is not only apparent, but real—no one denies that it is there. In a true marriage a man and his wife are both two and one, in a true home several make a real unit, in a true nation unity defies the multiplicity of millions, and so on. Nor is the unity either make-believe or artificial. Theology makes its own additions to the list of instances. This is not to be denied it on the mere ground that it cannot explain the antinomy. It has as much right to unexplained phenomena as other studies.

It is sometimes said that in early Israel, for instance, the concept of 'corporate personality' has nothing spiritual about it, since it bases on physical unity. It is undoubtedly true that a kinsman's claim, for example, for help from another kinsman, derived from the fact that the two were of one blood. Yet this is an incomplete account. The Book of Ruth shows that sometimes the nearest kinsman did not do his duty to a kinsman's family. It was not this man, but Boaz, who chose to do it. This shows that the will of individuals always played its part, as well as the societary concept. Again, to use our terminology, Boaz had the 'spirit of the clan' to a greater degree than the nearer kinsman. The physical phenomena do not furnish a complete account of the facts. It would be interesting to trace the different ways in which, period by period, the physical and spiritual elements interacted in the societary concept in the history of Israel, but a single instance from later times must suffice. When the Jews returned from the Exile, every man returned because he was a Jew by race, yet he also returned because, unlike many of his neighbours, he *chose* to do so. In other words, the loyalty of the individual to the spiritual unity of his race played here a decisive part. The voluntary element in corporate life is here clearer than of old. When the New Testament is reached, we find a society called the Church which has no physical basis, but which every man joins by his own choice, yet it would be quite wrong to say that the concept of 'corporate personality', if that phrase has to be used, is lost. On the contrary it reaches its climax in the Christian Church. Is not this the 'body of Christ'?

We now come to the ominous word, 'vicarious'. Sometimes

it is used as if it meant merely 'in place of', but in fact it always means also 'on behalf of', and this is the more important part of its meaning. It denotes the fact that one man may do something for another man. When a father, for instance, saves money for his son, he is doing something vicarious. When Columbus found the way to America, he found it for others as well as for himself—he did something vicarious. Only philologists know what millenniums of other men's diligence were needed to produce our alphabet. Every educated English child inherits the treasures of English literature. If there were nothing vicarious in human life, home and nation and Church would lose their meaning. In brief, without the vicarious there could be no human life at all. Outside theology the word denotes a commonplace. Further, the corporate or societary element in human life involves the vicarious. The one requires the other. It is unnecessary here to inquire whether every instance of the vicarious involves the societary, though this is probably true. It is enough to note that, wherever the societary occurs, there too is the vicarious. A mother practises the vicarious every hour for her baby. A teacher studies a subject that his scholars may vicariously enjoy the fruits of his study. It is for the benefit of the millions of his fellow countrymen that a statesman makes a treaty. Wherever there is the organic, indeed, there too is the vicarious. It follows that the vicarious is an inevitable function of the societary.

Why, then, do many find the word 'vicarious' almost repulsive? It is because it has generally been used only in two phrases, 'vicarious suffering' and 'vicarious punishment', and both phrases seem to denote something unjust. Since both phrases commonly occur only in theology, some feel a kind of animus against that study. The two phrases need examining separately.

There is no doubt that, as a matter of fact, vicarious suffering permeates human life. If a boy does wrong, his mother suffers. Indeed, her shame may be so great that she suffers more than the boy himself. Or, to take an instance where he is not to blame, she suffers vicariously when she gives him birth. A whole nation may suffer because of the financial policies of its Ministers, or a whole army through the honest follies of its commander, or a ship's company because its captain misinterprets the boom of a bell in a mist. Indeed, one cannot see how vicarious suffering could be excluded from human life unless it became altogether individual and ceased to be societary. And this suggests the other side of the picture. Men often gird at vicarious suffering, but rarely at vicarious benefit. 'I don't deserve it', cries many a man bitterly when he suffers through another's fault, but the same man usually takes it for granted when he benefits through another's excellence. A boy who has taken a dozen holidays by the sea for granted sometimes feels it hard if a year comes when his father is too poor to give him one. It seems to be true that the advantages of the societary and its disadvantages must go together, and that if we are to have vicarious benefits we must also accept vicarious loss. Perhaps most people will agree that, on balance, the advantages of the societary nature of human life outweigh its disadvantages. Without the societary we should have neither language nor law nor nationality nor home. It would be out of place here to pursue the subject further. A believer in the goodness of God will say three things: that while he cannot fully explain the mystery of vicarious suffering, he is still sure that the benefits of the societary will in the end be found vastly to outweigh its disadvantages; that ultimately suffering will not be the lot of any good man; and that meanwhile vicarious suffering, if it is lovingly borne for the sake of others, will ennoble the character of the man or woman who bears it. In other words, while a hedonist may condemn it, it serves the purposes of a God for whom character is more than happiness.

There is more to be said in defence of the animus against the phrase 'vicarious punishment'. It seems quite arbitrary and unjust to punish one man instead of another. To take an instance outside the realm of theology, the founder of an English noble house is said to have been 'whipping boy' for Charles I in his early years. That is to say, when the young Prince did something wrong, the other boy was whipped! It is easy for us to smile at the custom, but it is better to try to understand it. It belonged to the days when the kings of Europe believed in their own 'divine right' and did their best to practise it. Even though absolute monarchies often meant arbitrary monarchs, there were those who declared that a thing was right because the king willed it. If the heir apparent did something wrong, obviously there ought to be punishment, but to punish the heir would be to break in upon the 'divinity that doth hedge a king', so another must be punished instead—and, if the king willed it, rightly punished! The point is that men did this seriously. It is perhaps not an accident that the theory of 'vicarious punishment' flourished in Christendom at the time of the absolute monarchies. It made three mistakes. First, it interpreted the Atonement too closely on the analogy of the law court. It asserted without qualification that 'Justice must be done—on somebody!' This was supposed to be Paul's teaching, but it will appear in the sequel that this is not so. Next, it is supposed that God's will stands above His reason—that is, it justified the arbitrary. Third, it mistook the nature of the Divine punishment. Human punishments usually take the form of suffering, but this is because they are clumsily imperfect. As seen above, with God the core of punishment is degeneration of character. A young prince could not pass this on to another boy. If he lied, he, and no other, was thereby a worse lad. Strictly speaking, it was suffering that was passed on, and not punishment. On a true definition of punishment 'vicarious punishment' does not occur. If a man suffers for another and his own character is degraded thereby, it is because he does not bear it aright—that is, he is punished for his own fault. No doubt here, as elsewhere, there are societary elements in the whole situation, but it is not these that bring degradation of character.

Another religious term that is out of favour with non-religious people intrudes here, the term 'save'. Yet it is plainly part and parcel of the societary idea. This will appear if we turn to the question: From what can one man save another? Clearly he may save him from error. Every teacher, for example, saves his scholars from error many times. If he so much as says to a youngster, 'That letter is V, my lad, and not U,' he is using his knowledge vicariously to save the boy from making a mistake. Again, it is plain that one man may save another from toil. The compiler of a concordance does almost endless vicarious work so as to save others from tedious toil. The inventor of every labour-saving device does the same. Once more, it goes without saying that one man may save another from disaster. Every swimmer who rescues a drowning man does so by vicarious skill. Again, one man may save another from pain or sorrow. Lister has saved multitudes from pain. A man who pulls a child from under the wheels of a speeding motor saves the boy's mother from sorrow. Yet once more, one man may save another from some of the results of his sin. The Prodigal's father did so, and many prodigals' fathers have done so. The societary idea carries with it the concept 'save'. Yet the problem most germane to the present study remains: Can one man save another from sin? Or, to put the question more carefully, can one man save another from the punishment of sin, in the sense of 'punishment' discriminated above? Can one man save another from the degradation of character that is the result of sin? Or, if the degradation is already a fact and a man is already bad, can another man help the bad man to become a good man? The psychological phenomena here need closer attention.

Many years ago I read a story about the Chief Engineer on a steamship. It was his turn to be 'off duty', but some one in the engine-room failed in his duty and at once a stream of scalding and blinding steam filled the room. Every one in it fled. Yet, unless certain taps were turned, it was likely that there would be an explosion and the ship might sink. The Chief Engineer thrust his way resolutely through the steam, seized the hot taps with hands already scorched to the bone and turned them off. By so doing he saved the ship and its company, he saved himself, he saved the culprit. He saved them all from the results of another's fault, but did he save the culprit, as we say, 'from himself'? Did he do anything to change the man's character—to make him a braver man than he had been? The story, as I read it, did not say. Possibly the Chief Engineer 'gave him the cold shoulder' forthwith and dismissed him at the next port. Or was the man ashamed of himself, and did the Chief Engineer stand by him in his repentance? Was he from that moment 'his best friend'? If so, it is perhaps likely and certainly possible that the man's character changed, and presently he too was such a man as could be brave even in such a crisis. In that case, the Chief Engineer 'saved' him in a deeper sense. Usually we should say that he did this by his 'example' and 'influence'. When these words are examined, they are found to build on the societary. Even if we stick to 'example' alone, surely the culprit could only follow the other's example if he said: 'I too am a man'. And if we add 'influence' and ask what that word means, we find that we can only say that there is a way by which one man can 'get at' another man and change him and that we call this 'influence'. In other words, we are just back at the mystery and fact of the societary.

Another illustration may be found in a story of Schamyl, the chief of the fierce heroes of the tribes of the Caucasus in their long struggle against the Russians.[1] On one occasion some one unknown was giving away the secrets of Schamyl's little band to the enemy and he issued an order that the next person found

[1] I owe this story to Dr. P. T. Forsyth.

communicating with them in any way should be scourged.
Presently a culprit was discovered and it was Schamyl's mother.
For two days he disappeared into his tent. Then, haggard and
worn with his shame, he came out, bade his men strip him and
bind him to the stake, and he was scourged instead of his mother.
The physical pain would be terrible, but would not the struggle
of mind be worse? Had there not been an almost unendurable
tension in his heart between loyalty to his mother and loyalty to
his band? In other words, the societary tore him in two, for he
was at once 'one with' his mother and 'one with' his patriots. And
the depth of his suffering came just because he could not be
altogether like his mother. It was not in him, as it was in her, to
be treacherous. For this reason, he would feel the evil and the
shame of her deed far more than she herself could. I don't know
what effect his vicarious suffering had on her, but one would
think that she could never be treacherous again. If so, the fact
that he insisted on still being 'one with' her made her again 'one
with' him. Yet the individual element in human nature would be
there as well as the societary, for, as it was by her own choice that
she had been disloyal, so now it would be by her own choice that
she became again loyal. If this is what happened, he 'saved' her—
not merely or chiefly from physical pain, but from a degradation
of character that had set in.

The story of Father Damien furnishes an illustration that comes
nearer still to what Christians mean, or ought to mean, by 'salvation'. When he went to the leper settlement on Hawaii, he knew
that it was very likely that he would take the disease. We know
that this did happen. But he did not go that he might be a leper.
He was set on a spiritual quest. When he reached the settlement,
no doubt he found that the lepers took various attitudes to religion.
Some probably were strong in faith; others would be feebly
Christian; others, no doubt, simply ignored God; it is so likely as to
be almost certain that there were others who cursed God and all
His ways. What would Damien do for these last? It was much
that he shared their physical lot—that he was 'one with' them in
their dread surroundings. But if he were to win them for Christ,
he would need to understand their minds, too. He would even
need to be tempted himself to turn upon God with a curse.
Physically, he could not save them, but, if he were to lead them
to that 'change of heart' that is change of character, he must face
and conquer their temptation. In other words, paradox though

it is, he must at once be like them and not be like them. None the less, if any one of them were to be saved, he must use his own will—the individual element in human nature must come into action. If this choice were made, then the man who made it would become 'one with' Damien and so 'one with' Christ. The societary element, therefore, is also there. Many readers of the story of Father Damien fix their minds almost wholly upon the physical side of his heroism. This is an integral part of it, but it is not the whole. If it is an error to treat man as wholly soul, it is a worse error to treat him as wholly body. For religious men a leper who rails at God comes to be 'saved', not if he ceases to be a leper, but if he learns to love God. Yet they would add that there is a sequel —that in the Hereafter he is a leper no longer. At last the whole man is saved.

It would be easy, if it were necessary, to multiply illustrations. Instances could be found, for instance, in the stories of St. Francis and Kagawa.[1] I have given other examples elsewhere.[2] It will be enough, however, to state simply four of the psychological phenomena that have emerged: first, if any man is to do anything to save another, in the sense of changing his character, he must identify himself with that other, he must 'be with him where he is'; next, at the point where he seeks to change his character, he must do an altogether paradoxical thing—he must know what it is to be like that other man, yet not be like him, or, to use other words, he must at once identify himself with that other and not identify himself with him; third, just because of this tension in his experience, he will feel the horror of that other man's sin more than the man himself; and, fourth, that other man must himself consent to be 'one with' his saviour.

It is the purpose of this book to try to show how there is here the key to the Bible doctrine of Salvation. One remark perhaps needs to be repeated and another to be added. First, it is admitted that there is here only a description of the psychological phenomena in question, and not an explanation. None the less, the description is a description of facts. Second, while it is convenient to prefix this description of certain psychological phenomena to the main discussion, it must not be supposed that they were first gathered and then thrust upon the Bible. In fact, for the writer there came

[1] See especially the chapter headed 'A Header into the Slums' in William Axling's *Kagawa*.
[2] See the volume entitled *The Christian Experience*, p. 140.

first a long pondering of the teaching of the Bible and particularly of the New Testament, and then the discovery that this teaching bases, as he thinks, more or less consciously upon certain truths about human nature that this introductory chapter seeks to describe.

THE OLD TESTAMENT

CHAPTER II

SOME PERMANENT CONCEPTS

In the history of Israel, as of all other peoples, the individual and societary elements in human nature were always present and always inseparable. It would be possible to represent this history as the story of great individuals—Moses, Joshua, Gideon, David, and so on. Yet in every case it is clear that they are part and parcel of a race and that their greatness depends on what they did for the race. They were societary men in an outstanding way. Gideon, for instance, contrasts with his son Abimelech just because he fought for Israel, while Abimelech 'fought for his own hand'. Again, it is sometimes said that Jeremiah 'discovered the individual' when he declared that 'every man shall die for his own iniquity' and went on to proclaim a 'covenant of the heart' that by its very nature is individual (Jeremiah xxxi. 29–34). Yet in other parts of his prophecies Jeremiah treats the nation as a unit. It is true that before his time there had been no clear declaration that God deals with every man separately. It is true, too, that for Christian men this is the ground of the assertion of 'the ultimate value of personality', to use a modern phrase. It is also true that Jeremiah's assertion marks a great advance in Hebrew religious thought, yet none the less it had never been possible before his time, either in Israel or elsewhere, to deal with men as though they were altogether 'corporate', just as it has never been possible to treat them as altogether 'individual'. In such an elementary matter as food, for instance, every man must have the right to eat for himself if he is to live, yet the bread that he eats is the product of a corporate effort that has lasted for millenniums.[1] The real difference between different periods here is in *emphasis*. It is true, for example, that from the days of Luther till yesterday the emphasis in Protestant Europe was on the 'individual' element in human nature, and equally true that in early Israel, as in other ancient races, the emphasis was on the societary. Before Jeremiah the Hebrew habitually thought in terms of the family, the tribe and the nation, rather than in terms of individuals. After his time

---

[1] I have tried to trace the development of individualism in Israel in a volume entitled, *The Bible Doctrine of Society*. See its Index, *sub voce*.

while societary concepts never ceased to be important, the individual came more and more 'into his own'. The importance of this for the present subject will appear below.

The ruling idea of the whole Old Testament is the idea of Covenant. The term is found in the documents of all periods, but even where the term is absent the idea is present. Apart from one or two such small books as the Song of Songs, it is the presupposition of every book in the Old Testament. Without this idea, no Hebrew story would have a *motif*, no Hebrew prophet a message, no Hebrew psalmist a plea. The fundamental concept throughout is that there is a Covenant between a given god and a given people. Even when the Written Prophets preach on the assumption that Jehovah[1] is God of all the earth, they do not abandon the earlier idea, but only deal with it in a new way. Always the Hebrew race and the Hebrew god go together.

To English minds the word 'covenant' has often suggested the idea of a bargain, but this is only because we are a commercial people. The Jews, too, are now a commercial race, but this has not always been so. They only became commercial when other races left them little choice to be anything else, and this phenomenon did not begin to occur till the Exile at earliest. Indeed, it was not pronounced till far into the Christian era. From the days of Joshua onwards, the great majority of the Hebrew race were peasants, and it is in the concepts of peasants that we must seek analogies for the notion of Covenant. In a Hebrew village the dominant social unit was the family. This is based on marriage, and in every true marriage there is a covenant, though we may not use the term. It is implied in such a phrase as 'pledge their troth either to other'. If a marriage approximates at all to a bargain, in that degree it ceases to be a true marriage. Now, it is common with the Prophets, particularly Hosea and Ezekiel, to compare the relation of Jehovah to Israel with that of a husband to his wife. The bond is loyalty rooted in love. Similarly the relation of Jehovah to Israel is occasionally compared to that of a father to his family. The covenant that permeates family life is not usually expressed in words at all, as it is in marriage, yet it is none the less fundamental. It would not be easy, indeed, to define its scope in words, for its scope is as wide as life. It is altogether unlike a bargain, for there is no question of getting as much as one gives.

[1] I use this current English name for the God of Israel, though 'Jahveh' or 'Yahweh' is nearer to the probable pronunciation of the Hebrew word.

Yet it bases all the time on mutual love, mutual trust, mutual service. Again, while Jehovah is not usually called the King of Israel, yet that is what He is, the earthly king being only 'The LORD's anointed', ('Jehovah's Messiah', to come nearer to the Hebrew), and so His vicegerent. At an English coronation there is a covenant made, the king giving pledges to his people, and his people, through the nobility that once upon a time represented them, giving pledges to him. It would be quite unfair to compare the covenant of a coronation to a monetary transaction. But the king was much more to the Hebrew people, as to all early peoples, than he is to the English peoples to-day. He not only 'reigned', but 'ruled'. More, if he were a true king, his life and theirs went together. One can perhaps best reach a right idea of the relation between them by trying to feel the pulse of the people who told and loved the stories of David. Perhaps the nearest English parallel would be with Alfred the Great. To reach the right Hebrew idea of Covenant, one must ponder the covenant of husband with wife, of father with children, of king with people. The Covenant of Jehovah with Israel was no theoretical thing. It was the postulate of life. It was based on loyalty, trust, and love. Whether the words are used or not, the ideas are essential in Covenant.

This is only to say that Covenant was a societary or corporate idea and that Jehovah was a societary god. For centuries it was impossible to think of one without the other—as impossible as to think of a husband without a wife or a king without a people. When at length some of the Prophets suggest that Jehovah and Israel might be separated, it is because through the disobedience of the people the Covenant has been dissolved, just as marriage may be dissolved by a wife's unfaithfulness—and even then the typical Prophet maintains that the Covenant holds between Jehovah and a faithful 'remnant'. There is no more thoroughly societary concept in all history than that of the Covenant between Jehovah and Israel. For the Hebrew mind, He and His people go together till this day.

The concept of the unity of a god and a people is found also in other early races, yet there is a difference. Usually there is some physical connexion between the two—the god being the physical father of the nation's ancestors or of its line of kings—but this is not so in Israel. From beginning to end, the Old Testament has no suggestion of any such bond. If one seeks a phrase to express the nature of the connexion, one can only use some such modern phrase as 'spiritually organic'. It is true that Israel had no such phrase, but this is only an instance of the way in which men practise a principle long before they enunciate it. It would be easy to give instances from the life of a child. In the practice of its daily life, love and home and speech, for example, occur long before it could give any account of their nature. Indeed, there is much to be said for the contention that in human life practice always precedes the elucidation of the principles on which it rests. The relation of Israel to Jehovah was 'spiritual', for it had no physical basis. Yet it was also 'organic', for it was the basis of Israel's distinctive kind of life, and where there is life there is organism. It is too often assumed that only the physical can be organic.

If the origin of the relation between Jehovah and Israel was not thought of as physical, how was it conceived? It was conceived as founding on the choice of Jehovah, and on nothing else. This is clear if the Call of Abraham is considered. 'Now Jehovah said unto Abram, Get thee out of thy country. . . . So Abram went' (Genesis xii. 1, 4). Similarly, in the days of Moses it was of Jehovah's mere choice that He remembered and renewed His Covenant. There is no mention of merit either in Abraham or in the Hebrew race enslaved in Egypt. The merit of the latter, indeed, is explicitly denied (e.g. Deuteronomy ix. 4 f.). Even if the Deuteronomist sometimes says that Jehovah chose Israel because 'He loved [its] fathers' (e.g. Deuteronomy iv. 37), this is only to put the choice further back. No doubt it is possible to say that such a choice is caprice, for why should Jehovah 'love' Jacob and 'hate' Esau? Yet there are many things in the ways of God that may be called capricious. For instance, if one looks at the extent and resources of the British Empire to-day, one might tend to agree with Milton that God 'has a special favour for His Englishmen', but it would be difficult to give good reasons why this should be, or why one child should be born British and another Abyssinian. Yet it is not usually Englishmen who raise the problem, but men of other races. So Israel did not trouble itself about the reasons why Jehovah chose to make Covenant with it and not with other races. It just accepted its happy lot with joy.[1] From its point of view, Jehovah was

---

[1] There is, of course, much else to say here. I have tried to deal with the problem of God's choice of Israel from the modern, as distinct from the Hebrew, point of view, in chap. i of a book entitled *What is the Old Testament?*

'gracious', and in the pervasive idea that Jehovah of His own free will blessed it with the blessings of the Covenant there is implicit one form of the doctrine that has now long been called 'grace'.

If the Covenant be considered from the side of Jehovah, other facts emerge. If He was in some sense a part of the society called Israel, He was its absolute lord. It was His will that ran, or ought to run. He gave commands to Abraham or Moses; Israel's Law was His law; her king was 'Jehovah's Messiah'; His shrines were her shrines; every Hebrew prophet based his message on the conviction, 'Thus saith Jehovah'; Hebrew 'wisdom' was fundamentally His wisdom, and so on.

It was also a part of Jehovah's share in the Covenant to be His people's active Providence. It fell to Him, again of His own free will, to give His people a land, plentiful crops, a way of worship, a knowledge of Himself, and many other good things. It was for Him to 'save' Israel. This brings us closer to our particular subject, and it requires a more detailed consideration.

There are three Hebrew terms that are frequently used to describe Jehovah's deliverance of Israel. Two need little exposition. The first of these may be translated 'save' (*yasha*), the corresponding noun being rendered 'salvation'. The root idea here is to be 'placed in freedom', so as to 'live in abundance'.[1] The second term (*padhah*) is best rendered 'ransom', for this English word uses the same metaphor. The original use is of a slave or prisoner set free by money payment. It would have been well if the English translations of the Bible had uniformly used 'ransom' to translate the word, both because of the underlying idea and because English readers would then have been able to distinguish it from the third term, whereas both are often rendered by 'redeem'. This third term (*ga'al*) has no exact English equivalent, and 'redeem' has to be used. It has other translations, however, in the Old Testament, and of these 'to do the part of a kinsman' (Ruth iii. 13) is nearest to the Hebrew. One could wish that there were some such English verb as 'to kinsman'. The Book of Ruth is largely based on the idea. It implies that it fell to a dead Hebrew's kinsman to redeem his mortgaged land and, if he died childless, to save his family from extinction by marrying his widow. Elsewhere the Old Testament implies that if a Hebrew were murdered, it was his kinsman's duty to 'avenge' his death—

---

[1] See Brown, Driver, and Briggs' *Hebrew and English Lexicon, sub voce*. All statements about Hebrew terminology are based on this volume.

or, more exactly, to see that the murderer paid the just penalty of his deed (e.g. Deuteronomy xix. 6, where the Hebrew word for 'avenger' means 'he who does the part of a kinsman'). But, while only a few of a kinsman's duties chance to be mentioned in the Old Testament, there were many more. The best way to understand the word is to recall the full meaning of kinship among the Arab tribes or the old clans of Scotland. Here it would be difficult to find any limit to the claims of one kinsman upon another. It was the duty and pride of every loyal member of the 'kin' to help another in every possible way. The obligation or duty (both are far too cold words) went with the common blood. In other words, there is here a leading instance of the practice of the societary idea. To an Arab of to-day, a Highlander of yesterday, or a Hebrew in Old Testament times, it seemed as natural for one kinsman to stand by another as it seems to us for one of our hands to help the other. In the Old Testament there is no law to this effect, for law and history alike take it for granted. The 'kin' is a living unit. But the word to denote this is used about Jehovah. He is said to 'kinsman' Israel. Of course, as seen above, there was no idea that He was one with them in blood, but this makes this use of the term more remarkable still. His relation to Israel is described by a societary word. It is used literally about human kinsmen right through Old Testament times; so this derived use did not lose its full meaning. The comparison between Jehovah and a kinsman was consciously made. The term is used of Him frequently from the seventh pre-Christian century onwards, as will appear later, but there are one or two earlier instances (e.g. Exodus xv. 13). If Jehovah is in Covenant with Israel, He is thereby like a *go'ēl* to Israel, and so He will 'do a kinsman's part' and redeem Israel.

Here the question arises: 'From what did Jehovah save His people?' The commonest answer by far is: 'From all kinds of physical misfortune—from slavery in Egypt; from drought, famine and pestilence; from enemies; from exile in Babylon, and so on.' Only at the very end of Old Testament times did another answer occur (to use modern terms) : 'From the degradation of character that is the result of sin and may itself be called "sin".' This will appear later.

Another question ensues: 'On what grounds did Jehovah save His people?' There are here, too, several answers. In early times the answer sometimes was: 'Because they *are* His people; because

He and they are in Covenant', no question of their righteousness or sinfulness being raised at all. For instance, this is the reason why Jehovah delivered Israel from Egypt under Moses. Nothing is said whatever about their moral state. Similarly, while the 'Deuteronomic framework' of the Book of Judges declares that Israel fell into disaster because it sinned and was rescued when it repented, this is not so in the early stories of that book themselves. Jehovah there saves Israel, for instance, from the Canaanites through Barak just because she is Israel. Yet quite early another answer to the question appears: underlying the story of the Destruction of Sodom there is the idea that Lot ought to escape because he is righteous (Genesis xviii. 23–33). It is the same with Noah in the story of the Flood (Genesis vii. 1). Through the greater part of the Old Testament, however, and particularly in the Prophets and Deuteronomy, two ideas cling together: if Israel is suffering, it is because Jehovah is punishing her for her sins; if she will repent and turn from her sins, Jehovah will save her. Many examples could be quoted from Deuteronomy (e.g. Deuteronomy xxviii), and this is the burden of many of the Prophets. When, however, the problem was seriously faced, 'Why do the *righteous* suffer?' the answer in effect was: 'We do not know, but in the end Jehovah will save righteous men because they are righteous.' This is so, for instance, in the story of Daniel's rescue from the lions, and in the last chapter of the Book of Job. But it is only at the very end of the Old Testament, and hardly there that the dominant New Testament problem is as much as posed: 'If a man has sinned, and if he repents of his sin but cannot himself escape from the degradation of character that has resulted, will Jehovah save him?' In other words: 'Will Jehovah turn a repentant sinner into a good man?' To the question, therefore, 'On what grounds will Jehovah save Israel?' there are several answers: (1) He will save her from *suffering* merely because she is His people. This answer is confined to early documents. (2) He will save her from her *suffering* if, when she is suffering for her sins, she repents. This is the dominant Old Testament answer. (3) He will save righteous men from *suffering* just because they are righteous. This answer is sporadic, but is not confined to one period. (4) He will save a repentant sinner from his *sinfulness*. This is an answer that only begins to appear in the deeper Old Testament thinkers, as will be seen later. The reason is that so long as sin was defined principally in terms of outward act, and not of outward motive, it was taken for granted that a man could, if he chose, give up doing such acts, and so there was no need that God should save him from 'sin'.

It will have been noted that, in discussing the last question, we have passed beyond it, and this in two ways. The question runs: 'On what grounds did Jehovah save His people?' In the instance of Daniel, for example, He saves an *individual* Israelite. The idea underlies, too, such an earlier story as David's escapes from Saul. Similarly, the Book of Ruth presupposes that Jehovah will save a Hebrew *family*, the story of Sennacherib that He will save a Hebrew *city*, and perhaps the story of the Benjamites in the Book of Judges that He will not allow a Hebrew *tribe* to become extinct. The concept, therefore, is a broad one. It does not merely mean that Jehovah will save the nation. Here the most important instance is the assertion of the Prophets from Elijah onwards that Jehovah will save what we call 'the godly remnant'—that is, the righteous part of Israel.

But does Jehovah save anybody who is not a Hebrew? The instances of Noah and Lot show that this idea is not altogether absent in early times, and it is to be remembered that it is practically certain that these stories were told and re-told 'in the gate' of Hebrew villages through all the history of Israel. Yet the idea remained for centuries like a seed that does not germinate. In and after the Exile, however, the belief that Jehovah will save *righteous* or repentant Gentiles appears clearly, notably in Deutero-Isaiah and Jonah. In the former of these, the Servant of Jehovah is 'for a light of the Gentiles' (Isaiah xlii. 6), but this implies that through this illumination they 'turn from their evil ways', for it is a postulate with the Written Prophets that the Gentiles are sinful—and that therefore Jehovah judges and punishes them. The idea that He will save Gentiles if they repent is explicit in the Book of Jonah.

The word 'sin' has been used several times and the question ensues: 'What did the Hebrews mean by "sin"?' An examination of the different Hebrew terms for 'sin' is interesting, but it doesn't help much in the present investigation. One idea is perpetual in the Old Testament—that to sin is to do something that Jehovah forbids. The first illustration, of course, relates to such a seemingly unimportant matter as the eating of the fruit of a given tree. But with the deepening and purifying of the concept of God in the course of Old Testament times there goes a change in the concept of the things that He forbids. It is enough here to name two well-known facts. One of the chief accounts of Israel's developing concept of the will of God lies in the law codes. These are of different dates, but through them all there is no clear distinction between what we call 'ritual' and 'moral' commands.[1] It is contrary to the will of Jehovah that an Israelite should either 'commit adultery' or 'seethe a kid in its mother's milk', so both are indistinguishably 'sin'. The other fact is that the Prophets made the distinction between ritual and moral offences clear to the world once for all. There is no need to illustrate or emphasize this. At the same time, it ought to be remembered that the ritual and moral do not exhaust religion. There is a third element, best called the 'spiritual', which, however little it is defined, is present in all true religion. Its essence is that there is fellowship between God and man. If God is Himself conceived as righteous or moral, it will follow that He will require His worshippers to be righteous or moral. The ritual element in religion is also related to the spiritual, though in another way. If rightly used, the ritual is the expression and vehicle of the spiritual. There is, therefore, no necessary conflict between ethics and ritual. Through the spiritual both have a place in a complete religion.[2]

Throughout almost the whole of the Old Testament, as has already been implied, it is proper to speak of 'sins' and not of 'sin' (in the sense of 'sinfulness', i.e. the degradation of character that results from sinning). For a very long time, sin was thought of in terms of outward act and not of inward motive. Even when evil motives began to be considered, it did not at once follow that they were thought of as resulting in a sinful character. The idea that there is an evil racial quality that passes somehow from man to man has no more than the dimmest beginnings, and these belong to the latest period of Old Testament history. The idea was not enunciated until the Christian era was very near, if so early. It is a mistake, in particular, to read it into the story of what has long been called the Fall. Probably several elements entered into the story of Adam and Eve before it reached its present form, but one

[1] This is true even of the Ten Commandments, for, while we look behind the letter of the first four to the spiritual principles that they exemplify, it is unlikely that the Hebrew, at least at first, did this. He took them just for what they say, and this belongs to the 'ritual', not the 'moral' realm. Those who defend their value often weaken their case by treating them as if they belonged to the 'moral' realm. In defending the use of the Lord's Day, in particular, many forget that it must be defended, as it quite well can be, on ritual grounds.

[2] On this subject there is a chapter in my book entitled *What is the Old Testament?*

C

of its *motifs* was to explain why men have to 'live by the sweat of the brow' and women bear children in agony. These evils were universal, and, under a thoroughly societary procedure, they were traced to the sin of Adam and Eve. But it is not the sin that is societary, but the consequent woes. To 'visit the sins of the fathers on the children' is not to make the children sinful, but to make them suffer.

Something should be added on the Old Testament concepts of 'punishment', 'wrath' or 'anger', and 'vengeance'. In the earliest stories there are one or two traces of the notion that Jehovah might bring disaster upon men capriciously (e.g. 1 Samuel xxvi. 19), but the ruling concept from the first, and the only concept during most of the Old Testament times, is that Jehovah punishes men, not capriciously, but because men have sinned. This idea appears, for instance, both in the story of the Flood and in that of the Destruction of Sodom. In other words, punishment goes with justice. In ancient thought, as distinct from modern, anger and vengeance properly go with punishment. In God these are the righteous reactions to sin. To-day men, rightly anxious to secure justice for all, hold that a judge ought to be the calmest of men, but this is not the ancient idea. When Nathan, for instance, told David the story of the rich man who had seized the poor man's one ewe lamb, he expected the king to be angry and to take 'vengeance'. Yet the anger was not thought of as incompatible with justice, but as its complement, and to take 'vengeance' was to vindicate justice, not to overpass its limits. It is quite easy to see why men to-day distrust emotion in connexion with punishment and justice, but there is no inevitable incompatibility, and it is the standing concept, both of the Old Testament and the New, that with God justice and punishment and wrath and 'vengeance' all go together. Indeed, it is hardly an exaggeration to say that the four are all elements in one idea. A single illustration must suffice—the early story of Abraham's plea with Jehovah before the Destruction of Sodom (Genesis xviii. 16–33) illustrates the ideas, though it does not use the terms.

A commonplace needs to be remembered in dealing with the Bible. Some writers seem to take it for granted that at a given period all Jews held the same opinions and that current thought was logically consistent. Of course, neither of these things is true. The second perhaps needs specially to be remembered. Probably there has never been a time anywhere when the 'man in the street' has held altogether consistent opinions. Indeed, this is rare, even with thinkers. Many think that an altogether logical man would be a nuisance or worse! An illustration or two for Israel may be given. It is said that for early Israel Jehovah was 'a local god', and this was the dominant opinion, yet all the while the tales of the Hebrews told that Jehovah had called Abraham in Babylon, saved Israel from Egypt, and overwhelmed the whole world in the Flood. Similarly, while common opinion thought of Jehovah as a 'national god', it was also believed that He had made Adam, saved Noah and confused the tongues of Babel. Or, again, in Hebrew thought both the 'breath' and the 'blood' were identified with a man's life, but little seems to have been done to correlate the two ideas. Or again, sometimes the 'angel of Jehovah' seems to be Jehovah Himself and sometimes distinct from Him. Yet such phenomena are only to be expected, for the silent assumption that the thought of a people is consistent is, of course, mistaken. On such a subject as the present one, therefore, some inconsistency in current thought may be expected. Instances will appear later.

CHAPTER III

FROM MOSES TO ELISHA

It is difficult to exaggerate the importance of the Exodus in the history of Israel. It was the birthday of the nation, but it was far more than a birthday. From the days of Moses till to-day, Jehovah has been for the Hebrew 'Jehovah, our God, who brought us up out of the land of Egypt, from the house of bondage'. This way of the making of a nation is perhaps unique in all the annals of man. For Israel it has never been a mere distant memory, but always the basis of life. Illustrations could easily be given from the records of every part of Old Testament story. For Israel, in every vicissitude since, Jehovah has been the saviour, the deliverer, and in every dark day the Hebrew has based a 'sure and certain hope' on the Exodus. His whole history, indeed, is just a history of deliverance, of salvation, and as he has looked into the future, however sinister it has seemed, he has always said, 'Jehovah will save, for He has saved'. If there be a Prophet or two, such as Amos, who has despaired of the future of his people, this is one of the exceptions that illuminate the rule. A doctrine of salvation underlies all the thought of Israel, and its foundation has been the story of the miracle of the Exodus. For the Hebrew it means what the Buddha's moment of illumination means for the Buddhist or the revelation to Mohammed in the Cave means to Islam. While no Christian can admit that anything can mean to any other faith what the Life and Death of Jesus means to Christianity, the Exodus comes next to it in significance. The Old Testament, like the New, is a Book of Salvation.

Yet, while for Israel Jehovah, in the ultimate sense, was and is the only saviour, He saved her in the Exodus through one man, Moses. First Jehovah commissioned him on Horeb to deliver Israel from Pharaoh, and then, again on Horeb, taught him that he might teach Israel.[1] For from the beginning onwards 'to teach' meant for Israel no theoretical teaching, but to teach a way of life—to forbid the wrong and to command the right. In other words, 'to teach' was 'to save', for an obedient Israel or an

---

[1] Here it is to be remembered that we are concerned with the thought of the Hebrews and not with the historical facts, whatever they may have been (see pp. viii. f.).

obedient Israelite learnt through 'Torah' how to turn from sin and
to practise righteousness. Moses, under Jehovah, was the saviour
of Israel. In other words, he was a mediator between God and
man. He cannot be understood on any other terms. For modern
historians he may be the maker of a nation; but for Israel he was
this because first and foremost he was 'Moses, the man of God'.

This introduces the vicarious idea in two ways: Moses spoke for
God to Israel, and he spoke for Israel to Pharaoh. But the
vicarious idea roots in the societary idea. In the vision of the
Burning Bush the behests of Jehovah base on the declaration, 'I
am the God of thy father, the God of Abraham, the God of Isaac,
and the God of Jacob' (Exodus iii. 6)—in other words, Moses was
commissioned to save Israel because he himself was an Israelite.
It was because he was one with his people that he did everything
that he did and was everything that he was. Moses was a societary
man or nothing—and therefore his work was vicarious, and for
him the vicarious meant self-sacrifice and risk in Egypt and a
long agony with the very people that he was saving in the desert.
The idea pervades the whole story, but Moses' unity with his
people reaches poignant expression in a famous passage: 'And it
came to pass on the morrow, that Moses said unto the people, Ye
have sinned a great sin; and now I will go up unto Jehovah;
peradventure I shall make atonement for your sin. And Moses
returned unto Jehovah, and said, Oh, this people have sinned a
great sin, and have made them gods of gold. Yet now, if thou
wilt forgive their sin—; and if not, blot me, I pray thee, out of thy
book which thou hast written' (Exodus xxxii. 30–2).

For our purpose Moses' work for Israel in the desert is as
important as the deliverance from Egypt, for in the desert he
saved Israel from itself. Whenever he and the people disagreed—
and they often did—it was Moses who was right and the people
who were wrong.[1] He saved them in spite of themselves. He
shared with them the hard lot of the desert in order that he might
so save them, and he succeeded. When he climbed Pisgah to die,
Israel was at the gate of the 'land flowing with milk and honey'.
Moses was a successful vicarious sufferer.

From what did Moses save Israel? Clearly he saved his people

[1] Even in the story of Moses' sin in the Striking of the Rock, the people are not in the
right (Exodus xvii. 1–7), and it is only in the later account that Moses is said to have
done wrong (Numbers xx; cf. Deuteronomy iv. 21). Perhaps the best explanation here
is that this was an instance of 'water-divining' and that in time this came to be thought
wrong in Israel (like many other such things: Deuteronomy xviii. 10–12).

from suffering—from slavery in Egypt and from perishing in the desert. Again, he saved them from sinning—for he taught them the will of Jehovah, and thereby they not only knew His will, but sometimes did it—for instance when they kept the Passover and 'forsook Egypt'. Again, sometimes when they had sinned, Moses saved them from sinning again,—for instance, we don't find that in the desert they made a 'calf' to represent Jehovah a second time. He did not altogether save them from punishment—for the forty years' wandering in the wilderness is conceived as a punishment— yet he did save them from the uttermost consequences of Jehovah's justice and 'vengeance', notably in the passage quoted above, where Jehovah proposes to destroy them altogether. Moses did lead them to 'the promised land'. But did he save them from 'sin' in the sense of a sinful disposition? The answer is that, while modern readers might argue that he partly succeeded even here, the records themselves give no answer to the question because this conception of 'sin' was not yet current.

There is no need to take the stories of Israel from Joshua to Elijah in detail. Some of the ideas just enumerated plainly recur. For instance, if the contents of the Book of Judges (particularly chaps. ii–xvi) be considered, a better name in English would be 'The Book of Saviours', and indeed the phrase 'to save Israel' occurs in the story of Gideon. Like the heroes of all peoples, the great 'judges' of Israel were societary men, and they saved their people from various kinds of disaster. Yet they were also men of Jehovah. This comes out in various ways, but the idea is always present—for instance, Barak is called to his work by a prophetess of Jehovah and Gideon by 'the angel of Jehovah', Jephthah fights his battle under a vow to Jehovah, and Samson sets himself to his exploits when 'the spirit of Jehovah' begins to 'work mightily upon him'. Indeed, Samson, grinding at the mill, suffers for his people, though he does not thereby save them. All the other Judges are mediators of victory, and this means that they are societary men. Behind the threefold concept Jehovah-Judge-Israel there lies the Covenant, with all its corporate meaning.

With the coming of the kingship these ideas took another form, but they were still paramount. With many peoples in many ages there is a sense in which the king *is* his people. In *King Lear* for instance, Lear cries, 'Call France. . . . Call Burgundy, Cornwall and Albany', meaning 'Call the King of France and the Dukes of Burgundy, Cornwall and Albany'. In a modern historical novel

Cleopatra is called 'Egypt' more than once. This is not mere compliment or convenient brevity. Behind the use there lies the idea that a king and his people are one. It is true that the ground of the unity is not stated nor ever clearly defined. It is quite certain that this unity was not conceived in any modern way as a mere matter of convenient arrangement for government. If a word must be found that means more than 'societary' one can only say that the 'organic' idea is there, or even the 'spiritual', in the sense that a king and his people have 'a common spirit'. But early thought—and thought in many later ages, too—found the idea so natural that explanation was needless. Though no Hebrew king was ever called 'Israel', yet the idea is not absent. The characteristic Hebrew phrase brings out the characteristic Hebrew idea— the king is 'The LORD's Anointed' or 'The Messiah of Jehovah'. It is true that this phrase is not used of any king except Saul and David explicitly (though it is implied in 2 Kings xi. 12), but it is used in the Psalms of Israel's king (e.g. in Psalm ii), and the notions that went with it in the stories of Saul and David were permanent, for these stories were current in Israel all the time. A Hebrew king's chief business was to defend his people from their foes and to see that justice was done in the land. In both he was Jehovah's vicegerent, and in both, too, he was the head and embodiment of Israel. There is no need to trace, detail by detail, the different ways in which, however imperfectly, a good king's life illustrated the ideas of covenant, salvation, justice and punishment named above.

In the historical books of the Old Testament Elijah ranks next to Moses. There was a time when he was thought of chiefly as a great worker of miracles. When the historicity of these was discounted, some students tended to depreciate his importance. Now he takes his old place, but not chiefly as a worker of miracles. It is his importance in the story of the religion of Israel that is drawn out. First, he is important as a Prophet and a leader of Prophets.[1] The word is printed with a capital letter, because we have here to do, not with the prophets of Israel on the side of ecstasy, where they can be paralleled among other early peoples, but on the side of their message, where they have no true parallels, especially if their message be taken as a whole. Some things may

---

[1] Moses may rightly be called a prophet (cf. Deuteronomy xviii. 18), but in the earliest documents he is rather thought of as greater than a prophet (Numbers xii. 6-8).

be said about them all. They were sure that they were the mouth-piece of Jehovah, and their characteristic phrase is, 'Thus saith the LORD'. Other Hebrews were always sure of this, too, or the stories and oracles of the Prophets would not have survived. On the other hand, they were 'one with' their people, for their whole purpose was to save their people from their sins. They were not men who could see Israel sinning and stand aside and 'wash their hands of the whole matter'. Even if one or two of them, such as Amos, foresaw that they would ultimately fail to save, yet they counted themselves bound to try, and even Amos did not utterly fail, for his oracles were treasured by some 'faithful few' to come down to us. Three ideas cling with them so constantly together that we may fairly speak of the Jehovah-Prophet-Israel concept. The Prophets are societary and vicarious men, and they are this in the specific sense of 'mediators'. In their stories and oracles the word 'save' may or may not occur—and the connotation of the idea may vary—but without the idea there could have been no Prophets. It was the Prophets from Moses onwards that made Israel great in religion, and it was the ground of their message that Jehovah wills and longs to save His people. It is chiefly through them that the Old Testament is a Book of Salvation.

When we turn to Elijah in particular, it is necessary to recall the historical situation. Scholars have made it clear that ever since Israel burst into Canaan, it had run the risks of what is called 'syncretism'. They point out that on the Conquest Israel did not exterminate the Canaanites, but that the two races mingled, and that the conquered greatly influenced the conquerors, not least in religion. A cultus therefore arose that contained both Hebrew and Canaanite elements. According to the records, Jeroboam, the son of Nebat, in particular, coun-tenanced and encouraged this process, at least in the Northern Kingdom. The records tell us that there were two Prophetic protests,[1] but these seem to have been ineffective. So far as we can judge, even Prophetic protest ceased, for it is not against this particular form of syncretism that Elijah and Elisha cried out. It seems that at the 'high places' before Elijah's time the god was at least called 'Jehovah' (e.g. I Kings iii. 4 f.). Under the House of Omri, however, a further danger appeared. Ahab, in particular, under the instigation of Jezebel, built shrines for the Phoenician

[1] I Kings xiii and xiv. If the story of Exodus xxxii is ascribed to this period, as is done by some scholars, this would mean that there was a third protest.

Baal. He does not seem to have proposed to abolish the worship
of Jehovah, but to have tried to institute the worship of another
god, with separate temples, alongside those of Jehovah. In other
words, here was unmistakable polytheism.[1] No doubt this may
have been but the climax of a process that had long been afoot,
but it is common in human life for an insidious disease to pass
without much notice until it emerges in obvious and flagrant form.
At any rate, Elijah denounced Ahab's policy, and denounced it
as the leader of a party of protest among the Prophets. Ahab, in
consequence, seems to have slain every Prophet he could catch.
He seems also to have destroyed at least some of the shrines of
Jehovah (1 Kings xix. 14).

Elijah won his real victory not on Carmel but on Horeb. On
Carmel he indeed won a momentary triumph, for the people
cried 'Jehovah, He is god', and the drought ceased. Yet the
Prophet knew well that Jezebel was more than a match for the
people and at her threat he fled alone to Horeb. There can be
no doubt why he made for Horeb. It was there that Jehovah had
made covenant with Israel, and there that Israel had bound
itself to serve Jehovah. Now, as Elijah thought, the Covenant was
dead. The solitary survivor of a plighted people came to report
to its God that all was over—'The children of Israel have forsaken
thy covenant, thrown down thine altars, and slain thy prophets
with the sword; and I, even I only, am left' (1 Kings xix. 10).
There follows a kind of repetition of the ancient theophany of
Moses' day—tempest and earthquake and fire—but it is not a
theophany now. Then there follows 'a sound of gentle stillness',
and this marks the begining of the dominance of a certain idea
in the thought of the Prophets. It cannot be called an altogether
new idea, for it is perhaps best defined as the idea that Jehovah
worked His will through ordinary history, and this idea can be
found in earlier days. But hitherto Jehovah had been chiefly a
God of wonders, and of this idea the old story of the Burning
Mountain of the Covenant had been the greatest instance. He
does not cease now to be God of wonders, for this idea recurs often
in the Prophets. The change is a change of emphasis. There were
hereafter to be Prophets of whom no miracles were told, whose

[1] The question whether previous syncretism had involved polytheism, or how far it
had done so, is here left on one side. There was sometimes an 'Asherah', at any rate,
in the shrines, and this was the emblem of a goddess. In other words, there was another
god 'before [Jehovah's] face', but at least He was the principal god of the shrine, and,
so far as the records go, there was always some protest against the 'Asherah'.

whole message was to be that Jehovah is master of history. When He seems to be doing nothing—when there is no token of His doings but mere 'stillness'—He is none the less ruling the world of nations. As first instances, Elijah is sent to 'anoint' Jehu and Hazael. It was Elisha who carried out the behest, and the way in which he did so is significant. He waited till, as we should say, events had matured. Then, at the right historical moment, he summoned Jehu to destroy the Baalism of the House of Omri and Hazael to be the scourge of Israel's sins. Yet it is not in these acts that the chief importance of Elijah lies, and we need not stay to ask how far the whole people forsook Baalism. It has often been pointed out that with the words 'Yet will I leave me seven thousand in Israel, all the knees which have not bowed to Baal, and every mouth which hath not kissed him' (1 Kings xix. 18) a new idea emerged that was to mean much in the future. There were a faithful few, however obscure, all the time, and Jehovah willed to be a Providence to them. The Hebrew term rendered 'leave' is of the same root as the term rendered 'remnant'. On Horeb the history of the faithful, suffering Remnant began. Already the idea that Jehovah would save the Remnant is clear.

It is remarkable that the Old Testament does not tell that any of the great Prophets of Israel died for his faith, though this is told of obscurer men (1 Kings xix. 10; Jeremiah xxvi. 23; cf. 2 Kings xxi. 16). On the contrary, the story ran that Elijah did not die at all (2 Kings ii), and, at least on one reading of the Hebrew, that Jehovah Himself 'buried Moses' (Deuteronomy xxxiv. 6). Indeed, there is evidence that by the time of Jesus there were Jewish stories that told that Moses did not pass at death, like other men, to Sheol or Hades, but went to be with God.[1] Neither he nor Elijah died for his people. It is true, of course, that both men, like later Prophets, risked death—Moses, for instance, in his long struggle with the Pharaoh, and Elijah in his defiance of Ahab (1 Kings xviii. 4, 10, xix. 1 f.). Yet it is not here that the most significant fact for our subject lies. The horrors of death by violence are not the monopoly of saviours. The significant suffering of Moses' life appears in the story of his attempt to 'make atonement' for his people. When he climbed the mount on this enterprise, he was as a man who is torn in two. His unity with his people was so vital that he was ready to die for them; yet he could not forsake Jehovah with them. It is the tension between these

---

[1] See for instance, Hastings' *Dictionary of the Bible*, vol. iii., pp. 448–50.

two passions that is the hall-mark of saviours. Similarly, on Horeb Elijah was, as it were, two men in one and the two struggled with each other. If the Prophet had not been 'an Israelite indeed' he would never have bearded Ahab at all, yet he was also, if one may use the phrase, Jehovah's man. It is his distinctive agony that his two loyalties were at war. Both Moses and Elijah were one with their people, and yet not one with them in their sin, and this is how they saved them. As we shall see, this explains the story of their appearance on the Mount of Transfiguration.

CHAPTER IV

THE HEBREW MESSIAH

THE growth of the 'Messianic idea' in Israel concerns us here because of its bearing upon the doctrine of salvation. It should be remembered that the use of the *term* 'Messiah' for a *future* king is not found in the Old Testament, but appears first in non-Canonical Jewish literature.

In the Old Testament the term is used of *past* and *present* rulers, and usually of kings. The first striking use applies the term to Saul. For David he is 'the LORD's Anointed', or 'The Messiah of Jehovah', and therefore sacrosanct. Both Saul and David, as well as later kings of Judah, were literally anointed (1 Samuel x. 1, xvi. 13; 1 Kings i. 34; 2 Kings xi. 12). It looks as if any king of Judah might be called 'the LORD's Messiah', however evil he was, but he ought to be of the House of David (cf. 2 Kings xi). At least as early as Deuteronomic times, he could also be called 'the son of Jehovah' (2 Samuel vii. 14). After the Exile, the High Priest was literally anointed, and we don't know how far back this ceremony went (e.g. Leviticus iv. 3, 5, etc.). The term could also be used metaphorically of prophets (e.g. 1 Kings xix. 16; Isaiah lxi. 1), and in later days, of the Patriarchs, of the people Israel, and even of Cyrus (Psalm cv. 15, lxxxiv. 9; Isaiah xlv. 1).

For the present subject, it is best to begin with the instance of David, for the many stories about him that passed 'in the gate' of Hebrew villages generation after generation show the place that he held in the memory of Israel. It is clear first that kingship was counted a religious office, for the king was 'the Messiah of *Jehovah*'. It is plain, too, that the king was appointed by Jehovah to fulfil the will of Jehovah for the people of Jehovah. In other words, the idea of Covenant is here very strong, however absent the word chances to be. This means that the societary idea is strong. There is no reason to think that the general ancient idea that the king and his people are one—and that, in a sense, the king *is* his people —did not obtain in Israel, but rather the contrary. This is why either the king or the people might be called Jehovah's 'son' (for the latter see, for instance, Hosea xi. 1). The nature of the king's holy office is not difficult to discern. He had two chief duties: to subdue enemies and to do justice. Of David's success in conquest there is a brief account in the eighth chapter of 2 Samuel. He succeeded to the House of Saul when the fortunes of Israel seemed desperate, and he handed on to Solomon a united, prosperous and secure people. To prosperity David added justice. The last chapters of the Book of Judges show what internal evils might befall when 'there was no king in Israel'. In the East it has always been a mark of a good and true king that he should be the 'Protector of the Poor'. There are two chapters (2 Samuel xii, xiv) that tell how parabolic stories were told to David, and in both cases the presupposition is that David would care for the poor among his people. Otherwise the tales that Nathan and the Woman of Tekoa told him would have had no purpose at all. Both of them assume that it was his habit to do justice and mercy to 'the poor and needy'. In other words, David, being a true king, was, in a given sense, a saviour of his people, in the sense that he saved them from such outward evils as defeat and injustice. In the stories of Israel's hero-king the people cherished an ideal, however much the stories were 'idealized' in the telling, and the chief elements in the ideal were that the king was chosen of Jehovah to give victory, prosperity and justice to His people. Yet the king's tool was largely force. So far as the rule of force can save from outward sin by establishing the ways of outward righteousness, a true king might be called a saviour from sin, but no farther. One more idea of importance needs to be added: the Hebrew believed that Jehovah Himself would give such a king success, or, to quote the Hebrew phrase as it is used of David, Israel believed that 'Jehovah was with him'.

In modern times the word 'Messianic' has been used of many passages in Hebrew and Jewish books. These passages fall into three classes. Sometimes all passages are called 'Messianic' that foretell or expect that at some time in the future God will establish righteousness and prosperity among men. At other times the word is confined to passages that envisage the righteous and happy future under the form of a kingdom. Finally, the word is sometimes used in a narrower way still, being kept for passages where the term 'Messiah' itself occurs as a name of the perfect future king. As already stated, there are no Old Testament instances of the last use. How far are the other two found in the Old Testament?

The idea that God will in the end establish righteousness,

prosperity, and peace among men is all but universal in Hebrew thought. It is found alike in Deuteronomic and Prophetic writings. Again, the idea is frequent in the Psalms. Even the Psalms of the suffering poor presuppose that the God with whom they plead is able to help, and that, since He is righteous, He will in the end surely help. Again, the Apocalyptic idea would be meaningless unless the Apocalyptists counted on the ultimate realm of righteousness. They all declare that, however terrible the process, at the last God will vindicate Himself by making 'a new heaven and a new earth wherin dwelleth righteousness'. Their phrases may differ here, but the idea is constant. If the term 'Messianic' is to be used in this wide way, almost all the thought of Israel is explicitly or implicitly 'Messianic'. It is best, therefore, to keep the word for its narrower senses. None the less it is important to note that, however the content of the notion 'salvation' may vary, it is one of the axioms of Israel that Jehovah does and will 'save'.[1]

The second use of the term 'Messianic' may now be more exactly defined. Since monarchy has always been the usual form of society in the East, Hebrew writers often, either explicitly or implicitly, think of the perfect state that God will ultimately and inevitably establish as a kingdom in which God Himself is king. Usually, however, the notion is that Jehovah *will* be king in the perfect realm, because all the while He *is* king in this sinful and rebellious world. In other passages, the figure of a future earthly ruler, a kind of vicegerent of Jehovah, appears. It is of these passages that the term 'Messianic' in the second sense is used.

As we have already seen, the idea that a true king was 'the LORD's Messiah' is rooted in the past, and particularly in the stories of David. The Deuteronomic passage already named, the seventh chapter of 2 Samuel, looked for a continuous line of Davidic kings, and we know that, apart from the brief usurpation of Athaliah, the line did last for more than four centuries. The contrast with the repeated change of dynasties in the northern kingdom must have struck every thoughtful Hebrew. There was another contrast, too. According to the Deuteronomic editors of

---

[1] The 'Immanuel passage' (Isaiah vii. 14) may be called Messianic in the widest sense, for in it a young mother, in spite of the current perils of Judah, is so confident of Jehovah's help that she calls her newborn child 'God-is-with-us'. The Hebrew word rendered 'virgin', like the Arabic *bint* (*vide* Doughty's *Arabia Deserta*), could be used of a married woman who had not yet borne a child. It does not follow from this that Jesus was not born of a virgin.

the Books of Kings, there was not a single king in the north who
'did that which was right in the eyes of the LORD'. All were bad,
though in varying degrees. In the two centuries from Asa to
Hezekiah, however, it happened in Judah that on the whole good
kings ruled a long time, and the editors find that for three-quarters
of this period the Judaean kings, apart from the toleration of 'the
high places', 'did right in the eyes of Jehovah'. However much
this account may need qualifying when the first chapter of Isaiah
is studied, there must be some truth in it. If, therefore, there was
any hope of Hebrew kingship at all, it was in the Davidic line.
Consequently, even in Messianic passages where this line is not
specifically mentioned, probably the idea that the future king
would be of David's house is to be taken for granted. When the
line ceased to rule in 586 B.C., loyal Hebrews longed for its restoration. The way in which the editors of Kings finish their book with
a reference to some slight improvement in the lot of such a captive
king as Jehoiachin is a pathetic illustration of this hope.

Before the Deuteronomic school of writers, however, had
finished their work, the Prophets had already taken up the idea,
though the number of illustrative passages is not large. Some of
the most famous are found in the book named after Isaiah. One
speaks of a future king 'whose name shall be called Wonderful
Counsellor, Mighty God, Everlasting Father, Prince of Peace'
(Isaiah ix. 6). There seems to be no good reason for counting this
prophecy as later than Isaiah's time. To put the concrete Hebrew
phrases into the abstract terms that moderns prefer, the expectation was of a king who should rule in wisdom, power, fatherliness,
and peace.[1] Another passage (Isaiah xxxii. 1–8) develops this idea
further. There are two other passages of doubtful date. The first
(Isaiah ii. 2–4; cf. Micah iv. 1–4) looks for the universal worship
of Jehovah at Jerusalem and therefore for universal peace.
Probably the notion of a king at Jerusalem is implied, though this
may be disputed. Here there is a Hebrew account of a League of
Nations and it supplies the true basis of such a league in the
the worship of the one God (and therefore the common pursuit
of His policies). The other passage is in the eleventh chapter
(Isaiah xi. 1–9). This fine account of the Messianic Hope in the
widest sense of the term places an earthly king at the head of the

[1] The passage that speaks of 'Immanuel' (Isaiah vii. 14) cannot be taken as Messianic
in this more exact sense, and it does not seem to have been so taken by the Jews. If
the context is considered, the most that can be said is that the Prophet expected that
within a few years Ahaz would be succeeded by a righteous king of David's line.

coming kingdom, and he is to be 'of the stock of Jesse'. Out of this 'stock' a 'shoot' or 'branch' is to grow. The metaphor is anticipated in the story of the Call of Isaiah (Isaiah vi. 13), but there the nation, and not the House of David, is compared to the stump of an old tree, out of which a new shoot persistently grows. No doubt there is here a parable of the 'godly remnant', and behind the figure there is the silent certainty that God will not let Israel altogether perish, but will yet make her into a true and flourishing kingdom. In the eleventh chapter the parable is transferred to the House of Jesse. Whatever its date, it tells of a coming kingdom when there shall be universal prosperity and peace under a righteous king, for 'the earth shall be full of the knowledge of the LORD as the waters cover the sea'.

This parable of the shoot occurs also under the term 'branch' in the oracles of Jeremiah (Jeremiah xxiii. 5, xxxiii. 15). In both passages there is explicit reference to the House of David, to the re-uniting of the two Hebrew kingdoms, and to the righteous realm that is to be. In the second a true priesthood takes its place in the future beside a true kingship. In both the certainty that Jehovah will establish the future realm is emphasized. The metaphor of the branch has a further illustration in the prophecy of Zechariah (Zechariah iii. 8, vi. 12), but here the shoot or branch seems to mean Zerubbabel, who was apparently of David's line.[1] A similar metaphor appears in the New Testament phrase, 'The Root of David'.

There is another famous Messianic passage in the Book of Micah (Micah v. 2–15), though its date, too, is doubtful. Here the future king is to be a 'shepherd' to his people. There seems also to be an anticipation of the idea that war may be a way to peace— as, for instance, David's victories had led to the peace of Solomon. There is also an animus against cities (verse 11). Unlike Isaiah, who was probably a citizen of Jerusalem and who was the hero of its siege by Sennacherib, Micah expected that its destruction would be so complete that its site would become a mere piece of ploughed land and the Temple area a 'forest' (Micah iii. 12). Similarly the oracle of the fifth chapter, whether by Micah or not, bases its hopes of the House of David, not upon the 'city of David', but upon his village. Jerusalem was not the birthplace of his line;

---

[1] As the phrase, 'My servant the Branch', occurs here, it is just possible that the two concepts of the Suffering Servant and the Messiah are combined. There seems to be no certain instance of this in Jewish literature before the rise of Christianity.

it was from Bethlehem in 'ancient days' that the origins or 'goings forth' of the House of David had come. It is from 'little' Bethlehem, therefore, and not from the capital city, that this Prophet expects the future king. There is here the concept of the 'shoot' in a different form.

In the book of Ezekiel the last chapters (chaps. xl–xlviii) describe the glories of a future city, but it is upon the Temple and the priesthood that the writer lavishes a loving detail. The 'prince' (not 'king') plays quite a subordinate part; indeed, he is little more than the lay servant of the Temple. In an earlier chapter, however (chap. xxxvii), both the term 'king' and the term 'prince' are used of a future ruler of the House of David (verses 24 f.). It may be noted, too, that the king and his people go so closely together that within two verses the phrase, 'My (Jehovah's) servant', can be applied to 'David', to the people (called 'Jacob'), and to 'David' again. Here both north and south are to be redeemed, under one king of the House of David, who is to be his people's 'shepherd'. This metaphor has its most detailed illustration in the thirty-fourth chapter. Here the rulers in Jerusalem, no doubt forming the 'house of David' (cf. Isaiah vii. 2), are denounced for their selfish care for themselves and their carelessness of the flock. Then there is promise of a future where Jehovah Himself will be their 'shepherd', and this passes into a promise that 'my servant David' shall shepherd them. There could not be a better example of the way in which Jehovah, Israel, and the King of Israel, all 'go together' in Hebrew thought. Under the concept 'shepherd', too, the idea of force is in the background and the idea of salvation in the foreground, for it is the one duty of a shepherd to 'save' his sheep from every kind of harm. It is made a charge against the false shepherds that 'with force and with rigour they have ruled over' the flock (verse 4), wheras they ought to have 'sought that which was lost', and so on. The idea runs through the oracle that a true shepherd is strong, patient, and pitiful. No shepherd here 'gives his life for the sheep', but the true shepherd—whether Jehovah or David—will spend his strength for the sheep and so 'save' them.

Yet there is no teaching that Israel's true shepherd will save the wicked. On the contrary, the Prophet declares that there are bad sheep who have shouldered other sheep away from the feeding-trough, and that God will 'judge' them (cf. chap. xxxiii). It is the meek and frail sheep who are to be saved, and no doubt the godly

D

'remnant' is here again in mind. There is no suggestion that sinners are to be saved from their sinfulness.

Similar concepts, without the comparison with a shepherd, are found in the remaining Prophetic passage (Isaiah lxi). Here, however, the word 'anointed' is used of a Prophet and not of a king. 'The spirit of the Lord Jehovah' has come upon him that he may 'preach good tidings unto the meek'—and so on through the famous phrases. The whole chapter is Messianic in the widest sense, and it is here that within Old Testament writings the *word* comes nearest to the New Testament concept. A prophet, unlike a king, did not wield a sword. Yet the idea of force is not absent. It is to be wielded by God and not by the prophet, yet the latter is sent, not only to preach 'deliverance to the captives', but 'the day of vengeance of our God'.

In the Psalter the Messianic concept in the widest sense is common. It lies behind every verse that expresses any kind of hope. If a single example is selected—and one will suffice—the Seventy-second Psalm perhaps serves best, for it lays out the concept of the Realm-to-be at large. At the same time, it illustrates the use of the term 'Messianic' in the second sense also, for it tells of a future king. Here the writer looks forward to the world-wide and everlasting rule of an heir of David's line. He is not, indeed, expressly said to be a 'son of David', but the first verse seems clearly to imply this idea. Again, the future, perfect king is to rule in righteousness, and the first verse expressly says that his righteousness is to be like God's own. In particular, he will show his righteousness by doing justice to the poor. Under Eastern despots, this has always been thought a wonder and it is specially emphasized. The king's universal righteousness is to bring universal peace and prosperity. The terms 'save' and 'redeem' ('do a kinsman's part') are both used (verses 13 *f.*). The societary idea underlies the whole psalm, for the king here, as in all Eastern thought about a true king, is part and parcel of his people. This, indeed, is the basis of his rule. There is, however, no hint of the concept that he will save bad men from their sins. He saves the poor because it is assumed that they are righteous. As for the wicked, who 'oppress' them, he will 'break them in pieces' (verse 4). Again, his rule over other nations is to be by force. 'His enemies shall lick the dust' (verse 9). The valuable concept is that the future universal realm is to base on righteousness—a righteousness that to the poor is very like mercy.

It is necessary to consider two other 'Messianic' psalms. The first of these is the second in the Psalter. It falls readily into four stanzas, as the Revised Version shows. In the first stanza the writer refers to a rebellion among subject states, and asks sarcastically what good they think a rebellion will do. Are they not setting themselves against 'Jehovah and His Messiah' (verse 2)? In the second stanza, Jehovah, in derision and wrath, asserts the folly of their attempt, for *His* might lies behind the Davidic king. In the third, the king speaks. He says that God has promised him victory. Here it is necessary to point out that no reader could ever think that the phrases, 'Thou art my son; this day have I begotten thee', refer to the king's physical birth. The phrases are metaphorical and mean that Jehovah will make it manifest that the king is His 'son' by the victory that He will give Israel through him. In the fourth stanza, the writer himself again speaks and gives the rebels sarcastic advice. Their wisdom is to submit.

This psalm seems to have been written about some reigning king, but, as we know, it was later applied to the king that was to come. It is plain that the king is to prevail by force. Though the word 'save' does not occur, the dominant concept is that Jehovah will save the king, and through the king the people of Israel, by His power. There is nothing about salvation from sin, but only from peril. The one element of value in the psalm is the concept that the Messiah, since he is Jehovah's Messiah, cannot fail but must prevail.

The remaining psalm is the Hundred and Tenth. Apart from the obscure last verse, which need not detain us, the underlying concepts are the same as in the Second Psalm. There are, however, three details that call for notice. Here the king is not said to be the 'son' of Jehovah, but to 'sit at His right hand', sharing His power. This emphasizes the notion that the king's rule is derivative—it is Jehovah who is the sole source of his strength. Secondly, the king is here called a priest as well as a king, or, rather, like Melchizedek, in the ancient tale, he is king-priest. It is the everlastingness of priesthood, rather than of kingship, that is emphasized. Thirdly, the part the people play in the victory is here specially named. They come forward to fight as 'freewill offerings' (verse 3). Here the ancient custom by which warriors 'sanctified themselves' for war, as war was a holy cause, is in mind. Here, again, the underlying idea is that the king-priest cannot fail, for God is with him.

To-day it is usual to count three Apocalypses in the Old Testament—the Book of Joel, the Book of Deutero-Zechariah (chaps. ix–xiv), and a large part of the Book of Daniel (chaps. ii and vii–xii). All these books seem to have been written in the Grecian period. Here there is no need to illustrate the prevalence of the Messianic idea in the most general sense, for it is a postulate of Apocalyptic that Jehovah will in the end set up a universal realm of righteousness, prosperity, and peace. There is in these three books only one notable example of the Messianic idea in the second sense. This is in the ninth chapter of Zechariah. This illustrates the concept that peace is to be the outcome of successful war. There is nothing remarkable in this when one remembers that from Alexander onwards the world of which Palestine formed a part knew no long period of peace for centuries. It was by successful war that Persia had brought the Jew two centuries of almost unbroken peace; surely now it was Jehovah's purpose, through the wars that raged, to bring in a better and nobler peace. What other account could a monotheist give of the state of the world? But the remarkable part of the passage for our purpose is the verse that tells of a Hebrew king who shall be 'righteous and having salvation; lowly, and riding upon an ass, and upon a colt, the foal of an ass'. While the context requires that Jehovah is the warrior-god, here alone clearly the coming king is not to be a warrior-king. It is a surprising concept. In effect the writer says, 'The true king will not be an Alexander'.[1]

The concept of the Messiah in Jewish books outside the Canon will be considered later. For the Old Testament itself, the chief ideas are most of them constant. The future king is an idealized David. His kingdom is not to be small, like David's, but world-wide. Again, he is to rule, like David, righteously, but 'righteousness' is conceived now in the deeper sense that the great Written Prophets had made current. His kingdom is 'to have no end', but here probably the reference, as in the seventh chapter of 2 Samuel, is to the perpetuity of a line of kings, for there is no hint that the Messiah is to be anything but human and mortal. Again, the future king, like David, is to be God's vicegerent, a link between Jehovah and His people—that is, he falls under the idea of

---

[1] It may be added that Daniel ix. 25 f. is not to be taken as Messianic, for the phrase 'an anointed one, a prince' in verse 25 seems to mean Cyrus, and 'an anointed one' in verse 26, the high-priest Onias. See the commentaries.

'covenant'. He, like David, is to conquer all the enemies of Israel, or, alternatively, when Jehovah has conquered them, Jehovah is to give him the kingdom. He is to conquer by force. His own people, however, considered as a righteous people, he is to rule like a shepherd. As conqueror and ruler, he may be said to 'save' them. There is no idea of saving from sin, but only from trouble and oppression. Of the concept that the future king will turn bad men into good men—and in this sense 'save' them—there is no hint whatever. At best, as in the exceptional passages found in the sixty-first chapter of Isaiah and the ninth of Zechariah, he is to be the meek saviour of the meek. This is a valuable idea, but it is not the characteristic Hebrew concept, and, while it anticipates in some ways the New Testament doctrine of salvation, it fails to do so at the crucial point, the salvation of sinners. For anticipations of this, we must study the Prophetic books from another angle. Meanwhile it is abundantly clear that, while there is no instance of the use of the *term* 'Messiah' to describe the *future* king in the Old Testament, the *idea* that underlies this concept is frequently found.

CHAPTER V

THE WRITTEN PROPHETS

For the world at large, the books of the Written Prophets are the most significant part of the Old Testament. They begin with the oracles of Amos (c. 760 B.C.) and culminate in those of Deutero-Isaiah (c. 550 B.C.),[1] though the list of prophets extends to about the middle of the fifth century B.C. or even later. We have here to do, not with their general teaching, but with a particular element in it. From the point of view of their contemporaries generally, most of them were men who failed, but there must have been a minority who believed their message or their oracles would not have survived. In other words, there was a Remnant all the time.

Some of the psychological phenomena of salvation appear with Amos. Some writers present him as a hard man, and it is probably true that all his genuine oracles speak of unrelieved doom, yet this is only part of the truth. Amos denounces destruction upon Northern Israel, as well as on other nations (e.g. in i. 3–ii. 16), because they have been cruel to the poor. It is passionate sympathy that makes him hard. It is because he is sure that Jehovah cares for poor people, and because he himself is so closely 'one with' the poor, that he hurls his thunderbolts. In other words, he is, in his degree, a societary man. This is the secret of his outbursts at Bethel.

Hosea is plainly a broken-hearted man. It seems clear that it was his pitiful home that made him a Prophet. His wife Gomer was habitually an adultress and fornicator. It is not difficult to see how a tender-hearted man would react. One cannot make Hosea's prophecies logically consistent, for how could a loving but wronged husband achieve consistency? Yet there is no psychological difficulty here. Almost in one breath, Hosea cries out against Gomer and pleads with her. In the literal sense, he is distracted—divided against himself. His faithfulness to Jehovah drives him one way and his love for his wife another. Just because he loathes impurity, he suffers as his wife herself cannot. No doubt he cried out many a time in his distraction, 'How shall I give thee

---

[1] This term, of course, is conveniently used for the unnamed author of chaps. xl-lv in our Book of Isaiah.

up?' He is a Prophet because he sees in the tragedy of his home the tragedy of Israel, for to him, as to some other Prophets, Jehovah is the husband of Israel. It follows that he thinks of Jehovah Himself as suffering because the Israel whom He loves sins and sins and sins. The one phrase already quoted would be enough to prove this. 'How shall I give thee up?' (Hosea xi. 8) is Jehovah's cry as His righteousness struggles with His love. Can this be called anything but vicarious suffering, and vicarious suffering rooting in the corporate idea of Covenant? The concept of Covenant, indeed, is fundamental with Hosea, a Covenant in some ways like marriage. Whether Hosea saved Gomer we do not know, but he is sure that somehow Jehovah will save Israel. 'I will heal their back-slidings, I will love them freely' (Hosea xiv. 4). Yet we need to say 'somehow' for Hosea does not tell us how the heart of Israel is to be changed, how the character of the nation is to lose its love of sin. Yet he has come nearer the truth than any before him. He is sure that Jehovah will do a kinsman's part for Israel (Hosea xiii. 14).

There is no need to show in detail how every one of the greater Prophets, in his own way and degree, shares this strange antinomy of the soul. Only some leading passages will be named. For instance, it throbs behind the first oracle in our Book of Isaiah. With him the idea that most of his people will perish because of their unrighteousness, yet a few will be saved, is specially clear. For insatnce, he called one of his sons 'Speed-spoil-haste-prey' (Maher-shalal-hash-baz) and another 'Remnant-return' (Shear-Jashub). But it is the story of his Call (Isaiah vi) that is most significant. The societary concept appears in his cry when once he has seen the Holy One: 'Woe is me! for I am undone; because I am a man of unclean lips, and I dwell in the midst of a people of unclean lips.' A new idea appears when he is told his message: 'Hear ye continually, but understand not; and see ye continually, but perceive not. Make the heart of this people fat, and make their eyes heavy, and shut their eyes; lest they see with their eyes, and hear with their ears, and understand with their hearts, and turn again, and be healed.' A modern would sum the truth here stated under 'the law of atrophy'. He would say that if a man steadfastly refuses to use one of his faculties, the time comes when he cannot use it, for an unused faculty atrophies. He would say that this is one of 'the laws of life' or 'the laws of Nature'. If he were a theist, he must needs add that God made the 'laws of

Nature', and works through them. This means that if a man steadily refuses to see, he gradually blinds himself, and that God so made him that this will happen. In effect, Jehovah says to Isaiah, 'You are to preach and preach and preach and men will heed you less and less'.[1] No wonder the Prophet cries out, 'For how long?' but there is little to comfort him. His beloved Judah is to be 'waste without inhabitant'—it is to be like an old tree, of which time after time everything perishes except the stump. Yet the stump will not altogether die, for it is not altogether unholy. To change the figure, the Prophet is to prophesy through forty years of darkness, yet in the darkness there shall shine one little star. In other words, Isaiah looks forward to a lifetime in which his mind is to be torn between love of his nation and love of his God. By this vicarious agony, a few will be saved.

There is no need to show in detail that Jeremiah is rent by two strong passions—the passion for righteousness, or, as a Hebrew would prefer to say, the passion for God, and a passionate love for his sinful people. It is this that makes his story so poignant. It is this that made him for forty or fifty years a Prophet in spite of himself. If the second of these passions had been absent, he would have been able to stand aside and watch events, but this he could not do. If, on the other hand, he had not been consumed, like Jehovah Himself, with a passion for righteousness, he would not have inexorably demanded it. For the wicked he has no pity. There is an instance in the twelfth chapter. In its first verses he pleads with Jehovah, just because He is righteous, to spare the wicked no longer, for they are the curse of his people. Yet he harbours an ultimate hope, for he believes that the day will come when Israel will be righteous and therefore prosperous. For instance, it was this happy hope that once filled his dreams and made his 'sleep sweet unto' him (Jeremiah xxxi. 26). Only a man who is deeply in love with his people, fundamentally one with them, can rejoice in a hope that he does not himself expect to share (cf. Jeremiah xxix. 4–14). Up to this point, however, this Prophet does not carry the teaching of his predecessors much farther. He makes his own great contribution to the development of the doctrine in another way. There was a current proverb in his days that ran 'The fathers have eaten sour grapes and the children's teeth are set on edge' (Jeremiah xxxi. 29). It is not clear what the common people meant by this proverb. It may

[1] There was a brief, exceptional period in the crisis of Sennacherib's invasion.

either be, 'We are suffering for the sins of our fathers, and we cannot help ourselves', or 'We are suffering for the sins of our fathers, and this is not as it ought to be if Jehovah is righteous'. Perhaps the latter is the more likely meaning. In either case, however, Jeremiah gives an original answer to the complaint: 'Every one shall die for his own iniquity; every man that eateth the sour grapes, his teeth shall be set on edge' (Jeremiah xxxi. 30). In other words, here he revolts against the societary or corporate account of human nature and asserts its individual side. It is true, as seen above, that room has always to be found for both concepts, however difficult this may be, and if the rest of Jeremiah's prophecies are taken into account, he can be accused of inconsistency, for he has also hope for the nation, and this is an example of the societary idea.[1] But, since no one has even yet succeeded in logically or even psychologically reconciling these two truths, Jeremiah is not to be blamed for failing to do so. His achievement is that he asserts the truth of individualism. Yet this does not mean that he claims that Jehovah will save wicked men, so long as they remain wicked, for, as already stated, he holds unwaveringly that Jehovah will punish the wicked. The sequel in his greatest chapter is different. He declares that Jehovah is going to turn wicked men into righteous men. This is the teaching of the prophecy of the New Covenant, which follows the quotation of the proverb (Jeremiah xxxi. 31–4). It is clear that this change of heart must come to men one by one, and the Prophet says this in set terms (verse 34). To use a later phrase, Jeremiah teaches the need for individual conversion. Again, the passage implies a deep concept of sin. To use later terms once more, Jeremiah says that no mere attempt to alter outward behaviour will serve, for a man can only give up sinning if his heart is changed. There is still something lacking, indeed, for Jeremiah does not say how this change is to come about, apart from the assertion that God will make it: 'In their heart will I write [my law].' In other words, he asserts the certainty of the change, but leaves its method open. He goes on, however, to make two other assertions: that this New Covenant is eternal, and that change of heart will bring prosperity and happiness to wicked Jerusalem (verses 35–40). In other words, the Prophet makes righteousness fundamental, and happiness its sequel. To return to the main point, Jeremiah carries forward the

---

[1] E.g. in the same chapter Jeremiah has a great oracle of the restoration of Ephraim, considered as a whole (Jeremiah xxxi. 15–20).

doctrine of salvation in two ways—two, yet so closely related as almost to be one—he sees that there is a problem of the individual that God must and will meet, and he sees that there is no salvation without a change of character.

The ideas that mark the earlier Written Prophets recur in Ezekiel. There are, for instance, few examples of the combination of love for Israel with devotion to righteousness (that is, to Jehovah) so moving as the passage that tells of the death of the Prophet's wife and its sequel (Ezekiel xxiv. 15–27, xxxiii. 21–33). When suddenly 'the desire of [his] eyes' is taken from Ezekiel he does not mourn, in order that this may be an example to the captives in Babylon that they are not to mourn when Jerusalem, their beloved city, falls. There is no hint that the Prophet's wife was a wicked woman, but there is to be no mourning for Jerusalem because she is so vile. Yet, on the other hand, the presupposition of the story is that the captives and Ezekiel himself so love Jerusalem that the news 'The city is smitten' would naturally strike them down with sorrow. Indeed, Ezekiel's love for Jerusalem is so intense that he can only think of a restored nation in terms of a restored city, lying around a restored Temple (Ezekiel xl–xlviii). Similarly, Ezekiel repeats and expands Jeremiah's individualistic teaching as though there were no such thing as a societary element in human nature (Ezekiel xviii), yet elsewhere the societary idea is almost universal in his oracles. For instance, he has long chapters that symbolize Ephraim and Judah as Jehovah's adulterous wives, and this would mean nothing without the societary idea. Yet this Prophet, like Jeremiah, makes his own contribution to the doctrine of salvation. Jeremiah avoids the phrase, 'the Spirit of Jehovah', perhaps because the false prophets used it to describe the origin of their ecstatic utterances. Ezekiel, on the other hand, uses it frequently. For the present purpose, the important passages are those that carry forward Jeremiah's doctrine of the changed heart (Ezekiel xi. 19 f., xviii. 31, xxxvi. 25–7). Here there is a dual use of the term 'spirit'. The Prophet promises that Jehovah will give men each a 'new spirit' and that He will give them His Spirit. It is implied that the second gift carries with it the first. It may be noticed that Ezekiel also uses the notion of the gift of the 'Spirit of Jehovah' in a societary way, for this is to be the secret of the life of the new Israel (Ezekiel xxxvii. 1–14). It is to be noted, too, that there is here a new use of the term 'Spirit'. In earlier Israel the 'Spirit of

Jehovah' is given to some particular man that he may 'work mightily' for Israel (e.g. Judges xiv. 19), and the ecstatic state of prophets is also ascribed to this gift (e.g. 1 Samuel x. 10–13). Ezekiel says that it is by this gift that bad men are to be made good men, and he does not limit the gift to particular men. Both these ideas mark a great advance in the doctrine of the Spirit.

There are two other features of the situation in which Ezekiel found himself that should be mentioned. He was the pastor of a flock of Hebrews who had been 'carried captive' in the first deportation of Judah in 597 B.C. With these men, the societary or corporate sense must have been very strong. Even more than the 'remnant' who had been faithful to earlier Prophets, they must have been faithful to their God and their race, or they would not have been steadfast in exile. They would, in consequence, feel a special solidarity with each other. Again, these men would join Ezekiel's flock each by his own choice. It is very unlikely that every Israelite in exile was faithful. Even among Ezekiel's hearers there were those who came to hear his sermons in the mood in which men go to concerts (Ezekiel xxxiii. 30–3), a very common phenomenon still. Of the faithful hearers each man, or at most each family, would be faithful *from choice*. In other words, the mere historical situation imposed individualism upon Israel. It has imposed it, in greater or less degree, ever since. In Ezekiel and his flock both the societary and individual elements in human nature were strong, and it was thereby that they survived. To use Old Testament phrases, it was to such a flock that the promise came that Israel should be 'cleansed' from its iniquities and be 'saved' (Ezekiel xxxvi. 29, 33, xxxvii. 23). From this it is not a very far cry to the notion that it was through the faithfulness of a few that all Israel was to find this cleansing and salvation. In other words, the way was ready for Deutero-Isaiah.

It is necessary here to distinguish between what these Prophets *said* and what they *were* and *did*. Their message has often been briefly summed: they taught that there is one almighty and righteous God, that He punishes the sinful and blesses the righteous, that the only way for the sinful to escape punishment is to turn from sin, and that prosperity is the inevitable sequel of righteousness. Jeremiah and Ezekiel's additions to this teaching have just been named.

But there is something more than this in what the Prophets *were*

They were men who were faithful both to God and to Israel. They loved the righteous God *and* their sinful people. The two passions tore their hearts and made them 'men of sorrows'. This leads to what they *did*. Through this double faithfulness they saved the Remnant and through the Remnant they saved Israel unto this day. They agonized that they might save. This is mere fact of history. The truth that salvation is by vicarious suffering—suffering that is vicarious because it is societary—was not yet enunciated, but it was practised. The time had now come when it was to be enunciated.

There is a contrast between the teaching of Deutero-Isaiah and that of his predecessors, but it is only a contrast of emphasis. While they had taught that Jehovah would save His people, their emphasis had been upon the truth that He was punishing and would punish the sinful nation (and all other nations, because they too were sinful). While Deutero-Isaiah teaches, like them, that Jehovah punishes the wicked (e.g. in chap. xlviii), his emphasis lies on the salvation of the righteous. At the beginning of his prophecies he declares, indeed, that Israel has paid twice the penalty of her sins (Isaiah xl. 2). Punishment, therefore, is over and now Jehovah will save. It is this reiterated message that gives its peculiar sweetness to the general teaching of Deutero-Isaiah. It is no accident that so many of the scripture passages in the *libretto* of Handel's 'Messiah' are chosen from the oracles of this Prophet.

There is a corresponding change in the meaning of Jehovah's 'righteousness'. In three passages the word is used along with 'salvation' (Isaiah xlv. 8, xlvi. 13, li. 5; cf. lvi. 1, lxi. 10), not in the modern way of contrast, but as expressing complementary truths. Indeed, the two together almost make a single idea. When Jehovah cries, 'My righteousness is near. My salvation is gone forth', he is saying the same thing twice over—He is declaring that because He is righteous He will save. What else should a righteous God do for a faithful Remnant?

The use of the three terms 'save', 'ransom' and 'redeem' (or 'do a kinsman's part') is here important. The term 'save' had been used of deliverance from external evils (e.g. Judges ii. 16; 1 Samuel xiv. 23) and it is so used by Deutero-Isaiah (e.g. Isaiah xliii. 11–13), but it is at least doubtful whether it had so far been used about deliverance from moral evils,[1] and it is not used in this way

---

[1] Ezekiel xxxvi. 29, xxxvii. 23 come nearest.

by Deutero-Isaiah.[1] The second term, 'ransom', had been used of the Exodus (Micah vi. 4; Deuteronomy vii. 8), and it is now used of deliverance from Exile (Isaiah li. 11), but not deliverance from sin. The uses of the third term 'redeem' ('do a kinsman's part') are more significant. The word is rare before Deuteronomy (Genesis xlviii. 16; 2 Samuel xiv. 11), but it had been used of the deliverance from Egypt (Exodus xv. 13) and of deliverance from Exile (Micah iv. 10). Deutero-Isaiah uses it in the latter sense (Isaiah xliii. 1, xliv. 22 f., xlvii. 4; cf. lx. 16), but also in close connexion with deliverance from sin (Isaiah xliv. 21–3). As this last use marks a stage in the development of the doctrine of salvation, the passage may be quoted in full: 'Remember these things, O Jacob; and Israel, for thou art my servant; I have formed thee; thou art my servant; O Israel, thou shouldst not forget me. I have blotted out, as a thick cloud, thy transgressions, and, as a cloud, thy sins; return unto me, for I have *redeemed* thee. Sing, O ye heavens, for the LORD hath done it; shout, ye lower parts of the earth; break forth into singing, ye mountains, O forest, and every tree therin; for the LORD hath *redeemed* Jacob, and will glorify himself in Israel' (Isaiah xliv. 21–3; cf. lxiii. 9). The nature of the connexion between the forgiveness of sins and the truth that Jehovah is Israel's Kinsman is not examined in this lyrical passage, yet a connexion is made. It goes without saying that for a prophet who enunciated more clearly than any earlier prophet the doctrine of ethical monotheism, there can be no physical reference when he says that the LORD 'kinsmans' Israel. Jehovah will save Israel from her disasters, as a kinsman should, but more—this Kinsman blots out sin.

Whether the four famous 'Songs of the Servant' (Isaiah xlii. 1–9, xlix. 1–6, l. 4–9. lii. 13–liii. 12) were written by Deutero-Isaiah or not, it is best to treat them separately, especially as they bring the doctrine of salvation in the Prophets to its climax. While there are some problems about them that are still warmly debated, happily their main burden for this doctrine is plain. While the phrase, 'the servant of Jehovah', had been used earlier of such heroes as Abraham, Caleb, and David, its use of Moses had been peculiarly common in the recent writings of the Deuteronomists.[2]

---

[1] The Editors of the *Oxford Hebrew Lexicon* think that the corresponding noun 'salvation' approximates to this in such a passage as Isaiah lii. 7–10 (cf. lx. 18), but this seems doubtful.

[2] It occurs seventeen times in the Deuteronomic parts of Joshua. There are earlier instances in Exodus xiv. 31; Numbers xii. 7 f.

Again, Jeremiah, also a comparatively recent writer, had been the first to use the phrase of the people Israel (xxx. 10, xlvi. 27 *f.*). Deutero-Isaiah has this last use, both of Israel as sinful (e.g. Isaiah xlii. 19) and as redeemed (e.g. Isaiah xliv. 21). In the Servant Songs, however, the phrase is used, neither of the sinful, nor of the redeemed, but, as in the older stories, of a redeemer. It is possible that this use was immediately suggested by the almost contemporary Deuteronomic use of the term for Moses, who had been Jehovah's 'servant' in the rescue of Israel from Egypt. It has been seen above that the story of Moses illustrates in no slight way the doctrine of salvation, and that the societary idea is the key to the story. In any case, the idea of redemption is the *motif* of the Servant Songs.

In referring to the Servant Songs one by one, the Servant may be spoken of as an individual, since this is the Prophet's own method, without thereby deciding whether the phrase stands for an individual or the Hebrew nation or a part of that nation. In the first Song (Isaiah xlii. 1-9) two or three points may be noted. The Servant is unlike the earlier Written Prophets in two ways: in the first place, he is not to be clamant, but quiet, yet, through the Spirit of Jehovah, he is to succeed in saving the 'dimly burning wick' of Israel; and in the second place, through him the righteous Jehovah will save not Israel only, but the Gentiles, too. The nobility of this doctrine appears when we remember that Israel at the time was under the heel of the Gentiles.[1]

In the second Song (Isaiah xlix. 1-6) the truth that Jehovah will give 'salvation' both to Israel and the Gentiles is more fully drawn out. In addition, there are the ideas that the Servant was born to be Jehovah's weapon of salvation but had seemed to fail, that now he is to succeed, and that in this success Jehovah is to be 'glorified'.

The third Song (Isaiah l. 4-9) stresses the fact that the Servant suffers persecution, yet that, in spite of his meekness, he 'sets his face like a flint' to his God-given task, and that Jehovah will see to it that by this method he will succeed.

The fourth and greatest Song (Isaiah lii. 13-liii. 12) falls readily, as the Revised Version shows, into five stanzas. The first announces the subject of the whole Song, the 'prosperity' or success of the Servant. This is sure, even though it is a wonder of

---

[1] It is possible that the idea of the salvation of the Gentiles had been anticipated (Isaiah ii. 2-4, xi. 1-9, xix. 19-25), but many scholars think that these passages are post-Exilic.

wonders that will astonish nations and their kings. In the second stanza the thought is developed that the ground of this wonder is the Servant's present plight. Is he not 'a man of sorrows'? Does not every one turn from him as men turn from a leper? The third stanza is the most famous description of vicarious suffering in the literature of the world. The Servant's suffering is vicarious in two ways: he suffers for others' sins, and thereby he saves others. His 'chastisement' is others' 'peace'; his 'stripes' wound him, but heal others. The fourth stanza dwells upon the Servant's submission to this fate. Unlike Job, for instance, he does not writhe under sufferings that he himself has not deserved. On the contrary, he 'humbles himself' even unto death, without a word of complaint, and men think that now he is just 'dead and done with'. But the last stanza returns to the subject of the first: this is Jehovah's way of success. The Servant's suffering is like the pain of travail; it is the strange path to joy. But the nature of 'prosperity' or success appears now more clearly than in the first stanza; to save is success. Jehovah's 'righteous servant' sets many right with God, for he 'bears their iniquities'. They are now no longer bad men, but righteous.[1] This is joy, for this is success. As is well known, there are three current answers to the question, 'Whom did the Prophet mean by "The Servant of Jehovah"?' Some think that the writer is describing an individual—as Moses, or Jeremiah, or the writer himself, or even Jehoiachin—or some such individual idealized. Others think that the Servant personifies the Godly Remnant, faithful even in Exile. Yet others think that, as in the rest of Deutero-Isaiah, the Servant is the whole Israelite people. This question leads to another: 'Whom does the Servant save?' If he is an individual, the answer is that he saves his own people, Israel. Yet, if the earlier Servant Songs are taken into consideration, it seems necessary to add that he saves the Gentiles, too. Similarly, if the Servant stands for the Godly Remnant, the Remnant is to save the rest of Israel and the Gentiles. If the Servant be the whole of Israel, it would seem that the underlying idea is that this one nation is suffering to save other nations. Recent exposition, however, suggests that to insist on sharp alternatives is here a mistake, for the thought of a Hebrew writer would readily pass

[1] It seems to the writer that this is the meaning of the Hebrew term translated 'justify' required by the context. Possibly it should be 'vindicate the cause of, save', as in the *Oxford Hebrew Lexicon*, but to explain the word in the sense, 'treat as righteous', seems alien to the context. The main lines of the exposition of this Song are clear, in spite of the difficulties of the Hebrew text.

from an individual Hebrew to the Godly Remnant to which he belonged, and again to the whole nation of which the Remnant was part. When one remembers the strength of the societary concept in Israel, this is perhaps closest to the writer's own mind. 'A single Hebrew or the Remnant or the people Israel?' he might have said, 'I don't think of them separately like that!' It is important, however, to notice that on *any* interpretation, the societary idea is the dominant one. To revert to the Prophet's own use and speak of the Servant as an individual, it is plain that, like St. Paul, the Servant is a 'Hebrew of Hebrews'—that he is so loyal to his people that for their sakes he has 'great sorrow and unceasing pain in [his] heart, for [he] could wish that [he himself] were anathema' for his 'brethren's sake' (Romans ix. 2 *f.*). Indeed, he feels like this even for the Gentiles! He is both 'one with' his people and 'one with' all mankind—so much so that he feels that their sins are his. On the other hand, he is loyal also to the righteousness of God, for his very name is 'The Servant of the LORD'. It is the tension between these two loyalties that is his deepest pang. If, like some exiled Israelites, he had just given up his worship of Jehovah and merged in the general Babylonian population, he would neither have borne the outward sufferings that befell the faithful Israelite nor the deeper sorrow of the broken heart, for his heart broke under the tension between his love of God and his love of men. But—and here is this Prophet's climacteric discovery—the Servant submitted willingly to this fate, for he knew that thereby he would save others, even though they are sinful. In the Servant Songs the belief that by vicarious suffering—vicarious, because it is integral to the societary concept —the Servant will succeed in saving, is the root of the whole matter. Is this to be called 'vicarious punishment'? If by 'punishment' the outward plight of the exiles is meant, one might say that the faithful exiles bore the wrongs that for unfaithful Israelites were punishment. If, however, the distinctive suffering of the Servant—the tearing of the man in two between loyalty to God and loyalty to Israel—is considered, this cannot so easily be called 'punishment', and it was this suffering that made him great. If, finally, by 'punishment' we mean degradation of character, it is clear that this did not fall upon the Servant at all. On the contrary, his submissive suffering ennobled his character. It is better, therefore, to speak of 'vicarious suffering' and not of 'vicarious punishment'.

After Deutero-Isaiah, the prophets add nothing on the present subject to the truths already enunciated. It has often been pointed out that they don't all maintain the lofty teaching of Deutero-Isaiah about the salvation of the Gentiles. In a famous passage in Trito-Isaiah (Isaiah lx)[1] the Gentiles are to be saved, but they are to be 'hewers of wood' and 'drawers of water' for Israel. This is a kind of mitigated Universalism. In a passage that has somehow been pieced into Trito-Isaiah (Isaiah lxiii. 1–6) the societary idea appears in a conqueror that 'cometh from Edom, with dyed garments from Bozrah', but here, however legitimately the passage may be spiritualized by Christian writers, the original description depicts a warrior who saves Israel by butchering its hated foe. On the other hand, Universalism is, of course, the burden of the great Book of Jonah. For the rest, the only outstanding passage in these Prophets on the present subject is one that some ascribe to Deutero-Isaiah (Isaiah lxi). Here there is an 'anointed'[2] Prophet who has 'the spirit of the LORD' to 'bind up the brokenhearted'. Even this Prophet, however, is also to tell of 'the day of vengeance of our God', apparently against the Gentiles. The element of value, and it is considerable, is that the concept of 'the spirit of Jehovah' is connected with the societary idea. It is this that binds the Prophet to God and this that informs his message to 'the meek'. The contrast with an earlier concept of men of the Spirit is very marked (e.g. Judges xiv. 19; 1 Samuel xi. 6 f.).

If the exposition of the last two chapters is correct, we have in the Hebrew Prophets a striking example of a common phenomenon. Often great principles are imperfectly practised long before they are clearly understood and plainly enunciated. The history of democracy in England would give an instance. In the case of the Written Prophets, in particular, attention has not sufficiently been given to what they *were*, in distinction from, or rather in addition to, what they *said*. From Moses onwards they *were*, each in his own way and degree, saviours. They saved Israel because they were both 'men of God' and men of Israel. As time went on the concept of what they saved their people from grew deeper, but always they saved because they could neither be separated from God nor from Israel. They were the victims of a twofold passion, and this duality was the secret of their success. It was at once their agony and their glory. At last, in Deutero-Isaiah, the

---

[1] 'Trito-Isaiah' is a convenient title for the oracles gathered in Isaiah lvi–lxvi.

[2] The verb corresponds to 'Messiah'.

E

principle that underlay their whole lives from the beginning was enunciated. It was the principle that, since man is societary, man may be saved by vicarious suffering. Even Deutero-Isaiah did not fully draw out all that the principle involves, as will appear later, but the three great Prophets of the sixth century mark the zenith of Old Testament teaching on the subject of salvation.[1] Jeremiah saw that salvation means salvation from *sinfulness* and that this demands a change of character; Ezekiel declared that this change would be wrought by the *Spirit* of God; Deutero-Isaiah taught that men may be saved, even from sin, by *vicarious suffering*, if it be willingly borne. Even here, however, it is God, and not the Servant, who saves, or rather, it is God's good pleasure to save through His Servant. 'Behold, *my* servant shall succeed.' In the last of the Servant Songs, whether the writer was conscious of it or not, there is a poignant description of the ideal prophet. Every prophet, in some degree, realized this ideal.

[1] For the references in Deutero-Isaiah to the 'lamb' (Isaiah liii. 7) and to the sin-offering (or rather the guilt-offering—Isaiah liii. 10) see pp. 82 *ff*., below.

CHAPTER VI

THE PSALMS OF SUFFERING AND SIN

AMONG the psalms that deal most closely with the subject of salvation those that relate to the Messiah have already been discussed. Others will be named at a later point. Here some psalms are considered that connect more or less closely with the doctrine of the Written Prophets about sin and salvation. These fall broadly into two groups that may be called respectively 'Psalms of Sufferers' and 'Psalms of Sinners' (or Penitential Psalms). It is fairly well agreed that all these psalms are post-Exilic. They therefore naturally follow a chapter on the Written Prophets.

As is well known, there are Hebrew terms (*'anav, 'ani*) that may be translated either 'poor' or 'meek'. The reason is that under Persian and Hellenistic rule those who were faithful to Jehovah would usually be 'poor'. Occasionally a righteous man, such as Mordecai or Daniel, might succeed at Shushan, but this would be an exception there, and probably still more exceptional at the local court at Jerusalem. There it would be the supple, the fawning, and the unscrupulous that would 'get on', and the righteous, who would not descend to these arts, would be left in poverty. This fact lies, for instance, behind the Book of Ecclesiastes. The term 'meek' therefore rightly combines the idea of the 'righteous' with that of the 'poor'.[1]

A number of the psalms express the appeal of the 'meek' to God. Their plea is that a righteous God ought to save righteous men. This means that, for the writers of these psalms, as for Deutero-Isaiah, the concepts of righteousness and salvation are not contradictory but complementary. In the psalms, as in Deutero-Isaiah, the two terms are very frequent. Psalm after psalm bases upon the idea that a righteous God ought to punish the wicked and save the righteous (e.g. Psalms xxxv, lxxi, xcviii). 'The LORD hath made known his salvation: his righteousness hath he openly showed in the sight of the nations' (Psalm xcviii. 2) is a typical instance of the connexion between the two ideas. Similarly, the future King of Israel is to be righteous, and therefore he will 'deliver the needy' (Psalm lxxii).

[1] For a further discussion of the subject of this paragraph see the writer's *Bible Doctrine of Society*, pp. 189 ff.; cf. pp. 200, 372.

But from what will Jehovah save the 'meek'? Here we come to the three terms that commonly describe salvation. There is no doubt that the first of them, 'save' (with its noun 'salvation'), is frequently used of deliverance from trouble and suffering. The editors of the *Oxford Hebrew Lexicon* think that 'spiritual ideas' are sometimes included, but they don't clearly indicate to which passages they refer. The prevalent idea is that the good man is to be saved from trouble, not that the bad man is to be saved from sin.

Of the two terms, 'ransom' and 'redeem', the latter term is not so common in the Psalms as one might expect. Some will think that the idea of the great Redeemer or Kinsman is the ruling concept of Psalm ciii (verse 4). There is, however, only one clear instance of the use of either of these terms for salvation from sin (Psalm cxxx. 8). This will be named later. The ruling concept for both is deliverance from trouble and sorrow and the threat of death.

In the Psalter there is traceable a change in the concept of the word 'holy'. Originally the term had meant 'religiously separate' or 'numinous', but when, through the testimony of the Prophets, the truth that Jehovah is 'righteous' had been firmly established in the minds of the better Israelites, the two concepts were bound to react on each other. In the psalms the old use is still the common one, but such psalms as xv, xcix, and ciii show how the concept of 'righteousness' and the concept of 'holiness' began to lie side by side and to influence each other. The idea is not distant that God is 'holy' and separate, at least in part, because He is altogether 'righteous' and pure. We ourselves use the word 'holy' both in a ritual and an ethical sense, as a consideration of two such phrases as 'a holy place' and 'a holy man' would show, though with us the idea of the awesome is often almost altogether absent. The two concepts fuse in Psalm li, as will appear below.

It is remarkable that the doctrine of the Suffering Servant has left few clear traces in literature that belongs to the post-Exilic period. The nearest approximation to the doctrine is in some of the Psalms of Sufferers. It is doubtful whether their writers were thinking of the Songs of the Servant, for it seems likely that if they were, they would have come nearer to a complete expression of their teaching. There are, however, a few psalms where some of the ideas in this doctrine appear more or less plainly. In Psalm xlix the writer is a sufferer speaking to the world of successful sinners and telling them that in the end they will be punished and the righteous will triumph.[1] Incidentally he declares (verses 7 f.) that the wicked cannot pay the costly price needed to ransom a brother. One phrase has even been translated, 'Cannot give wer-gild to God'. This might be taken to imply that a righteous man can do so. The societary concept is certainly present, for it seems that the writer's experience of wicked men was that their families stood by them in case of need, and he declares that they will find that they cannot do this when God takes them in hand.

Some particular 'Psalms of Sufferers' may be mentioned. Psalm lxix falls into four parts. In the first stanza (verses 1–12), while the sufferer admits his sin, he claims to be faithful, yet he is sinking in the mire amid the scoffs of his people, and even of his kinsfolk. He sums up his faithfulness in the phrase, 'The zeal of thy house hath eaten me up'. In the second stanza (verses 13–21) he pleads with God to save him from his misery, using the terms for 'do a kinsman's part' and 'ransom' (verse 18). The third stanza cries out for punishment of his persecutors (verses 22–8). In the fourth (verses 29–36) he sings of his sure salvation and with it the salvation of all other meek men. Here (verses 27, 29) 'righteousness' and 'salvation' are synonyms, and the meek are called God's 'servants'.[2] There is here, too, the suggestion that the ultimate deliverance of one meek man will be the lot of all the meek.

Psalm xl seems to fall readily into three parts. In the first (verses 1–8) a 'poor man' describes the way in which Jehovah has delivered him, apparently in the past; in the second (verses 9 f.) he declares that he has proclaimed this gospel of salvation to every one; in the third (verses 11–17) trouble has again come upon him and he pleads for a further deliverance, and, while confident that it will come, he pleads that it may come speedily, for the wicked are now jeering at his gospel of deliverance: 'Make no tarrying, O my God.'

There is here no doctrine of salvation from sin. On the contrary, the writer asks that the wicked, who persecute him, may be 'ashamed and confounded together' by the evidence of his second deliverance. He himself has found the secret of righteousness; its source is not in the ritual system, but in obedience to the will of God (verses 6–8). For himself, he quite honestly thinks that he

---

[1] In describing this triumph, the writer adds: 'God will ransom my soul (or life) from the hand of Sheol. For he shall receive me' (verse 15). This *may* be a reference to a resurrection (cf. xvi. 10), see pp. 94 f.

[2] This term is used of the righteous some fifty times in the Psalter.

has yielded complete obedience, as the record of 'the book' of men's actions which God keeps will show. For him, Jeremiah's prophecy that God will 'write his law' in men's hearts has been fulfilled (verse 8), but this has been by his own delighted and willing consent. The two poles of his confidence are 'The LORD thinketh upon me' (verse 17) and 'I delight to do thy will, O my God' (verse 8). The word 'covenant' does not occur, but the concept that there is a sure bond between Jehovah and every single righteous man, however poor, is fundamental. Here, too, the meek are taken as a class. The gatherings of the faithful in the synagogue seem to be implied; for instance, a Hebrew might 'proclaim the glad tidings of righteousness in the great congregation'. This man, a preacher who can tell of his own deliverance, is a kind of mediator of righteousness to his spiritual kin.

It is plain that if there is any hint of vicarious suffering in these psalms at all, it is no more than an implied suggestion that if a meek man suffers faithfully, it will redound to the blessing of other *meek* men. There is no idea that the righteous may suffer to save sinners; on the contrary, the writers cry out for the punishment of the wicked. There is a psalm, however (xxii), where the last idea is absent. So far as the future of the writer's persecutors is thought of at all, it is conceived as a future of worship (verse 29). The writer also comes nearer to the *assertion*, as distinct from the *implication*, of the idea that one man's suffering has a vicarious result for other righteous sufferers. This appears if the structure of the psalm is considered. Its turning-point is the phrase, 'From the horns of the wild-ox thou hast answered me'.[1] Before this the writer pleads that he is righteous, for he has 'committed himself unto the LORD' from birth. He does not deserve to suffer, yet he suffers as if he were a 'worm and no man'. So he cries out from the midst of his persecutions, 'My God, my God, why hast thou forsaken me?' He is delivered just when the 'wild-ox' is on the point of goring him to death. Forthwith he breaks out in unrestrainable praise 'in the midst of the congregation'. Thereupon the meek rejoice with him, and there is a joyful expectation of the universal worship of God, and of the perpetual witness of the 'seed' that shall 'serve him'. After the final Servant Song, this psalm comes nearest to an enunciation of salvation by vicarious suffering.

---

[1] Readers of Sienkiewicz' *Quo Vadis* will remember the scene where a wild ox is goaded into the arena with a fainting and naked Christian girl bound between its horns, and a gigantic Christian slave grasps the horns and breaks the wild ox's back.

Of the 'Penitential' psalms (Psalms vi, xxxii, xxxviii, li, cii, cxxx, cxliii) two (vi and cii) do not contain any express confession of sin and might therefore be classed with the Psalms of Sufferers. They exhibit an early form of a certain attitude to Sheol or death, but this is discussed later. The writers of the other five all confess their dire sin, though some of them plead for salvation from persecution as well as from sin. In two psalms (Psalms cii, cxxx) the sense of the writer's solidarity with Israel is explicit. All plead with Jehovah to forgive and save. Psalm xxxii, in particular, is a great Psalm of Forgiveness. Here, too (verses 7 f.), the idea of Psalm xl recurs: that the secret of religion is complete obedience. It seems probable that the 'forgiveness' for which the writer longs does not mean the mere escape from the trouble that sin brings, but something deeper. In the *De Profundis* (Psalm cxxx) there is no mention of persecution or trouble at all and here the idea of salvation from sin itself seems quite clear (verses 3 f.) Indeed, the psalm ends with the one undoubted instance where the word 'ransom' (*padhah*) is used in the Old Testament for salvation *from sin*: 'O Israel, hope in the LORD; for with the LORD there is mercy, and with him is plenteous redemption [ransom]. And he shall ransom Israel from all his *iniquities*.'

In these five psalms there are certain common ideas. The writers all confess their sins, yet at the same time they love God. It is the combination of these two things that makes true repentance. Again, behind their plea for salvation there is a sure confidence that, however plainly God may seem to have deserted them, He has not really done so. The writers are sure that He will save. Again, the opinion that in these psalms Israel is personalized, and that it is the deliverance of the nation and not of individual men that is meant, seems almost incomprehensible, for there are few more personal poems in all literature, and after the Exile the concept of personality was well developed in Israel.[1] The most that can be said is that behind the writer's own experience of trouble there lies the concept that other 'meek' men are suffering, too. The kind of trouble meant is chiefly persecution. This defines also the kind of salvation meant. The concept of deliverance from sin itself, however, has begun to appear.

At this point, however, Psalm li almost stands in a class by itself. The writer only once refers to trouble, and then he thinks of it, not as due to persecution, but as God's own act. It is God who has

[1] See, for instance, the writer's *Bible Doctrine of Society*, chap. iv.

'broken his bones' (verse 8). For the rest, he writes wholly of sin, not of trouble. There is no limit at all to his sense of sin. He confesses that he has been sinful from birth.[1] He confesses that he is sinful through and through. He knows that sin is no mere matter of outward acts, but of inward nature, and his nature is altogether contaminate. He looks for joy, but for him the ground of joy is not prosperity, but purity. He pleads with God to make him over again: 'Create in me a clean heart, O God.' The recurrence of Jeremiah's discovery that the only hope for the sinful is change of heart is clear. The psalmist does not say much of the way by which God will re-create his heart, but what he does say is significant. Here he, like Ezekiel, adds the word 'spirit' to the teaching of Jeremiah. Again, like Ezekiel, he uses the word both of God and man almost in the same breath (verses 10–12). The adjectives that he uses with the word are all significant: 'stedfast', 'holy', 'willing'. Here is one of the two passages where the word 'holy', which is the characteristic description of the Spirit of God in the New Testament, appears in the Old (cf. Isaiah lxiii. 10 f.). At last we have a plea that God will change a bad man into a good man. This writer knows the true definition of salvation.

From the second part of the psalm (verses 13–17),[2] it appears that the writer is a preacher. He is convinced that a man who does not himself know the miracle of a new heart cannot effectively preach its need and possibility to others. And he feels that until he does so preach he is guilty of the blood of his hearers. There is here explicitly a form of the societary concept that we found to be only implicit in others of the Penitential Psalms. The writer is sure that when he himself has been made over again, he will be able to lead other sinners to the same experience (verse 13). Finally, writing in the post-Exilic days, when the Temple was the centre of Hebrew life, he sobs out the truth that what God demands is not mere Temple ritual, but a broken heart. This God 'will not despise'. It is a humble phrase, but at the heart of it there is a 'sure and certain hope' of salvation, and of the kind of salvation that he has asked for. In this psalm the Old Testament tells at last the whole truth about sin. Yet it is not a pessimistic psalm. It might even be called 'The Psalm of the Successful Preacher'.

[1] This, and not any assertion of 'original sin', is the meaning of verse 5.
[2] There is general agreement that verses 18 f. are a later addition. See p. 65.

CHAPTER VII

THE POST-EXILIC SACRIFICES

IN order to understand certain New Testament passages, it is necessary to examine some parts of the post-Exilic sacrificial system in detail. It is best to begin, however, with some general subjects. The first relates to the meaning of the term 'sacrifice', for the word is used to-day in many different senses.[1] In religious terminology, it usually means that a worshipper denies himself in order to give something to his god, or to do something for his god, or to suffer something for his faith. In brief, anything in religion that 'costs' is called 'sacrifice'. In this sense there was very much 'sacrifice' in Judaism in and about the time of Jesus. To keep the Jewish law in Rome cost unpopularity and sometimes persecution; to maintain the local synagogue would often mean self-sacrifice; to husband resources to pay for a journey to Jerusalem to keep Passover would often mean self-denial; often it would cost a poor man more than he could easily afford to pay tithes or to contribute to the Temple the half-shekel required from every Israelite. It is not in this sense, however, that the word 'sacrifice' is used here. It is plain that it has no special reference either to ritual or to the Jews. Here the word is used of offerings made in the Jewish Temple, and of their significance apart from their cost.

For the present purpose—the discovery of the New Testament doctrine of salvation—it is necessary to describe the sacrificial system, or rather certain parts of it, in the period that preceded the Birth of Christ, and then to ask: 'What was the *meaning* of these parts of the system to the devout and intelligent Jew in the first Christian century?' For the facts there is fairly abundant evidence. For the *meaning* of the ritual there is hardly any direct evidence at all, and we need to fall back on the implications of the facts.

This limitation of theme excludes happily any discussion of the *origins* of sacrifice, either in the ancient world at large or in Israel itself. Our questions relate to the intelligent Jew after the Exile.

---

[1] For instance, sometimes 'sacrifice' means 'suffering for others', sometimes 'dying for others', and sometimes it is almost a synonym for 'worship', as in the phrase 'sacrifice of praise and thanksgiving', which recalls the *literal* meaning of the word. Under some definitions *all* doctrines of the Atonement are 'sacrificial'.

A man who had learnt to think of God as 'the high and lofty One that inhabiteth eternity', could not permanently entertain ideas that were obviously inconsistent with this concept. It is common in history for a ritual to be retained, or largely retained, long after the ideas that originally gave rise to it have been outgrown. For instance, some experts tell us that in Christian Churches the altar is usually on the east because originally men faced the east in worship in order to greet the rising sun. Again, it is surely incredible that when such a man as Gamaliel or Saul of Tarsus joined in the eating of a 'peace-offering', he thought that he was eating his God! Again, while there are traces in the earliest of the Old Testament documents that once upon a time Jehovah, like other gods, enjoyed the reek of a burning animal (e.g. Genesis viii. 21; 1 Samuel xxvi. 19), there is no hint of such an idea after the days of the Written Prophets. Again, the best Jews surely did not think of the priests, when they ate parts of the sin-offering, as 'sin-eaters'. Or, again, whatever be the truth of the suggestion that there was a totemistic element in the sources of Hebrew sacrifice, it is incredible that the idea survived, for this would mean that Israel had a complex of totems—both animal and vegetable—and this is consistent neither with totemism itself nor with the final Jewish concept of God. Some modern writings make it necessary to say these rather obvious things.

Again, it seems plain that for an intelligent Jew the ritual was now symbolic—that is, when rightly used, it was an 'outward and vivible sign' of spiritual worship. It is hard for us to accommodate the concept of spiritual worship with the killing of animals, but this is just an extreme example of the difficulty most men have in entering into the meaning of a ritual to which they are not accustomed. Nothing is easier than to ridicule other people's ritual, few things harder than to enter sympathetically into it. If, however, any one makes a sustained effort to do so, it is possible for him to feel the real value of such a ritual as that of the Day of Atonement. There is good evidence that many devout Jews rejoiced in their ritual. The last of the psalms, for instance, could not have been written by any one who did not delight in the music of the Temple, and the earlier part of the fiftieth chapter of Ecclesiasticus thrills with joy in the splendour of a worthy High Priest on some great festival day. In the period in question, at least for the better kind of Jew, the sacrificial system was in the true sense symbolic. There is good evidence in the Jewish literature of the period that such Jews did not think that it availed *ex opere operato*.[1]

It was also sacramental—that is, it nourished the spiritual experience that it expressed.[2] It is usually thought that the last two verses of the Fifty-first Psalm are a later addition. Why did some one, after having read the psalm, add them, and why did others accept the addition? Not, surely, just because he and they wanted to push ritual in somehow, but because they felt that, when the experience so poignantly described in the psalm was theirs, they could go on to use the sacrifices of the Temple sacramentally. There were men who, having cried out for 'a clean heart' and 'a right spirit', knew that the right use of ritual would help them to find it, as on the same spot it had helped Isaiah himself (Isaiah vi).

Again, there is no need here to discuss whether the origin of sacrifice lay in the idea of gift, or communion, or propitiation, for, long before this time, the Hebrew had a master-concept that included all three—the concept of Covenant. Without the belief that Jehovah was Israel's God, and that there was or ought to be some link of fellowship between Him and every Israelite, there would have been no Temple nor any Jewish *cultus* at all. It was because they believed that Jehovah was their God that they brought Him gifts, that they joined in the sacred meal of the 'peace-offerings', that, when they felt that sin had marred their fellowship with Him, they brought sin-offerings and guilt-offerings to express their longing that fellowship might be restored. No doubt, as the centuries passed, the connotation of the concepts of gift, communion, and propitiation—particularly the last, as will be seen later—changed, yet there was continuity as well as change. It is hardly too much to say that under the concept of Covenant with a holy and benevolent God all three ideas were bound to occur.

When, however, we turn from a ritualistic system considered as a whole to its details, difficulties begin. A particular detail of an old ritual may mean one thing to an earlier generation and another to a later one, or it may even mean different things to two contemporary worshippers. When, as in the Jewish documents of the Priestly school, hardly any explanation of the symbolism is given, it may be hazardous to venture on one. Further, the reason for some details is just custom, without any explanation.

---

[1] See, for instance, Walker's *Jesus and Jewish Teaching*, pp. 249 ff.
[2] For this see chap. ii in the writer's volume on *The Sacramental Society*.

This is true even in the West, where we are accustomed to ask 'Why?' For instance, much of the religious ritual of an English coronation is followed century by century merely because 'it has always been so'. Antiquarians may try more or less successfully to explain 'the reason why' some part of this ritual was first practised, but this is not always the reason centuries later. It goes without saying that in the East the power of custom is or was much stronger than in the West, and perhaps it has always been strongest of all in religious ritual. With the Jew, a further factor needs emphasis. The sacrificial system was a part of a larger whole, the Pentateuchal Law, and every orthodox Jew believed that he should keep every one of its commands just because Jehovah had so willed it. Modern democracies expect to know 'the reason why' before a law is made, and they abandon any that seem useless, but Eastern peoples were used to obeying their rulers without requiring any explanation. 'Theirs not to reason why.' Doubtless their ruler had some reason for his behests, but they did not expect him always to explain it. This was the attitude of the Jew to Jehovah. A Christian follows the same rule more often than he thinks. He doesn't know why he is born to be a man and not a woman, an Englishman and not a Chinaman, poor and not rich, and so on. All these things he loyally accepts as the inscrutable, though doubtless wise, will of God. It was the same with a Jew when he was bidden to offer a bullock at one sacrifice and a goat at another, or when he circumcised his son on the eighth and not on the seventh day, and so on. He could no longer think of any reason why the reek of a burning animal or even the fragrance of incense should be a 'sweet-smelling savour' to Jehovah, but it was enough that the Law commanded it. People, therefore, who want to find a meaning in every detail of the ritual, for instance, of the Passover or the Day of Atonement, are probably wasting their time. The whole story of Judaism from Ezra till to-day is perhaps the greatest historical instance of unquestioning obedience to the will of God, explained or unexplained.

At this point it is necessary to examine certain items in the Temple ritual, for most of the New Testament passages that connect the Death of Christ with ritual refer to specific parts of the ritual and not to any general principles that may be supposed to underlie the whole.

The animal offerings formed the chief element in the Jewish sacrifices, and it is these that are the most important for New

Testament study. They were of three (or four) principal kinds; the 'whole burnt-offering' (often called the 'burnt-offering'), the so-called 'peace-offering', and the 'sin-offering' (with the 'guilt-offering'). In the ritual there was an important point of difference among them, and an important point of likeness. The difference lies in the answer to the question, 'What was done with the bodies?' In the 'whole burnt-offering' the whole was burnt on the great open-air altar of sacrifice; in the 'peace-offering' part was burnt on the altar, part eaten by the priests, and part eaten by the worshippers; in the 'sin-offering' and 'guilt-offering' part was burnt on the altar, and part given to the priests (Leviticus i–iii, vi. 8–vii. 38).[1] It is specially to be noted that, while the worshipper ate of his 'peace-offering', he did not eat of his 'sin-offering'. Feasting does not go with confession of sin. The point of likeness between all these kinds of sacrifice lies in the answer to the question, 'What was done with the blood?' While the worshipper himself usually slew the victim, two duties fell to the priest: to burn the whole or part of the body on the altar and to pour the blood upon or at the base of the altar (or, on the Day of Atonement, on the 'mercy-seat'). The blood always belonged to God.

Were the sin-offering and the guilt-offering only offerings for 'unwitting sins'? Many think that the Code of Leviticus implies this (Leviticus iv, v), and a passage in the Book of Numbers seems definitely to assert it (Numbers xv. 22–36). Here only two kinds of sins seem to be admitted—sins 'with a high hand' and 'unwitting sins'. The first phrase seems a strong one if it is meant to cover all known sins. There are facts on the other side. It seems impossible to hold that all the sins for which a guilt-offering was appointed were unwitting (Leviticus vi. 1–7). Again, a sin-offering was appointed for a leper (Leviticus xiii, xiv). It is possible to suppose that the leper was thought to be suffering from his fell disease because he had committed some sin of which he did not know, but it seems better, remembering that the Priestly Code makes no distinction between ethical and ritual offences, to suppose that the sin-offering was for his ritual uncleanness, and of this he would be very miserably aware. Again, a woman was held to be ritually unclean after childbirth (Leviticus xii), and she was to offer for her cleansing both a burnt-offering and a sin-offering. It is, of course, incredible that she should not know that she had borne a

[1] There was an exception on the Day of Atonement. See pp. 71, 73.

child. It is possible to suggest that there was here a memory of the story of Eve's sin (though in that story childbirth is not counted sinful, but the pains of travail are counted the penalty of sin), but the mother would not be ignorant of Eve's sin, though in no way responsible for it. Other examples occur in the fifteenth chapter of Leviticus. We are therefore driven to suppose either that the Priestly Code is here inconsistent with itself, or that in the passage in Numbers the reference is to 'high-handed' sin against *ritual* rules, the meaning being that, if a man knowingly followed some other ritual, he could not escape by bringing a sin-offering. The instance of 'high-handed' sin that concludes the passage—that of a man who worked on the Sabbath—would fall in with this interpretation, for, of course, while the observance of the Sabbath was a very valuable piece of ritual, yet it was a ritual and not an ethical observance. Probably, therefore, it is right to limit the rule of Numbers to ritual sins. In any case, it is very difficult to think that devout Israelites, generation after generation, went up to Jerusalem to keep the Day of Atonement, observed all its very effective ritual, heard the High Priest confess 'all the sins' of the Children of Israel over the 'scape-goat', and went away supposing that all this had nothing at all to do with the sins of which they were aware.

Was the *lamb* given any special significance in the Jewish ritual, as over against other sacrificial animals? There is no hint whatever that it had any pre-eminence, but rather the opposite. In the case of all the animals, the fully grown animal, such as a sheep, seems to have been reckoned more valuable than the immature, such as a lamb. In addition, the sacrifices seem to have been valued by their size and to have fallen into three classes: oxen, sheep and goats, birds (e.g. pigeons). The suggestion that there was a distinctive and valuable 'gentleness' about a lamb does not occur in the Priestly Code, though it does occur in a prophetic passage (Jeremiah xi. 19), but here there is no reference to the Temple worship. So many sacred associations have gathered round the word 'lamb' for Christians that it is not easy to rid the word of them. It will be maintained below that in the New Testament they are not derived from the ritual, but from another source. Meanwhile, it seems to be certain that in the ritual the lamb had no sacrificial eminence. Again, the phrase 'the Passover lamb' does not rightly reproduce the Old Testament phraseology. The word translated 'lamb' or 'kid' in the account of the institution of the Passover means 'sheep or goat' (*seh*).[1] The distinctive word for 'lamb' (*kebes*) does not occur. In the Deuteronomic code any animal from 'the flock or herd' might be offered (Deuteronomy xvi. 2). There is evidence that about the time of Christ either a sheep or a goat or a lamb or a kid might be offered.[2] If we wish to get as near as English allows to the ideas of a Jew of the first century, probably the phrase 'the Passover sheep' would be the best. For the rest, we need to remember that on the Day of Atonement no lamb was offered. If any one wishes to connect the lamb with the sin-offering, he can only turn to passages where a lamb is a sin-offering for a private person (e.g. Leviticus iv. 32), and there the preceding paragraphs imply that it is of less value than a bullock, or even than a goat. The most frequent use of the lamb was not as sin-offering but as burnt-offering, for a lamb was the burnt-offering every morning and evening. Yet there were other burnt-offerings, too. It is impossible to isolate the lamb in any special way in Hebrew ritual.

In considering the Passover, some reference must be made to several passages in the Old Testament. At some unknown date, this feast and the Feast of Unleavened Bread became practically one. All leaven was carefully removed before the Passover was killed and eaten. The story of the institution of the Passover in Exodus (Exodus xii) shows that for the Jew the feast commemorated the deliverance from Egyptian bondage, whatever may have been its real historical antecedents. The story tells that the Angel of Death, when he saw the bloodstains on the lintel and doorposts of a house, passed it by. It is generally agreed now that the blood was 'apotropaic'—that, in effect, it said to the destroyer: 'The people here are in covenant with Jehovah; therefore they are not to be touched.' Jehovah was taking vengeance on His Egyptian enemies, not on His own people. Probably in the earlier days of Israel there was no thought that the Egyptians were sinners, but only that they were enemies. Later on this notion was modified to mean that Jehovah spared righteous Israel, but smote wicked Egypt.[3] In either case there is no notion of saving any one from sin, but only of saving Israel from bondage and oppression. In later days, no doubt, when the Jews kept the Feast, their thoughts ran something like this: 'In the old days

---

[1] Exodus xii. 3–5, 21. So, too, Isaac's real question on Mount Moriah was: 'Where is the sheep [or goat] for a burnt-offering?'
[2] Buchanan Gray, *Sacrifice in the Old Testament*, pp. 344 ff.
[3] E.g. in the Book of Wisdom.

Jehovah delivered righteous Israel from her oppressors; He has delivered her to this day, and He will always deliver.' The idea of salvation *from sin* does not occur. The fundamental idea, here as elsewhere, is that of Covenant. This is borne out by later references to the Passover. The idea is peculiarly clear in the Deuteronomic account of the Feast (Deuteronomy xvi). In the historical books there are three accounts of special Passovers—two of a Passover kept by Josiah and one of a Passover kept by Hezekiah (2 Kings xxiii; 2 Chronicles xxx, xxxv; cf. 1 Esdras i). In all three accounts the Passover is a feast, *following* a purification. This is specially clear in the Chronicler's account of Hezekiah's Passover (2 Chronicles xxix. 20 *ff.*), and this probably dates from about 300 B.C. In the days of Jesus, of course, crowds flocked to Jerusalem to keep the Feast. One man out of each company took the sheep or other animal to the Temple. These men were admitted in relays. At a given signal, each man slew his own sheep, while a priest held a bowl for the blood. These bowls were passed along a line of priests to the altar, at whose base the blood was poured. The fat was burnt on the altar, but each worshipper took the rest of the sheep to his waiting comrades. All of them then joined in a prolonged feast, a number of cups of wine being drunk at intervals, an item for which the Old Testament gave no warrant.[1] It seems plain that in practice it was not the offering of the blood in the Temple that chiefly filled the popular mind, but the long feast that followed. In this there was no reference to sin at all. The emphasis was not on penitence, but on joy. Men fasted when they remembered their sins, but this was a feast. The same conclusion follows if the ritual itself is considered. While it is not exactly parallel to any one of the three main types of sacrifice distinguished above, it ranks as a special kind of 'peace-offering', for it is in this kind of sacrifice that the worshipper himself eats of the sacrifice. As already stated, in the sin-offering this did not happen. On the other hand, the Passover sheep is unlike a burnt-offering, for in the latter all the sacrifice was burnt on the altar. Again, the term *kipper* ('make atonement') which is used often of the sin-offering and occasionally of the burnt-offering and even of incense, as will presently be shown, is never used of the Passover. If one were to insist in finding some reference to sin in the ritual of the meal, one would need to turn to the leaven, which was

[1] For the Passover in the time of Christ, see Hastings' *Bible Dictionary*, art. 'Passover' (W. J. Moulton).

removed before the Feast began. It was not sacrificial. It is true, as will appear below, that some hold that wherever there is mention of 'blood' there is an implicit reference to sin, but in any case there was no blood at the Passover feast, for the blood had been left in the Temple. The ruling ideas at the meal were covenant, redemption from oppression, and thanksgiving.

Apart from the blood of the Passover sheep, however, according to the Book of Numbers (Numbers xxviii. 16–25), among the sacrifices that were to be offered at Passover in the Temple itself, there was 'one he-goat for a sin-offering' (cf. Ezekiel xlv. 22). The item recurs in the accounts of the ritual for Pentecost and Tabernacles that follow. It contrasts with the *ten* animals that are to be offered at Passover as burnt-offerings. The explanation of its occurrence is probably simple. If a form of *thanksgiving* is drawn up to-day, there is usually *some* reference to confession of sin, as well as to other proper elements in worship, but the *emphasis* is laid on thanksgiving and it is to this that most space is given. Similarly, when the Jewish ritual reached its maturity, on the great *Feasts* there was *some* place found for other items, but the *emphasis* was on rejoicing. In any case, it is impossible to equate this he-goat with the sheep that was taken away to be eaten. The conclusion seems inevitable that the Passover meal had nothing at all to do with the forgiveness of sins.[1] At most it might be said that those whose sins had been forgiven joined in eating it.

There is another part of the Jewish ritual that bears upon our subject. This is the ritual of the Day of Atonement. There is a detailed account of it in the sixteenth chapter of Leviticus.[2] An outline of the chief features may be given. There were five animals in all, a bullock, two goats, two rams (cf. Ezekiel xliii. 18 *ff.*, xlv. 18–20). The High Priest appeared, not in his usual splendid robes, but in 'holy garments' of linen; he presented the bullock, which he slew as a sin-offering for himself and his house; he then took a censer of incense and the blood of the bullock and entered the Holy of Holies, burning the incense so that it 'covered the mercy-seat' and so saved him from death, and sprinkling the blood seven times upon and around the mercy-seat.[3] The High

---

[1] This connexion could be most easily made at a point in Ezekiel's account of the future ritual, but a point also where his directions were not followed: he prefaces the holding of Passover by the holding of a separate ceremony for the Cleansing of the House (Ezekiel xlv. 18 *ff.*).

[2] Or, rather, two accounts, for the ritual is described summarily in verses 3–10, and then more at length in verses 11–28.

[3] Some think that he entered with the incense and blood separately.

F

Priest then returned into the open-air court, and slew one of the goats. He took its blood also within the Holy of Holies and sprinkled it on and around the mercy-seat seven times. This time he 'made atonement' for the whole people, and also for the shrine itself—the Holy of Holies, the Holy Place, and the great outdoor altar—since the uncleanness of the people had contaminated them all. Next, the High Priest confessed 'all the iniquities of the children of Israel, and all their transgressions, even all their sins' over the head of the other goat, on which he laid his hands. Here first confession of sins is mentioned. As already seen, it is difficult to think that the long phrase just quoted only refers to unwitting sins. This goat was not killed, but was sent into the wilderness 'to Azazel', which seems to be the name of an evil spirit that lurked there. The man who led it away was counted unclean. Next the High Priest put off the white linen garments of penitence, donned his usual coloured robes, and offered the two rams, one as burnt-offering for himself and his house, and one for the whole people. The bodies of the bullock and the slain goat were carried outside 'the camp', their fat having first been burnt on the altar. The man who removed them was unclean.

As in some other parts of the system, certain items were later added or altered in the ritual of this day, and a few may be mentioned.[1] There was no Ark in the Second Temple and therefore no mercy-seat, and a small stone took its place. Before slaying the sin-offering for the Aaronic house, the High Priest confessed their sins. The goat for Azazel was led to the edge of the wilderness and thrown over a precipice to certain death. A surmise may be added, for which there seems to be no evidence unless it be in the Epistle to the Hebrews. With 'the blood of goats and bulls', its writer puts 'the ashes of a heifer sprinkling them that have been defiled' (Hebrews ix. 13). It seems possible that the men who carried away the bodies of the dead sin-offerings and led away the goat for Azazel cleansed themselves with the 'water of separation' described in the nineteenth chapter of Numbers, for it was apparently mixed with the ashes of a 'red heifer'. These men's return would be the last item in the Day's ritual, and probably the people flocked to see it. This would account for the whole phrase in the Epistle to the Hebrews.

Some particular comments may now be made. First, there is

[1] For these, see article, 'Day of Atonement', in Hastings' *Bible Dictionary* (Driver and White).

no doubt that, at least for the better Jews, the ritual was not mere 'superstition' but had a spiritual meaning. The account in Leviticus ends with a paragraph where the Hebrews are told to 'afflict their souls' on the Day, and both Philo and the Mishna bear this out,[1] the latter insisting on the need for repentance. In view of this, it is difficult to accept the suggestion that the ritual merely meant that the blood in some way 'sucked out' the unholiness from the shrine. It was not sprinkled at all upon the worshippers; how, then, did it 'suck out' their sins? Second, on this one occasion the priests ate no part of the sin-offerings. This, however, only exemplifies the rule that the sinner for whom a sin-offering was offered did not eat of it, for on this day there was 'atonement' for the sins of the priests themselves. Third, there was no lamb among the offerings. There were, indeed, two rams, but these were not sin-offerings, but burnt-offerings, and rams are not lambs. Fourth, the goat for Azazel is an almost unique phenomenon in Hebrew ritual (cf. Leviticus xiv. 7). Many, therefore, think that it is an intrusion from an alien source. In any case, it is doubtful whether it is properly to be called a sacrifice at all. Its blood was not sprinkled in any part of the Temple, as was the blood of every other animal sacrifice, of whatever kind. The writer to the Hebrews, therefore, does not refer to it when he speaks of 'the blood of goats and bulls'. If it were a sacrifice at all, it would seem to be offered to Azazel and not Jehovah, and this is not likely at this period.

If once it is admitted that the ritual of the Day of Atonement had a symbolic or sacramental meaning, some parts of this seem to be clear. Two ideas, which are logically exclusive, are fundamental: first, that God is holy and therefore can have nothing to do with the unholy, and, second, that He is still the God of Israel. The whole arrangement of the Temple buildings exemplified the same two ideas. It was built on the principle of exclusion—as one approached from the outside, first the Gentiles were shut out, then Jewish women, then lay Jews, then the priesthood (save that one priest entered the Holy Place each morning and evening), and finally the High Priest (save that once a year he entered the Holy of Holies). For the rest Jehovah dwelt in the inmost shrine, awe-fully alone. None the less, all the time He was in Covenant with Israel. It is easy to see here an example of the two concepts that Otto calls the *mysterium tremendum* and the *mysteriun fascinosum*.

[1] See the article quoted above.

On the Day of Atonement the two ideas reached a symbolic climax. The ritual was inconsistent, or, rather, paradoxical, and rightly so. The High Priest cannot look upon God lest he die, yet he draws near. God is so holy that He can have nothing to do with the sinful, yet He is so merciful to Israel that He must have everything to do with them. Their penitence is incomplete, for He still needs to hide Himself in the Holy of Holies, yet, if it is sincere, He is not altogether separate from them. The High Priest's white garments of penitence give way to his glorious robes and the burnt-offering again rises to Heaven. The whole ritual is a culminant symbol of the antinomy of holiness and mercy in the character of God. When once sin has occurred, and so long as it exists, the antinomy is inevitably there.

Again, it is clear that on the Day of Atonement the High Priest was a societary man. On his first entry into the Holy of Holies he stood for all the priesthood, on his second for all Israel. When he entered with the blood of the goat, it was as if all Israel entered. There could not be a plainer example of the corporate or societary idea. Here, too, as shown above, the societary concept involves the vicarious one. The High Priest acts instead of all Israel, for he and it are one.

Again, it seems clear that when the goat for Azazel is said to have 'borne away' the sins of the people into the Wilderness, the symbolic meaning was 'Our sins have gone' (cf. Leviticus xiv. 7). However much some of the more thoughtful Jews regretfully regarded this as an ineffective symbol, there can be no doubt that this is what this part of the ritual symbolized. It was symbolized also in the taking away of the bodies of two of the sin-offerings 'without the camp'—an almost unique piece of ritual. As the goat for Azazel is said to 'make atonement' (Leviticus xvi. 10), it is plain that in this instance this last word, whatever its meaning, could be used where there was no shedding of blood. It seems clear, too, that here the root idea about sin is that it is an affront to God's holiness, not that it is an object of His wrath. There is no suggestion that God was angry with the goat, or that He was punishing it. This brings us to the question of the meaning of the term translated 'make atonement'.

The Hebrew word is *kipper*. Here the usual Old Testament translation 'to make atonement for' will be used as far as possible, for it is agreed that, if the English word 'atone' is taken in its literal sense of 'to make at one', this *at least* is meant by the Hebrew term. When atonement had been made, Jehovah and Israel were 'at one', for now the bond of the Covenant held between them. It needs next to be noted that, while the term is used most often of sin-offerings, it is also used, for instance, of burnt-offerings (e.g. Leviticus i. 4), of oil (e.g. Leviticus xiv. 29), of incense (e.g. Numbers xvi. 47; 1 Chronicles vi. 49), of all blood offered in sacrifice (e.g. Leviticus xvii. 11), and by Ezekiel for all the sacrifices (Ezekiel xlv. 17).[1] It will be noted that the making of 'atonement' is not always by blood.

There is still discussion about the original meaning of the word *kipper*. Some experts maintain that this is 'to cover' and that the original meaning was either to cover a god's face or to cover the sin, so that the god does not see it. Others claim that the original meaning is 'to wipe off', and that the thing that atoned was thought to wipe away the anger from the god's face. This difference of opinion, however, need not detain us, for there is little doubt or none that, as with many words in all languages, the literal meaning was ignored in course of time. It would be impossible to maintain that in all the examples given any one of these metaphors survives. For instance, as already noted, the word is used of the goat for Azazel. Could it be said that this goat either 'covered' or 'wiped off' sin? On the contrary, it 'bore' it 'away'. There is further evidence that the metaphor, whatever it was, had been forgotten in the use of another metaphor for what was done on the Day of Atonement—'On this day shall atonement be made for you to *cleanse* you; from all your sins ye shall be *clean* before the Lord' (Leviticus xvi. 30).[2] This metaphor had been anticipated in the Vision of Isaiah, where the Prophet's 'unclean lips' were scorched pure and his 'sin atoned' by a 'live coal' from off the altar (Isaiah vi. 1 ff.). The original metaphor, whatever it was, was forgotten.

There is no doubt that the word *kipper could* mean 'propitiate' or 'appease', in the sense of 'allay' or 'turn away' anger, for this is not only the natural meaning of one of the earliest instances of the term (Genesis xxxii. 20), but it occurs in the Priestly document itself in the story of the way in which Aaron, speedily burning incense, turned away the 'wrath' of Jehovah from Israel (Numbers

[1] For a more complete list of uses, see Buchanan Gray, *Sacrifice in the Old Testament*, pp. 75f.

[2] To 'clean' might possibly be equated with 'to wipe away', but this would require that it was not the face of the god that was 'wiped' but the faces of the people, and no one holds that this was the original metaphor.

xvi. 41–50; cf. Proverbs xvi. 14). The same story, however, forbids the notion that atonement was made and Jehovah's anger allayed by punishing either the sinners themselves or animals that might be said to 'represent' them, for it is impossible to say that the incense was punished, and the people did not suffer punishment, but escaped it. Indeed, could any Israelite ever suppose that the death of two animals on the Day of Atonement and the wandering away of a third represented due punishment for all the sins of Israel? Neither the notion of 'vicarious punishment' nor the concept of punishment itself occurs. Nor does the notion of 'vicarious suffering', for this phrase cannot be used of oil or incense, and if the sufferings of the animals had been a prominent idea, presumably they would have been slowly put to death. Nor is the *killing* of any animal ever said to 'make atonement'. Its *blood* does so, but, as will be seen below, the blood does not symbolize suffering at all.

While, however, there is evidence that the word in question could be used to mean 'propitiate', this is not the usual idea in the post-Exilic period. For if it were, such a phrase as 'to make atonement to Jehovah' would almost certainly occur, and there is no such instance in all the Priestly Code. The phrase runs 'to make atonement for' a man, the people, or the Temple. In other words, the prominent thought is not a change made in the temper of God, but a change made in the relation of the man, the people, or the Temple, to God. This brings us to the suggestion that *kipper* is best translated by 'expiate', for 'expiate' describes what man does to secure forgiveness for sin, while 'propitiate' refers to its effect on God. Here we may quote again from the story of Isaiah's vision, using the rendering in the Revised Version margin: 'Lo, this hath touched thy lips, and thine iniquity is taken away and thy sin expiated.' At once, however, we must beware lest the idea of paying a legal penalty is introduced, for if we say, for instance, about a criminal who has spent five years in Dartmoor Prison that 'he has expiated his crime', the notion of the bearing of punishment inevitably intrudes, and, as we have seen, this idea is foreign to the passages where the Hebrew term is used. When the 'live coal' touched Isaiah's lips, he was not being punished, but cleansed, and so made a man of God.

This brings us to the one account of the meaning of the word in the Priestly Code that covers all its instances. The root idea about God here being His holiness, there is need so to purify a man, the people, or the Temple, that their uncleanness may be taken away. When 'atonement' was made, this uncleanness was removed, and the man, the people or the Temple was hallowed.[1] In other words, the idea was that by the making of 'atonement' the Israelite could again enter into the fellowship of worship with Jehovah. In other words, there was literal 'at-one-ment', and it is best that this word should stand in the English versions. It is true that the Prophets and some of the psalmists knew that the Temple ritual could not effectively 'atone for' sin, but none the less this, and no more, seems to be what the ritual symbolized where this word occurs.

As we have seen, in the sacrificial system atonement was not always by blood, though it was mainly so. It has to be added that it was not necessarily by sacrifice at all. There is an instance in a story that is usually ascribed to an early document, where Moses seeks to 'make atonement' for the people by prayer (Exodus xxxii. 30). Again, in a passage in Proverbs 'mercy and truth' are said to 'atone' (Proverbs xvi. 6). Evidence from books outside our Canon is also considerable.[2] The Book of the Son of Sirach (Ecclesiasticus) probably represents the general Jewish point of view in the centuries just before Christ. His thirty-fifth chapter is perhaps the best single illustration. He has three things to say here: that every Jew should offer the sacrifices (as God has commanded this); that he must not think that the sacrifices will avail unless he himself is penitent and shows his penitence by good works; and that such good works are as pleasing to God as sacrifices. Indeed, unless the Jews were already thinking such thoughts, it is difficult to see how the observance of the Day of Atonement could have survived the Destruction of the Temple in A.D. 70. After that they must have accommodated themselves very soon to a non-sacrificial ritual, and the rabbis quickly said, 'Though no sacrifices be offered, the Day in itself effects atonement'.[3]

Why was blood used on the Day of Atonement? This is only to take the leading instance of a larger question: Why was blood used in the sacrificial system at all? In the Priestly documents themselves three things may be noted—in every animal sacrifice

[1] This idea is perhaps least apparent in the story of Aaron's standing with the holy incense 'between the living and the dead' (Numbers xvi), but even here the idea probably is that the holy incense sheltered the people who had just sinned.

[2] It is conveniently gathered in T. Walker, *Jesus and Jewish Teaching*, pp. 249 *ff.*

[3] *Jewish Encyclopaedia*, art. 'Day of Atonement'.

the blood was kept for God; there is the repeated explanation 'the blood is the life'; the blood is said to 'make at-one-ment'. It is fairly well agreed now by experts that emphasis was not placed upon the death of the victim, still less on its sufferings. It needed to be killed in order that its blood and body might be available for more significantly sacrificial acts, but its slaughter was not itself the central act. The central acts—the offering of the bodies and the pouring out of the blood—were kept for the priests, but not the killing of the victim (e.g. Leviticus i. 5, 11, etc.). In relation to the blood, the emphasis is on the fact that it 'is the *life*', not on the fact that it was the blood of a *dead* animal. The Hebrews for long, perhaps even in post-Exilic times, thought that blood was literally life, but surely the better Jews did not at that date think that in itself literal blood was of value to God. They would think that it *symbolized* the offering of their 'lives', in a deeper than a physical sense.

Yet there is something more. In early times, among many nations there was the custom of blood-brotherhood. It was commonly supposed that those who shared the same blood literally shared the same life. This is, of course, an instance of early societary ideas. In particular, covenants were often made by the sharing of blood. Here there might be transfusion of blood from one man to another, or both might drink the same blood, or the same blood might be applied to both.[1] They then shared a common 'life'. In the twenty-fourth chapter of Exodus we read that Covenant was made between Israel and Jehovah by the sprinkling of the same blood upon the altar and the people. Though this comes from an early document, it is difficult to think that the Hebrews ever thought that the blood was literally sprinkled upon Jehovah. Already a symbolic use of the ritual seems to be evident. It is likely that, when an intelligent Jew in post-Exilic times watched the blood being poured out at the altar in any sacrifice he thought of it as *symbolizing* the Covenant of God with His 'peculiar people'. They shared a common life with Him in a higher than physical sense.

Yet there is more still. The phrase 'to make at-one-ment' suggests that reconciliation needed to be made—in other words, that Israel by its sins had broken the Covenant and that this needed to be restored. The intelligent Jew, therefore, thought that, whenever in any sacrifice (cf. Leviticus i. 4) the blood was offered, it symbolized both the fact of Covenant, the truth that he had

[1] See article, 'Blood-brotherhood (Artificial)', in *E.R.E.*

broken it, and the further truth that, as he now came to God with a penitent heart and in His appointed way, the Covenant was renewed and was valid for him.

This leads to one more idea. In the ritual of the Day of Atonement, the blood is said to 'cleanse' the altar and the people (Leviticus xvi. 19, 30) from the 'uncleannesses' or 'sins' of Israel. It is clear that the altar itself was thought of as 'unclean' because of the people's sin. It is possible to maintain that the blood was held literally to cleanse it, though it is difficult to think that the better Jews had not got farther than this. But the blood was not sprinkled on the people, and yet it is said to 'cleanse' them. Here the *symbolic* sense seems to be unmistakable. It is likely enough that the idea that the worshippers needed to be 'cleansed' in a spiritual sense was present, not only when the blood was offered on the Day of Atonement, but, to a greater or less degree, when blood was offered in other sacrifices.

If this account be correct, it follows that a reason can be given for the connexion of the three ideas that went together with the use of blood in the ritual of post-Exilic times: the offering of life, the making of at-one-ment, and the concept of cleansing. All of them symbolize the idea of Covenant in one way or another. A Jew gave his life to his Covenant God; at-one-ment was the re-making of a broken Covenant; the Jew needed to be cleansed if he were to continue in Covenant or to re-enter it. It is likely, indeed, that not only in post-Exilic times, but from the earliest days of Israel, this three-fold concept had underlain every use of blood in ritual. After the Exile, however, for the better kind of Jew at least, blood did not *affect* any of the three purposes, but *symbolized* all. Indeed, the giving of the blood to Jehovah in *every* sacrifice probably stood first and foremost for the idea that Jehovah and Israel were in Covenant.

It needs to be added that, while these three ideas were symbolized, there is no evidence that any others were symbolized, however many Christian thought may have mistakenly added. In particular, here the word 'vicarious' should be carefully used. No doubt all the ritual, including the offering of animals, was practised 'on behalf of' or for the benefit of, the worshippers, but there is no hint, either on the Day of Atonement or elsewhere, of the idea that a victim suffered the sufferings that a worshipper ought to have suffered, or was punished with the punishment that was his due, or died the death that he ought to have died.

'How then,' it may be asked, 'could the goat for Azazel be said to "bear all the sins of [the children of Israel] into a solitary land" (Leviticus xvi. 22)?' Other uses of the phrase 'to bear iniquity' or 'sin' need first to be considered. The commonest use in the Priestly Code is of a man for whose sin the sacrificial system made no provision and who must therefore 'bear' it himself (e.g. Leviticus v. 17; Numbers v. 31, xiv. 34, xviii. 23). There are, however, a few places where one *man* is said to 'bear' another's iniquity (Exodus xxviii. 38; Leviticus x. 17; Numbers xxx. 15; cf. xviii. 1). This vicarious use is found also in passages that have nothing to do with ritual (e.g. Ezekiel iv. 4–6, xviii. 19 f. ; cf. Numbers xiv. 33).[1] In them the idea is that one man suffers the sufferings that are due to another man. Is it so in the vicarious uses of the phrase in the Priestly Code? In two of them the meaning seems to be 'take away' (Exodus xxviii. 38; Leviticus x. 17); but, whether this is so or not, the meaning there cannot be 'endure the sufferings' of another. The only instance that approaches this is when a man, who has been silent when his wife made a vow and subsequently wishes to annul it, is declared to be bound by it (Numbers xxx. 15). Even here to 'bear her iniquity' need not involve the offering of an animal sacrifice, for the woman's vow might not include this. In all these cases, too, it is persons and not victims that 'bear' the iniquity of others. There is no instance of the phrase being used of animals slain in sacrifice at all. Must the concept be found, then, in the phrase about the goat for Azazel? Even if this is done, it must be remembered that this goat was not slain in the Temple. But the probable meaning of the phrase 'bear upon him all their iniquities into a solitary land' is the literal one. The idea is not that the goat was suffering the sufferings that were due to sinners, but that it was carrying away their sins. Of course, spiritually minded Jews would take this symbolically. In any case it would be hazardous to base the notion of the vicarious suffering of animals on a single phrase. The concept that one *man* might endure the sufferings due to another's sin does occur in the Old Testament, notably in the last Servant Song, but, apart from the doubtful instance of a wife's broken vow, not in the accounts of the ritual system.

There remains the question of the meaning of the phrase 'Aaron shall *lay both his hands* upon the head of the live goat'

---

[1] For similar ideas, in Second and Fourth Maccabees, see Oesterley, *Sacrifices in Ancient Israel*, p. 264.

(Leviticus xvi. 21), and, standing so, shall confess all the sins of Israel. It would be difficult to give one account of all the ways in which this symbol is used in the Old Testament, except that it means that there is *some* connexion between the man who lays his hands on a thing (or person) and that thing. The kind of connexion depends on the context. For instance, to take an example from Leviticus, when a man was accused of blasphemy those who had heard the words were to lay their hands on his head before he was stoned (Leviticus xxiv. 14). Here the symbol means: 'I am prepared to say that *my* ears heard *this* man blaspheme.' In the absence of any hint to the contrary, it is well to keep to the simplest explanations where the phrase occurs in the Priestly ritual. It is used in the ritual of all three kinds of animal sacrifices—the burnt-offering, the peace-offering, and the sin-offering (e.g. Leviticus i. 4, iii. 2, iv. 4)—and it is best to seek an explanation that gives the same meaning in all three cases. This is done if the act be taken simply to mean: 'This is *my* sacrifice.' Similarly, when Aaron is told to 'lay his hands' on the head of the goat for Azazel, the meaning would be: 'Over *this* goat I, representing all Israel, confess all Israel's sins.' It may easily be that originally the sins were supposed to pass literally to the goat, but surely here, too, such a Jew as the Son of Sirach or Hillel or Saul of Tarsus took the act symbolically.

We are now ready to ask what part the sacrificial system played in the thought of Deutero-Isaiah, particularly in the Songs of the Servant, and most of all in the last and greatest of the Songs. Some general remarks may first be made. Many think that the unnamed Prophet lived in or near Babylon towards the close of the Exile. In that case, it is possible that he himself had never seen a sacrifice in the Temple. No doubt, as he foretold a return to Palestine, he thought of Jerusalem as the City of Jehovah and of the Temple as its glory, but he has only one clear reference to its ritual outside the Songs (xliii. 23 *f.*).[1] Here he contrasts strongly with Ezekiel, the earlier Prophet of the Exile, and even with other exiled Jews, for it is generally agreed that the documents of the Priestly School had their beginnings in this period and that the memories of past ritual were kept alive against an expected return. As has been seen, Deutero-Isaiah was heir to the

---

[1] Here he seems to say that while Jehovah had not resented the Exiles' (inevitable) neglect of the Temple sacrifices, He had been 'wearied' by their 'iniquities'—yet now He was ready to 'blot out' these.

thought of the Prophets and brought their doctrine of redemption to its climax—is there evidence that he was heir to the
Priests?[1]

Of direct references to the ritual system three have been found,
all in the last of the Songs. One is in the phrases, 'Surely he hath
borne our griefs and carried our sorrows', 'He shall bear their
iniquities', and 'He bare the sin of many'. But there is no
suggestion anywhere in the ritual system that the victims 'bore
griefs and sorrows' in the sense that they endured them, and in
the phrase, 'He shall bear their iniquities', the word translated
'bear' is not a sacrificial term, though it occurs elsewhere of
vicarious suffering outside the ritual (Lamentations v. 7). The
phrase 'bare the sin of many' might possibly be referred to the
goat for Azazel, yet the Servant, unlike the goat, was put to death,
and it is at least doubtful whether this part of the Jewish ritual
goes as far back as the time of Deutero-Isaiah. It is just possible
that the phrases borrow their metaphor from the ritual, but the
metaphor is used in the exactly opposite way to the commonest
use there. While, as we have seen, the latter speaks of offences
that the offender cannot escape, the prophetic phrases speak of a
way of escape from sin.

The second supposed reference to ritual runs, if the phrase is
translated literally—'He was oppressed, yet he humbled himself
and opened not his mouth; as a sheep that is led to the slaughter,
and as a ewe that before her shearers is dumb; yea, he opened
not his mouth' (Isaiah liii. 7). The word for 'lamb' does not occur.
Again, it is agreed that the reference to shearing does not fall in
with anything in the ritual. It is not true, again, that a sheep is
dumb when it is being killed or shorn. The Prophet is speaking
of a sheep *before* it is killed or shorn. Here, of course, we must not
think of the picture of a frightened animal being driven through
the strange streets of a modern town, but of an Eastern shepherd
leading in a sheep from the hills. The sacrificial system has no
reference to this at all. The nearest Biblical parallel is with a verse
in Jeremiah, where he says that, when the men of Anathoth were
plotting his death and he did not yet know it, he was 'like a gentle
lamb that is led to the slaughter' (Jeremiah xi. 19). This reference,
too, is to a lamb *before* it is killed. The comparison with an un-
resisting sheep suits exactly the tenour of Deutero-Isaiah's thought,

[1] The question whether the Songs of the Servant are ascribed to Deutero-Isaiah or
another author, does not affect what follows.

but it has no analogy in the sacrificial system, either before or after the Exile.

There are textual difficulties about the third passage, but if it is taken as it stands, it runs: 'Yet it pleased the LORD to bruise him: he hath put him to grief; when Thou shalt make his soul [life] a guilt-offering [or, 'when his life shall make a guilt-offering'] he shall see his seed, he shall prolong his days, and the pleasure of the LORD shall prosper in his hand' (Isaiah liii. 10). The English versions mistakenly turn the 'guilt-offering' into a sin-offering. The distinctive marks of a guilt-offering seem to have been that it was offered when some specific wrong had been done to God or man, and that so far as possible the wrong was to be undone before the guilt-offering was offered. The best illustration is perhaps in the opening verses of the sixth chapter of Leviticus. Here, for example, it is decreed that if a man has robbed his neighbour of something, he shall first restore it to his neighbour, adding a fifth of its value, and then 'come and offer' his guilt-offering. The priest is then said to have 'made atonement' for him and his fault is 'forgiven'. The restoration and fine are not the guilt-offering, though they must precede it. If now the *main* thoughts of the stanza in the great Song be considered, it is plain that the guilt-offering had nothing to do with them. Jehovah did not 'bruise' such an offering or 'put it to grief'; 'the pleasure of the LORD' did not 'prosper in' its 'hand'; it did not 'see of the travail of' its 'soul'. *At one particular point*, however, there is a parallel between the ideas of the stanza and the interpretation of the term 'make atonement' given above. It was there suggested that when blood (life) was offered in sin-offerings (and here guilt-offerings go with them), the concept was that there was restoration of fellowship between the holy Jehovah and unholy Israel. So in the Song, substituting the word 'righteous' for 'holy', the 'righteous Servant' restores unrighteous Israel to fellowship with God. At this one point there is a parallel between the ideas of this Prophet and a given idea of the Jew about 'atonement'. It does not at all follow, however, that this was so also with his other ideas. They are not ritualistic. Probably, therefore, in this instance the reference is just illustrative. It is not that the Prophet derives his teaching from the sacrificial system, but that at one point he finds that an idea, otherwise derived, can be illustrated from that system. The fact that even in the relevant stanza the sacrificial reference is limited to a single phrase supports this. The reference shows that for the

Prophet's doctrine of salvation the ritual system was of real, but very limited, value.

Returning now to the term 'vicarious', we may say that there is yet another way in which all the offerings, of whatever kind, might be called vicarious, for they were gifts, and every true gift is in a given sense vicarious. It stands for, or even instead of, devotion and love.

When a devout Jew brought any gift to the Temple—whether it were animal or vegetable or money or anything else—it might be called 'vicarious' in this sense. But another question ensues: 'When such a Jew brought a sin-offering or guilt-offering to be slain in sacrifice, was it vicarious in any other and distinctive sense?' Of this there seems to be no evidence whatever.

In the ritual of the Day of Atonement, the High Priest is much more clearly 'vicarious' than the sacrifices. As we have seen, on that day he was a societary man, and the vicarious roots in the societary. When the High Priest entered the Holy of Holies, it is not possible to speak of his vicarious death, or his vicarious suffering, or his vicarious punishment, but it is possible to speak of his vicarious penitence, though this would mean, not that he was penitent instead of the people, but penitent as representing the people and as being part and parcel of it. In effect he said: 'The people Israel, for whom I come, share my penitence and I share theirs; our penitence is one penitence.' About two centuries before Christ there was a High Priest whom men called 'Simon the Just' (cf. Ecclesiasticus l). When he entered into the Holy Place on the Day of Atonement, the people would think of him both as righteous and as identifying himself with their sinfulness. So far he would be like the Servant of Jehovah. But at one point the parallel signally fails: unlike the Servant of Jehovah, he was not wounded for Israel's transgressions; he did not enter the Holy Place 'with his own blood'. He failed to be a societary man at the crucial point.

Did the post-Exilic Jews think of the sacrificial system at all in terms of salvation? Here it may be significant that two of the three usual Hebrew terms to denote the idea do not occur in this system at all. These are the words 'save' and 'redeem'. The third, 'ransom', does occur, but in a clearly defined way, there being one instance from pre-Exilic documents (Exodus xiii. 13 f. (E), xxxiv. 20; Leviticus xxvii. 27; Numbers xviii. 15–17, iii. 40–51). In every case the term refers to the substitution of one offering for another in the ritual of the first-born. The first-born of men and of animals, like the first-fruits of crops, belonged to Jehovah. As the ass, for instance, was an animal that was never used in sacrifice, a lamb or kid was substituted for an ass's foal. Similarly, as the practice of offering human sacrifices to Jehovah was extinct in Israel, at any rate after the Exile, a lamb or kid was offered instead of a first-born child. There is here, of course, no suggestion that the ass's foal or the lamb or the kid or the child had sinned. The offering of first-fruits and first-born was not a sin-offering. In the last passage mentioned, there is a variant of this practice. Here the Levites are said to be accepted instead of the first-born Israelites, and, as this did not exhaust the number of the latter, a money payment was to be made in place of each of the surplus. There is here an idea of substitution, but not of substitutionary suffering, still less of substitutionary suffering for sin, and least of all of substitutionary punishment. Again, neither the sin-offering nor the guilt-offering is ever said to 'save' or to 'redeem' or to 'ransom'.

Was the *idea* present without the usual *words* for it? There is no suggestion anywhere that the sacrificial system saved Israel from the results of sin. Indeed, the facts of Israel's sorry plight after the Exile would forbid such a thought. The conviction was indeed current that if only Israel faithfully kept the Law of Jehovah, He would at last inevitably deliver her from her evil plight, and the sacrificial system was part of the Law, yet this means, not that the conviction was based on the system, but that at some points the system illustrated the conviction. As already suggested, under the term 'make atonement' there lay the idea of the restoration of a largely broken Covenant. It is here that the system is valuable for the doctrine of salvation, for the restoration of Covenant was a form, however imperfect, of the idea of the restoration of fellowship between man and God. Such men as the writer of the Fifty-first Psalm knew well that the system was woefully unequal to fulfilling this kind of salvation, yet an inadequate illustration of a great idea may have great value. Many a sincere Jew must have taken part in the ritual of the Day of Atonement, thinking, 'I am here to confess my sins in penitence; I am here in God's own appointed way; surely He will have mercy upon me and help me to fulfil His will better in the coming year than in the past year'. Who shall say that such a Jew did not leave the Temple a better man? None the less, the fundamental thing here is not the sacrificial system, but a 'broken and a contrite spirit'. The ritual was but the tool of the spiritual. Nor was it the only tool. The worship of the synagogue, particularly, no doubt often served just as well, especially for Jews in the Diaspora. It might be truly said that from the days of Ezra the keeping of the Law saved Israel from absorption by the Gentiles—but the keeping of the Law involved the reading of the Book, the observance of the Sabbath and of circumcision, dietary rules, and so on, as well as the sacrificial system. Since A.D. 70 the other observances have 'saved' Israel in this sense, without the system. And indeed, before that date, whether Israel knew it or not, the system was becoming an anachronistic survival, like the retention of the Khalifate in Islam till the other day. To some clear eyes, the system was perhaps already 'waxing old and nigh unto vanishing away'. It is the synagogue that has saved Israel—and the Book and the rabbi that go with the synagogue—yet here by 'saved' we only mean that at many periods Israel's level of life has on the average been higher than that of other peoples, and that in all periods she has survived. The Jews themselves, of course, admit that this is a very incomplete kind of salvation.

Finally, a distinction should be again noted that is not always made. It is one thing to say that a given idea *originates* with ritual and another to say that ritual *illustrates* an idea that has its origin elsewhere. Again, it is one thing to say that ritual illustrates a truth, and another thing to say that a given truth is peculiar to ritual. It will be seen that an attempt has been made above to show that the use of ritual in the Old Testament in relation to the doctrine of salvation is only illustrative, and that it exhibits truths that are neither peculiar to ritual nor derived originally from it. A similar attempt will be made below in dealing with the New Testament doctrine of salvation. Some writers seem to think that if they can show that a given idea is illustrated by ritual, this proves that ritual is essential to the idea, but this is far from being the case. There is probably no religious idea that cannot be expressed by ritual, but no particular ritual expression is essential to any religious idea.

THE OLD TESTAMENT AND AFTER

CHAPTER VIII

ESCHATOLOGY AND APOCALYPTIC

I⊤ is agreed that the subjects of Eschatology and Apocalyptic are important for the soteriology of the New Testament. The writers of that book often used phrases from this realm without explanation—that is, they assumed that their readers would know what the phrases meant. In order that we may understand their terminology, therefore, we need to know what this meant for people who lived in the first Christian century, and they, of course, inherited the thought of the generations just before them, however much or little they modified and changed it. It is impossible here to enter upon the whole subject, but a summary account needs to be given. When this has been done, the implications for the doctrine of salvation will be briefly stated.

Something needs first to be said about the use of 'literal' and 'symbolical' language. The distinction between the terms is plain enough, but it is often naïvely assumed that this distinction is kept clear in ordinary speech. This is far from the case. For instance, every metaphor involves the use of symbolism, yet the metaphor may either be consciously recalled, or partly forgotten, or altogether ignored. In the phrase, 'I *grasped* his meaning', the metaphor, and the symbol behind it, seem still to be recollected; in the phrase, 'I *saw* what he meant', probably few recall the metaphor; in the phrase, 'I *understood* him', there seems to be a metaphor that no one can confidently describe at all! There are multitudes of examples in proverbs. If any one says, 'A stitch in time saves nine', no doubt he believes it to be literally true, but it is the symbolic meaning that he has in mind. Again, we slip from the symbolic to the literal and back again far more frequently than we think. When the Prophet said to the Jews in Babylon, 'He hath *anointed* me to *preach* good tidings', he makes the transition, but perhaps few readers think of it. When Jesus quoted this passage, many readers take one phrase, 'He hath sent me to proclaim release to the captives', symbolically, and the next, 'Recovering of sight to the blind', literally, without being aware that they are doing so. On the Prophet's lips, on the other hand, the first phrase would be literal and the second symbolical!

As soon as these phenomena are pointed out, they are obvious, yet in discussing Jewish Eschatology and Apocalyptic many wish to distinguish clearly between the literal and symbolical. There are pronounced apocalyptic elements in Dante, in Milton, and in Blake. Is Beatrice a symbolical figure or not, or is the figure partly symbolical? How far did Milton think that his picture of Satan and Hell was literally exact? To quote Blake's best-known poem, it is plain that the 'bow of burning gold' is symbolical, but is not 'England's green and pleasant land' literal, and do not exponents dispute whether the 'dark Satanic mills' are one or the other? If any of these poets had been asked to give his own decision, it is likely that he would have said, 'What does it matter?' Probably a Jewish apocalyptic writer would have said the same. Yet since these writers deliberately put their message in symbolic form, the 'working rule' ought to be: 'Take everything symbolically until a detail is reached which for good reasons needs to be taken literally.' For instance, it is agreed that almost the whole of the seventh chapter of Daniel is symbolical; very good reasons need to be given before the figure of 'one like unto a son of man' coming 'with the clouds of heaven' is to be taken literally. Indeed, it ought not even to be *assumed* that while the figure is symbolical, the clouds are literal, though this is likely. In any case, it is the symbolical meaning that is of permanent worth.

Jewish Eschatology and Apocalyptic presuppose a certain account of the physical universe. To a large extent the Jews shared this with contemporary peoples, though, as we shall see, they modified it to suit their own distinctive convictions. Here we are speaking of the generally accepted account. It was not universally accepted, for a few Greek philosophers rejected it, but the exception only proves the rule. Only a few of the chief ideas need be named.[1]

The guiding principle is exactly the opposite to ours. The teaching of astronomy from Copernicus onwards has permeated popular thought, and we assume that the universe is *not* what it *seems* to be. For instance. we believe that the sun does not move across the sky, though it seems to do so; that the earth's surface is not flat, though it seems to be so; that, though the earth looks as if it were large and the stars small, the precise opposite is the truth.

---

[1] For a more complete account, see art. 'Cosmogony' (O. T. Whitehouse) in *H.D.B.* This article includes a diagram, which presents the whole cosmogony more readily than much writing.

For most men of earlier days the first principle was that the universe *is* what it *looks* like. They only modified this idea or added to it when they could not help it. Consequently they thought that the earth was the largest thing in the universe, and that its surface was a huge, flat disk with a great blue dome over it. The first chapter of Genesis calls this dome 'the firmament'. The sun, the moon, the planets, and even the stars seemed to move across the dome—but on this side of it—in different ways. The various complications that were introduced into this simple outline by more careful observers need not detain us.

Three other concepts that were not based on the direct evidence of men's eyes need to be named. They are particularly important in relation to the concept or concepts of evil beings. Popular thought seems to have placed the abode of the gods, more or less consistently, above the dome. But in the wide spaces between the dome and the earth—called by Paul 'the heavenly places', or more accurately, 'the heavenlies'—there were other superhuman beings. Some of these were connected, more or less closely, with the planets and stars. A few were beneficent, but most of them malign. Some, at least, of the Greeks called them by such abstract names as 'principalities' and 'powers'. This seems to mean that many Greeks—and some Jews, such as Paul—thought of them more or less symbolically. Sometimes they seem to have been conceived as organized under one ruler, who might be termed 'the prince of the power of the air'. Again, between the gods or God and men there might pass 'angels'—that is, messengers. Here, as in the realm of eschatology generally, Persian influence was great. The angels were usually beneficent beings, though the denizens of the 'heavenlies' seem to have been chiefly evil.

On the earth itself there were other evil spirits. These were called 'demons'. It is remarkable that this concept appears only occasionally in the Old Testament, though it is common in the New, for it is one of the oldest and most widely spread ideas in the world. It obtains to-day, for instance, alongside cosmogonies or theologies with which it is at most loosely connected, among the Chinese, the Hindus, and the Arabs. Many demons were thought miserable unless they could find some man or animal in which to dwell. Otherwise they roamed about 'seeking rest and finding none'. They were counted the causes of most diseases or even all. This means that moral evil was conceived as the cause of physical evil. There is no clear account of the 'demons' ' origin, but their proper habitat was the 'deep' or 'abyss'. This was the name for a giant mass of water, on which the earth floated, and which came to the surface in the sea and in lakes. Springs even might be thought of as coming up out of it through the earth. It was a mighty chaos, in which lurked a mighty monster or monsters always seeking to overwhelm the earth. Demons had escaped from it and hated to return to it. The demons of Gadara asked to be sent into swine rather than the abyss, yet they do not seem thereby to have escaped the abyss, but to have rushed down into it through the Sea of Galilee.

There was yet a third concept. While the earth's surface was flat, the earth itself was very thick, and in the middle of its solid mass—and not, like the abyss, underneath it—there was a vast hollow or cave. The Hebrews called it Sheol and the Greeks Hades. Usually, it seems, this was not thought of as the abode of evil spirits, but of dead men. Originally, at least, it was not a realm of fire or of punishment, but simply the realm to which every man, good or bad—apart from a few great men, such as Hercules or Elijah or a dead Caesar, who went to 'heaven'— passed as a matter of course when he died. Here he could hardly be said to 'live', but he went on existing in a bloodless, juiceless way, the 'shade' or shadow of his former self. Our nearest parallel is the popular concept of a ghost. Hebrew modifications of the idea of this underworld will be named later. Usually when the word 'death' occurs in the Bible, it does not mean, as in much modern speech, just a momentary physical event, but also the state into which the dead man entered. It includes existence in Sheol. Here, no doubt, some used words in a symbolical way, some in a literal, some without considering which of the two they were following, but to all the idea was a miserable and terrifying one. No account of what 'death' means in the Bible can be adequate that confines it in the modern way to the mere physical event. It was under this ancient concept that men 'through fear of death' were 'all their lifetime subject to bondage'. Sheol or Hades might be called 'evil', not in a moral sense, but in the sense of 'horrible'.

When the Jew of the latest centuries before Christ brought his great concept of 'ethical monotheism' to bear on these ideas, he did not completely harmonize the two, for the Jew was no master of philosophical consistency, yet he did not accept the ideas unmodified. His concept of the universe is expressed in the first passage in Genesis. This is remarkable both for what it says and what it leaves unsaid. It enunciates three permanent truths of religion: that God is Creator, that all that He does is good, and that man is made 'in the image of God'. The exact meaning of the last phrase need not detain us. The writer himself seems to find it in the limited 'dominion' by which man uses the universe for his own purposes (cf. Psalm viii). On any interpretation, it is the Hebrew account of what we mean by 'the value of personality'. On the other hand, the passage omits all reference to evil of any sort. It tells neither of its existence nor its origin. The subject of sin, however, belongs to our next chapter. In the passage in Genesis, while there is one reference to the 'deep' or 'abyss', there are none to death or to Sheol. Yet for a believer in ethical monotheism these concepts raise a serious problem.

It is not certain at what time the Hebrew came to believe in Sheol. Some think that in the earliest times he was content with the notions that a good man would live to a ripe old age, 'see his children's children' and finally 'sleep with his fathers'. Others identify this 'sleep' with Sheol. On either showing, however, the developed concept of Sheol was current by the Exile, for in the thirty-second chapter of Ezekiel the various nations, societarily considered, lie here and there in 'the pit'. This is clearly conceived as a place of misery, and the question follows: 'Can an omnipotent and righteous God allow this to be the last word about either a righteous nation or a righteous man?' Attempts to meet the difficulty were ultimately made in two ways. Some modified the concept of Sheol itself. It was now divided into two (or more) areas, one for the good and the other for the bad. The first was conceived as a happy place, and to describe it the Persian word 'Paradise' (that is, park or pleasaunce) was used. For the part reserved for the bad the term 'Gehenna', a Greek loan from the Hebrew phrase, 'The Valley of [the sons of] Hinnom', was common. This valley lay near Jerusalem and had been used for heathen worship. Josiah therefore 'defiled' it and made it into the midden of Jerusalem. Outside every Eastern city there was such a midden. All refuse, animal and vegetable, was flung into a heap there. The mass would breed vermin. A fire was kept perpetually burning so that the heap would smoulder away as fast as it grew. It would be a place where, quite literally, the 'worm dieth not and the fire is not quenched'. The midden of

Jerusalem is described by this phrase at the end of our Book of Isaiah. It came to be used for the area where the wicked were punished in Sheol. This seems to be the time when a realm in Sheol was first thought of as a place of fire. How far this is to be taken literally, however, rather than symbolically, is at least doubtful.

Yet there was another answer to the problem, that might either be held instead of the one just described or along with it. Its significant word is 'resurrection'. There are only two indubitable references to this in the Old Testament (Isaiah xxvi. 19; Daniel xii. 2), but there are more in the non-Canonical literature. In Jesus' day the concept was not universal, for it is said that the Sadducees repudiated it; yet it seems to have been general. As usual with the Jews, the idea arose, not by philosophical reasoning, but from the impact of events. In particular, when in the persecution of Antiochus Epiphanes men died for their faith, the Jew sprang to the sure belief that this could not be the end of the faithful. In the story of the Mother and her Seven Sons, for instance, in the seventh chapter of Second Maccabees, the second son, 'when he was at the last gasp', cried to the torturing king, 'Thou, miscreant, dost release us out of this present life, but the King of the world shall raise up us, who have died for his laws, unto an eternal renewal of life'. It seems to have been with this kind of story in his mind that the writer of the Epistle to the Hebrews, having referred to the stories of Zarephath and Shunem under the phrase 'women received their dead by a resurrection', adds, 'And others were tortured, not accepting their deliverance, that they might obtain a *better* resurrection'. Believers in a living and righteous God could now say no less.

The Resurrection was placed at the crisis that was to close the 'age'—a concept to be discussed presently. There was difference of opinion under the question, 'Who will rise again?' Some thought that all, good and bad, would do so, in order that they might be judged. The good then passed into the glory of the 'coming age', but the bad were consigned to punishment, apparently in the old or a worse Hades. Others thought that the righteous only would rise again. All seem to have been sure that the great majority of these would be Hebrews—and the fact that the Jews, generally speaking, were obviously better than their Gentile contemporaries needs to be borne in mind—but some held that the worst Hebrews would perish, but the best Gentiles, becoming Jews in religion, would rise again. Yet, amid these diversities, two ideas were constant: a righteous God cannot let righteous men remain in the misery of Sheol; He will bring them back from that underworld to *this* world—this world purified and perfected, no doubt, yet to *this* world. Sometimes, indeed, the good are thought of as joining the angelic powers in the upper regions of the air, but this still keeps the concept within the cosmogony described above. This state of the righteous is sometimes called 'Paradise'. For those who also believed in a Paradise in Sheol, there would be both a preliminary and a final Paradise. Once again it may be doubted whether any or all of those who held these notions took every phrase in the descriptions literally. Indeed, there is evidence on the other side. The writer of the Book of Wisdom, for instance, seems almost certainly to have interpreted all such concepts symbolically. How else could he have written the passage beginning, 'But the souls of the righteous are in the hand of God' (Wisdom iii. 1 *ff.*)?[1]

Another concept, also widely current, needs to be named alongside the current cosmogony. This refers, not to space, but to time. Probably most men to-day still think of time under the figure of an uninterrupted and never-ending line. Many peoples, on the contrary, have thought of it as divided into 'Ages'.[2] Here, too, it is only necessary to refer to some of the leading notions. The number of ages varied, but often four were counted: the age of gold, the age of silver, the age of bronze, the age of iron. Of these the first was the best and the last the worst. Each age was reckoned very long—for instance one account gives to each 60,000 years. The series recurs—that is to say, the course of time is more like a circle that continually repeats itself than an unending line. Each age is divided from the next by a crisis and an upheaval. None the less, the universe persists through all—persists in spite of cataclasmic change. The change is often presented as a great conflagration. Perhaps a parallel from metallurgy is the best: when a metal is cast into a furnace, the dross perishes, but the metal remains. Almost or quite unanimously, those who thought in these terms believed that they lived in the worst of the ages. This is not as pessimistic as it looks, for the best kind of age always follows the worst. The present age, for instance, might be called 'the age of iron', but then the 'age of gold', while very far away

[1] Only points salient for the purpose of this book have been mentioned. For a competent synopsis of the manifold and complex details of the whole subject, reference may be made to T. Walker, *Jesus and Jewish Teaching*, chap. vi.

[2] See art., 'Ages of the World' (various writers), in *E.R.E.*

in the past, would be the next to come in the future. It is clear
that no true idea of progress is compatible with this scheme of
things. The course of the universe is a never-ending cycle. 'What
has been is what will be.' The whole idea, too, readily suits the
concept of the Divine as mere Fate.

It is plain that the Jew, with the Old Testament in his hands,
could not take over these ideas as a whole. For instance, the
chronology of that book required that the universe—'the heaven
and the earth' as the Jew called it—had only existed about 4,000
years. Again, the Book did not allow of the concept of a series of
recurring ages, separated by crises and conflagrations. The
nearest thing to such an idea was the story of the Flood. This
was not a conflagration, and the Book expressly said that it
would not be repeated (Genesis ix. 11). Again, the idea that once
upon a time there lived one man and one woman in the Garden
of Eden was not commensurate with the notion of a vast and
happy mankind in a distant golden age. Most of all, the Jew
could not admit that the One Righteous God could allow a mere
repetition of good and evil ages. If He were omnipotent and
righteous, He must ultimately perfect His universe once for all.
Finally, for the Jew the universe was not eternal, but created.

None the less, there was a part of the concept—and that the
practically effective part—which fell in quite readily with Jewish
ideas. This was the concept that now there is an evil age, and
that after a great crisis this will be followed by a happy and perfect
age. Indeed, these ideas had a long anticipation in the Old Testament. It had been the constant teaching both of prophets and
Deuteronomists that the woes of Israel—and often the woes of the
whole world—were God's punishment for sin, that there would
come a 'Day of Jehovah' when He would vindicate His righteousness, and that thereafter He would set up a realm of righteousness,
peace and prosperity. It was natural, therefore, that the Jew
should speak of 'this age' and 'the coming age'. His own
experience of alien empires, from the day of Assyria onwards,
made it easy for him to believe that 'the days are evil'.[1] When,
however, he spoke simply of 'the age', he meant the coming age.
The Greek phrase translated 'for ever' in the New Testament
means literally 'into the age'. There are other phrases about the
future—such as 'the ages' and 'the ages of the ages'—but these
seem merely to emphasize the same idea as 'the age' and to bring

[1] See the writer's *Religion of the Hebrews*, chap. iii.

out the idea that it lasted and lasted and lasted, much as we emphasize the phrase 'for ever' by saying 'for ever and ever', and as children will sometimes say, 'for ever and ever and ever and ever. . . .' If any notion of a future succession of ages remains in these phrases, the ages are conceived as continually better and better, and not as recurrently good and bad. While there is no philosophical discussion of the nature of 'eternity', the common notion made the age unending. It was from this notion that the adjective *aionios* derived, and its *primary* notion is neither 'eternal' nor 'age-long', but 'belonging to the [coming] Age'.[1] What other ideas were added to this one by various kinds of thinkers need not here be discussed.

The chief and permanently valuable Jewish contribution to this set of ideas has already been implied, but needs to be made explicit. It was a certain concept of God. Over this whole complex of ideas both about space and time, the Jew set the one righteous and omnipotent God. It is not wrong to call the idea 'transcendent', for God is not immured in His universe or limited by it. Yet the concept is not 'deistic', in the sense that it teaches that God, having made the universe and set it on its way, now leaves it to run its course. On the contrary, He is very active in it. Still less, however, was the concept immanental. The notion of immanence is not altogether absent from Jewish books, but it is nowhere dominant and it is alien to Apocalyptic. Perhaps the nearest analogy to the true notion may be found in the empire of the time. Augustus, for instance, might have been called 'an absentee Emperor' in Palestine, but, while the phrase is literally true, it gives false suggestions. Augustus was master of Palestine, and so Asshur-bani-pal had been and Cyrus. A Theudas or a Judas of Galilee might rebel, and for a little time he might seem to the short-sighted to be prevailing in a little area, but presently the Emperor would act and crush. If this idea be purified and enlarged, we reach the Jewish conception of God's relation to His universe. No Jew, of course, believed that He lived at a kind of celestial Rome, though he might say symbolically that He was 'above the heavens'. Again, if challenged, he would have agreed that God is everywhere. None the less, while God could not be placed at this point or that, the dominant concept was that He was ruling all the time over a strangely confused and rebellious universe. In other words, the Jew believed in a *present* 'kingdom',

[1] Cf. Moulton and Howard, *Grammar of New Testament Greek*, vol. ii, p. 336.

or, rather, kingship, of God. This is the postulate of every apocalyptic book, and of Christians now.

Yet there was also another idea for which Augustus or Cyrus would not furnish an analogy. No one, for instance, thought that when Theudas rebelled, Augustus was all the while using the rebellion for his own ends. Yet this is what the Jew thought about God's relation to men and kingdoms who rebelled against Him, and it is clear that, while this idea does not meet all the difficulties about the possibility of rebellion against an omnipotent God, it does diminish them. The concept was an old one. It appears clearly at least as early as Elijah, for in his story and that of Elisha, Hazael, King of Aram, is thought of as Jehovah's tool for the punishment of Israel. Isaiah, again, taught that Assyria was merely the 'rod' of Jehovah's anger, and that when it had served His purpose of punishment, He would turn upon His tool (Isaiah x. 5–15). After Isaiah's day the concept is one of the commonplaces of the Prophets. It is true that the idea of punishment did not appear to cover the whole problem—as the Second Book of Esdras, for instance, shows—and that the Jew had no light to give upon the question, 'What other purposes has Jehovah in the strange vicissitudes that He permits for men and nations?' Here the *whole* of 'His ways' were 'past finding out'. None the less, the Jew believed that Jehovah had His own plan in it all, however inscrutable, and He would 'bring' His plan 'to pass'. Here, too, Christianity is the heir of Judaism.

As already several times stated, Judaism at large and apocalyptic *par excellence*, added a third postulate as it strove to give an account of the universe. In modern terms, it believed that Jehovah would turn the present chaos into a future cosmos. It believed that He would do this by a cataclasm—and a cataclasm that would be no inevitable event in a fated recurrence, nor the outcome of some process of progress in the universe itself, but a decisive and overwhelming act of His own power. In such a time as that of Augustus it might seem for a moment to a Virgil that a halcyon day had dawned on earth, but for the Jew no time when a heathen Emperor, tolerating popular polytheism and prescribing a State *cultus*, governed the world could seem halcyon. In other words, the Jew believed that the coming cataclasm would be a judgement. There is no need to depict the varying details that different writers added to this central idea. The apocalyptists, looking at the present chaos, all expected the 'end of the [present]

Age', with its cataclasm and judgement, soon. After this they all 'looked for a new heaven and a new earth wherein dwelleth righteousness'. In other words, when they considered the next age, the concept of the kingship of God suffered a certain change. In that age there would be no sin, no rebels, no misery, but all men and every man would gladly obey the will of God. In that age the kingship of Jehovah would have its proper correlative in a righteous and happy world—in the modern sense there would be a perfect 'kingdom' as well as a perfect king. If the apocalyptic symbolism be stripped away, this idea, too, is Christian. It will appear below that all this means that the Jews believed in the 'Kingdom of God' in at least two senses.

The concept of the 'Messiah' belongs to apocalyptic, but it is best left to the chapter on Mediation. The question remains: 'What bearing have eschatology and apocalyptic on the idea of salvation?' The answer has already been implied and needs only to be recapitulated. It is plain that the apocalyptists, like all Jews, believed that God would save the universe both from sin, misery, and every kind of trouble. It is plain, too, that they believed that in the end He would save every righteous man. It is plain, too, that they did not think it incongruous with their notion of God that He should leave the wicked to the miseries of Sheol or even of Gehenna. There is no doctrine of the salvation of sinners, no idea that God would find a way by which bad men might become good. While these writers no doubt shared the common concept of their contemporaries—to be discussed in a later chapter—that an evil man might at any time repent, and so become a good man, and therefore share in the realm of future bliss, yet the dominant idea was that God will save good men from trouble, not that He will save bad men from sin. Yet, paradoxically, the Jews now knew all the while that before God 'There is none righteous, no, not one'.

CHAPTER IX

MEDIATION

THE idea that Jehovah spoke *directly to His people Israel* seems to occur only once in the Old Testament. This is in the story of the theophany on Sinai (Exodus xix). Even here it would be more correct to say that Jehovah made ready to speak to the Israelites and that this proved too terrifying for them to bear. The ideas that Jehovah sometimes spoke direct to *individual men*, on the other hand, is found fairly often, from the stories of Adam, Noah and Abraham onwards. Here, however, the idea that He spoke through them to others is not found, or at most is in the background. With Moses there was a change. He was the first mediator in the stories of Israel. After this, as already shown, there were various examples of the idea. While Moses mediated law, good kings mediated rule and judgement, and prophets mediated teaching. While it is often silently assumed that God spoke directly to prophets, there are a few cases where this is directly asserted—for instance, Amos said to Amaziah, 'Jehovah said unto me' (Amos vii. 15). Yet there is also a passage where it is asserted that Jehovah spoke to no man 'face to face' except to Moses (Deuteronomy xxxiv. 10), and there are a good many where 'the Spirit of Jehovah' reveals His will to a Prophet. This phrase will be named again later, but the idea seems to be present that God is so terrible and holy that even a Prophet has not quite direct contact with Him. None the less, true Prophets were mediators between God and man, and, as has been seen, were thereby in some sense saviours. The High Priest should be added, for when such a High Priest as is described in the fiftieth chapter of Ecclesiasticus came forth from the Holy Place to bless the people, surely he was thought of as mediating forgiveness. Yet it must have been difficult to retain this idea in the generations before Christ. What were the feelings of a devout Jew when on the Day of Atonement he waited in the court of the Temple for a Jason, an Alexander Jannaeus, or a Caiaphas to come forth from the Holy of Holies? As to the other kinds of mediator—law-giver, king, prophet—all had ceased. Apart from priests, there were no human mediators left, unless one reckons the pseudepigraphic

writers of apocalypses. No wonder the Jew cherished the Book
that enshrined the mediations of the past.

Yet he could not believe in a merely absentee God. Nor did it
suffice to believe that God was working out His plans inscrutably
in current history. Surely He was still revealing Himself in some
way. The devout Jew found himself in the dilemma that has
examples in the devout men of other religions, too. He believed
at one and the same time that no man can 'see God and live',
and that no man can 'live' unless he 'sees God'. In this dilemma
he developed the idea of mediation in a new way, or, rather, he
developed, in an unsystematic but far-reaching fashion, an old
way. In doing this, he used various phrases, in part drawing on
passages in his own book and in part borrowing, so far as it suited
him, from current ideas. Some of these phrases must be
mentioned, though a full discussion of their origin and use would
take us too far from our immediate subject.

One of these is *shekinah*. This word does not occur in the Old
Testament, but it was used in the Hebrew of Jesus' day for the
glory of Jehovah that was manifested in the Tabernacle of Moses
and the Temple of Solomon. The word means 'dwelling' or
'abiding', and it was used for the splendour of Him that 'dwelleth
between the cherubim'. Was this Jehovah or only a manifestation
of Jehovah? The Jew hesitated about the answer. As the use of
Greek spread, it seems to have been noticed that the Greek term
for tent or tabernacle (*skēnē*) had a similar sound to *shekinah*. So
a Christian writer said that 'the Tabernacle—the *shekinah*—of God
is with men'. Did no Jew believe this? If not, why did he now
make use of the word? At any rate, it seems to be necessary to
put the idea that underlay the word paradoxically: the *shekinah*
was not Jehovah, yet it was.

Another term was 'glory'. Here neither the Hebrew term nor
the Greek means 'splendour' by etymology, yet both came to
mean this. The term goes readily with *shekinah*, yet it could be
used more widely. It was applied, not only to the 'glory' that
'dwelt' 'between the cherubim', but to such fiery manifestations
of God as the 'pillar of fire' that led Israel in the wilderness and
the flame of the theophany on Sinai. Such expressions were the
more suitable because 'smoke' went with 'fire'—that is, symbolically,
mystery went with manifestation. Or, to put this in another way,
the comparison with the sun was to hand, for many peoples have
used the sun as symbol for God. It illustrates the two underlying

paradoxes: if a man look at the sun, he is blinded, yet no man can see without the sun; again, the sun's brilliant rays may both be distinguished from the sun and identified with it. To-day the word 'glory' is either used without any apparent meaning at all or as a kind of pious interjection. It is time that the ancient meaning of the word was restored. 'Thine is the glory!' Both these words, though used literally in describing past events, were used symbolically of God's manifestation of Himself now.

In these instances the starting-point is something that can be seen. There was another such term—'face'. We all think that we can gather much of a man's character from his face. This notion, also rid of its imperfections, was transferred symbolically to God. It is easy to see how the idea of 'face' goes with the idea of 'presence'. There are terms both in Hebrew and Greek that may be translated by either word: 'Thy presence shall go with me' ; 'And they shall see His face'. In a passage in Deutero-Isaiah where the Hebrew has 'And the angel of His presence saved them', the Greek rendering suggests: 'No angel but His presence saved them' (Isaiah lxiii. 9). Here the idea of salvation (from suffering) is clearer than under *shekinah* or 'glory'.

There were also terms in use that drew analogies not from the eye but the ear. These are 'name' and *memra* or *logos*. It is the last term that lies nearest our subject.

A man's speech is a clue to the man. In consequence, the 'word' of Jehovah could be and was conceived as a manifestation of God. The idea is found in the Old Testament. For instance, the process of creation in the first chapter of Genesis is a consequence of a series of 'words' of God. 'And God *said*, . . . and it was so.' The idea occurs elsewhere, too: 'He *spake*, and it was done' ; 'The Ages were framed by the *word* of God'. The Jew had a term to express this—*memra*. Among the Greek-speaking Jews the idea was further developed. Here the term is *logos*. The writer of the Book of Wisdom uses it in a way that seems artificial to us; speaking of the destruction of the Egyptians in the days of Moses, he says: 'Thine all-powerful word leaped from heaven out of the royal throne, a stern warrior, into the midst of the doomed land, bearing as a sharp sword thine unfeigned commandment; and standing it filled all things with death; and while it touched the heaven, it trode upon the earth' (Wisdom xviii. 15 *f*.; cf. Hebrews iv. 12). Here the word is a king's word of doom to his enemies and deliverance to his subjects, and it only needs to be uttered to be executed. Elsewhere, however, in this book there is another idea: 'The creation, ministering to thee, its maker . . . ministered to thine all-nourishing bounty. . . . That thy sons, whom thou lovest, O Lord, might learn . . . that thy word preserveth them that trust thee' (Wisdom xvi. 24–6). There is no need to examine the use of *Logos* in Philo in detail. It connects rather with the second use named above than with the first. But now something akin to the concept of immanence can be traced, for Philo tried hard to identify the Stoic concept of a revelation that pervades all Nature with the Hebrew concept of a personal God. Whether he succeeded need not be discussed. But it is notorious that Philo found it difficult to say whether the *Logos* is to be identified with God Himself or not. At one place he says that the *Logos* is 'a sort of god'. He was on the horns of the characteristic Jewish dilemma. His doctrine of the *Logos*, however, is of a creative and sustaining 'word', rather than of a redeeming one.

Philo uses two other terms that with him are hardly more than synonyms for *Logos*: 'wisdom' and 'spirit'. Here, too, he seems to have moved further in an immanental direction than Jewish thought in general. The Hebrew word for 'wisdom' does not denote a merely theoretical quality, but a practical one. It could therefore be used for 'prudence'—or, again, it might rise insensibly from this to denote the manifold skill that is needed to practise the great art of life. This brings us to something that distinguishes this concept from that of *shekinah*. Like 'glory' and 'name', 'wisdom' is related to human nature as well as to Divine. A man can have wisdom if he likes. 'My delight is with the sons of men', says Wisdom, and she pleads with men to receive her. Yet the concept here is not that wisdom is inherent in human nature in any immanental way, whether men will or not. She is a gift that is offered to men. If one were to use spatial terms, she comes from outside him. For the Jew wisdom was a quality both in God and, by the gift of God, also in *good* men. Here Jewish thought comes nearest to bridging one of the two great gulfs that for him separated God and men—the gulf between the Creator and creation.

He came nearest to bridging the other great gulf—that between the holy and the sinful—under the concept 'spirit'. Here the Hebrew term, unlike the corresponding Greek and Latin terms (*pneuma* and *spiritus*), did not originally mean 'air' but 'rushing mighty wind'. For instance, when 'the Spirit of Jehovah' came

H

upon Samson, he went out furiously to slay Philistines. Before the Exile, the term does not seem to be used at all to describe a part or aspect of human nature, but later it could be so used. As we have already seen, it is so used, for instance, in the Fifty-first Psalm. Here, therefore, the later use is parallel to that of 'wisdom'. Man is not altogether unlike God, for 'Spirit' is an element in both their natures. Even here, however, the immanental concept is not worked out. Indeed, it is at least doubtful whether a clear-thoughted believer in immanence could ask: 'Renew a right spirit within me.' Yet it is perhaps here that Old Testament thought drew nearest to the concept of immanence. The tendency is carried further in the Book of Wisdom and in Philo. Here it is difficult to deny that immanence is taught. It is true that in the Book of Wisdom the concept of spirit is subordinate to that of wisdom and in Philo to that of *Logos*, yet it does occur, and it carries further the tendency to the immanental use of both terms. The greatest passage in the former is too long to quote (Wisdom vii. 22*b*–viii. 1), but it begins with the statement, 'There is in [wisdom] a spirit quick of understanding', and it teaches both that wisdom pervades the universe and that it 'maketh men friends of God and prophets. For nothing doth God love save him that dwelleth with wisdom'. Yet even here there is no concept that wisdom indwells *bad* men in any way. Elsewhere, indeed, the writer says that 'wisdom will not enter into a soul that deviseth evil' even though 'wisdom is a spirit that loveth man' (Wisdom i. 4–7). However inconsistent it may seem, immanence in the *whole* universe is clearly taught, but not immanence in *every* man. There is little doubt that in its teaching about wisdom and spirit this book had some influence at least on the phraseology of some New Testament writers.

It will be seen that while the ancient idea that the Spirit of God is mighty has not here been lost, yet there is no longer always the idea that the Spirit works by inruptive violence. Power and violence do not necessarily go together. The distinction between them is found in the Old Testament—for instance, in the early verses of the sixty-first chapter of Isaiah, or in the two passages where the phrase 'holy spirit' occurs in the Old Testament (Psalms li. 11; Isaiah lxiii. 10). As to the so-called Palestinian books in the Apocrypha, while there are parallels to the general Old Testament use, two particular uses should be named: sometimes 'spirit' is used as a synonym for 'angel', a term whose meaning is discussed

below; and there are instances of the use of the phrases 'the spirit'
or 'the holy spirit' without the addition of 'Thy' or 'of God'. For
example, Esdras prays: 'If I have found favour before thee, send
the Holy Spirit into me' (2 Esdras xiv. 22). It is sometimes said
that this is one of the passages where the 'Spirit' is 'hypostatized',
but if a Jew could have been brought to understand the modern
question, 'Is the Spirit here an influence or a person?' he might
have denied that this twofold classification is exhaustive. Even
to many modern readers, the sentence probably suggests something
more than an influence and less than a person. It is just another
case where the Jew tries at once to do justice to the separateness
and to the activity of God.

It is clear that if the terms just discussed are no more than
devout alternatives for the word 'God', they do not illustrate
mediation at all, but, if the exposition suggested be accepted, they
are examples of a kind of semi-mediation. Through them God
makes Himself known to men in order that He may help men.
With the term 'angel', the question, 'Is an angel God Himself or
not?' has a clear answer. There are indeed passages in the pre-
Exilic documents where it is difficult to say whether the 'angel of
Jehovah' is or is not Jehovah Himself (e.g. in Judges vi. 11, 14),
but after the Exile, when angelology developed under Persian
influence, it is quite plain that an 'angel' is an intermediary
between God and man, and is himself neither God nor man. For
the most part, he has little character of his own, but is merely a
'messenger' from God, as both the Hebrew and Greek terms
literally require. If, therefore, the whole series of ideas is examined, we find three kinds of mediators: men, such as Moses and
the Prophets; manifestations of God, hardly distinguishable from
God Himself, such as the *Shekinah* and the *Logos*; and 'angels', who
are distinctly separable both from men and God. All these
concepts obtained at the same time. It is true that human
mediators, with the exception of the High Priest, had ceased, but
this does not mean that they could never occur again. The way
in which the people called both John the Baptist and Jesus
'prophets' shows this. None of the ideas was worked philosophi-
cally out, but their very multiplicity and variety shows that the
Jews could not be mere Deists. On the other hand, their
connotation, in spite of some partial exceptions, also requires
that immanentism was not congenial to the Jewish mind. Under
every term, God comes to man from outside man in order to do

man good. Sometimes He so comes in order, in one sense or other of the word, to *save* man. It is only and always God who bridges the gulf between God and man.

The concept of mediation appears in the apocalyptic books in a distinctive way. To show this, there is no need to examine all the books, nor even to discuss any book in detail, for it is only the main ideas that are relevant to the present subject. In the book of Enoch there is a superhuman figure, sometimes called 'the Elect One', sometimes 'the Son of God', sometimes 'the Messiah'. 'Superhuman', of course, is not a synonym for 'Divine'. How far the figure is meant for a literal being is doubtful, but there is no doubt that there is a symbolical meaning. Nor is there any doubt that the figure denotes a mediator. But he is not a mediator *now* at all. He is 'reserved in heaven' for future mediation. In the cataclasm that is to end this age he will appear to conquer, to judge, and to reign. He is God's *future* vicegerent. In the cataclasm he will use force, whatever he may be conceived as doing in the age that follows it. This is the dominant concept in the apocalyptic books. The exceptions to it need not detain us. It should be noted, however, that sometimes the Messiah is human, not superhuman. Through him the kingship of God in a rebellious world will pass into the kingship of God in an obedient world. This future realm will be happy; the symbol of a 'Messianic banquet', where the righteous 'sit down' to feast in 'the kingdom of God' sometimes expresses this. When the Messiah is thought of as human, he usually belongs to 'the house of David', though in the first fervour of Maccabaean victory he could be thought of as belonging to 'the house of Levi' (in parts of the Testimonies of the Twelve Patriarchs). While the term 'Messiah' is by no means universal in the apocalyptic books, the use of the word in the New Testament seems to show that in the time of Jesus it was current among the people. How far this was also so with 'Elect One' and 'Son of God' does not so clearly appear. It is possible that in Mark (xii. 35 *ff.*) Jesus refers to the question, 'Is the Messiah human or superhuman?' In comparison with the Old Testament doctrine of the Messiah, discussed above, the chief novelties are that the *term* is now used to describe the expected *future* ruler and not for a living man, and that the coming king is now uniformly an apocalyptic figure.[1]

One or two notes need to be added about the use of the phrase

[1] For a full statement, see T. Walker, *op. cit.*, chap. iii.

'Son of God'. In the Old Testament it had been used of angels, of the people Israel, of the Davidic king, and of judges (e.g. Psalms xxix. 1; Hosea xi. 1; Psalm lxxxix. 26 f.; Psalm lxxxii. 6). In Sirach and the Book of Wisdom it is used, along with 'Son of the Most High', as equivalent to 'a righteous man' (e.g. Ecclesiasticus iv. 10; Wisdom ii. 18)—some would say, 'a suffering righteous man'. In Enoch it is used as a synonym for 'Messiah', and this may also be so sometimes in the New Testament (e.g. Mark xiv. 61; John i. 49). Under this phrase the human concept seems to have been more frequent than the superhuman one.

It seems to be agreed that both in Hebrew and Aramaic the phrase 'Son of Man' was used as a synonym for 'a man'. In the apocalyptic books, however, it is sometimes used in a distinctive way. Some think that in apocalyptic the antecedents of the phrase are Persian, but a Jew would not borrow ideas unless he could connect them in some way with his own writings. In the Book of Ezekiel God addresses the Prophet more than ninety times as 'son of man'. Even if the phrase here is equivalent to 'man', it seems unlikely that it has nothing distinctive about it. The clue can perhaps be found if the first use of the phrase (Ezekiel ii. 1) is taken in its context. In the first chapter there is a description of the way in which Jehovah showed Himself to Ezekiel. This theophany lies in the Prophet's mind throughout his prophecies, reappearing explicitly when they reach their climax (Ezekiel xliii. 1 ff.). It would be out of place to consider it in detail, but one or two of its very distinctive ideas may be named. Jehovah does not now show Himself hidden in a cloud, but half-hidden in a rainbow. Therefore He is both seen and unseen. What is seen is described in two phrases. One of these is: 'The appearance of the likeness of the glory of the LORD.' In the trailing phrase there is the sense of separation, yet not complete separation. One might almost say that God is seen at 'four removes', yet He is seen. When the Prophet saw even so much he 'fell upon his face'. On the other hand, upon 'the likeness of the throne' that is the summit of the vision there is 'a likeness as the appearance of a man'. It follows that God is not altogether unlike the human being lying prone before him. When bidden, Ezekiel can 'stand upon his feet'—or, rather, at God's first word 'the spirit entered into him and set him upon his feet'. In Ezekiel 'spirit' is a term used both of man and God (Ezekiel xxxvi. 26 f.). It has already been shown that this has a parallel in the Fifty-first Psalm, and that there is a similar duality in the use of the word 'wisdom'. Since it is also in this period that man is said to be made 'in the image of God', there seems to be no reason to deny that in Ezekiel the use of the term 'son of man' is related to the phrase used of God, 'a likeness as the appearance of a man'. In other words, when Ezekiel is addressed as 'son of man' both his insignificance and his worth are suggested. William Watson came near saying what is meant when he wrote of man:

> 'Magnificent out of the dust he came, and abject from the spheres.'

Nor is the phrase 'son of man' merely individual in Ezekiel. It is societary, too. The Prophet is aware that he is the mediator of a message, not just for himself, nor merely for Israel, but for all nations. It is not a great exaggeration to say that as Ezekiel lies on his face before God, he *is* mankind.

The same set of ideas appears in a different way in the Eighth Psalm. When its writer says:

> 'What is man that thou art mindful of him?
> And the son of man, that thou visitest him?'

it is clear that the parallelism requires that 'son of man' is a synonym for 'man'. It is clear, too, from the succeeding verses with their reference to 'dominion', that the first chapter of Genesis is in mind. Whether another phrase is rightly translated, 'Thou has made him a little lower than the angels' or 'lower than God', it is clear that man's greatness is asserted alongside his feebleness. Both are asserted because of the nature of God. He is creator of the universe; how small then is man! He 'visits' man—or, as Ezekiel would say, 'gives man His spirit'—and that means that man is tremblingly great. Finally, it is clear that the psalm applies both to individual men and to mankind. Here 'son of man' (like 'man') is both individual and societary in meaning.

In apocalyptic the phrase—or, rather, a variant of it—appears first in the seventh chapter of Daniel. Here it will be best to recall the historical situation and to put the writer's message in ordinary words. It is fairly well agreed that the passage belongs to the time of Antiochus Epiphanes, when faithful Jews were suffering and dying for their faith. For centuries the Jews had been under the rule or 'kingship' of alien empires—Babylonian, Persian, Grecian—which each in turn ruled the whole of their world. None the less, they believed that Jehovah was king all the time, however inscrutable His ways were. Presently the cataclasm of judgement will come, and then He will set up His kingship or 'kingdom' in the second sense described above, and in this realm the seemingly helpless 'saints of the Most High' will rule, as His vicegerents, over it. The use of the term 'the kingdom', without any such addition as 'of God', in this passage is noteworthy. In brief the writer is saying: 'The meek shall inherit the earth.'

The writer, putting all this in symbols, describes the alien empires under the form of wild beasts that come from the mysterious and evil chaos called 'the sea'. Clearly these wild beasts are societary concepts. Clearly, too, the idea of a universal realm is present. Next there comes the final judgement: 'One that was ancient of days did sit. . . . The judgement was set and the books were opened.' In other words, God asserts His kingship and ends all rebellions. Then: 'I saw in the night visions, and, behold, there came with the clouds of heaven one like unto a son of man.' This, too, is a societary concept. Indeed, later in the chapter this figure is identified with 'the saints of the Most High'. Again, unlike the wild beasts, the 'one like unto a son of man' comes from 'heaven'. And to him (that is, to the saints) there is given the final, universal and everlasting kingdom. The term 'kingdom' here, of course, implies both rule and realm. In it 'the saints' are to be the vicegerents of God.

It is clear that here too there is the concept that men—or, rather, in this instance explicitly (as implicitly in Ezekiel and the Eighth Psalm) righteous men—are both feeble in themselves and yet 'of worth for God'. What can a man do against a wild beast— or a faithful Jew against Antiochus Epiphanes? Yet all the time the saints have God behind them for they are righteous.

In later apocalyptic the phrase 'Son of Man', like the others named above, is far from universal. It is commonest in the Similitudes of Enoch. Here there are several differences as compared with the passage in Daniel. First the phrase 'the Son of Man' occurs instead of 'one like unto a son of man'. Alternatively the phrase 'that Son of Man' occurs and in Second Esdras 'the Man'. In the last book, and in the Book of Enoch outside the Similitudes, the Son of Man is called 'God's Son', while in the Similitudes the phrase is a synonym for 'the Elect One'. Again, in Enoch the 'Son of Man' is not only a superhuman but pre-existent being, a being older than the universe. His 'dwelling-place' is 'under the wings of the Lord of Spirits'. In other words, the symbol comes nearer being personalized than in Daniel. Again in Enoch the Son of Man is not only to rule for ever, but he is first to judge mankind, whereas in Daniel (as in some other Apocalypses) God Himself is judge. It is not so easy here to equate the figure with righteous men in their feebleness, but it seems still to represent them in their future power. In view of the whole account of the term, it seems hardly possible to claim that because 'son of man' is an equivalent of 'man' in Hebrew and Aramaic, the first phrase could not be used in these languages in any distinctive way. By some writers, at any rate, it was so used. Finally, it seems clear that the phrase 'Son of Man' was used from Daniel onwards because of the feeling that, however superhuman the final deliverer might be, and however close his dependence on God for his power, he must yet, if he were to deliver men, be societarily connected with them. Why else should the phrase persist? There were alternatives.

In the tenth and twelfth chapters of Daniel the current account of mediatorial angels has an apocalyptic development. Here there are angels, apparently in the upper regions of the air (rather than with God in 'heaven'), who represent Persia and Greece and Israel. The last is called Michael. He is said to have fought ith the other two and at length to have prevailed. Of him, unlike the others, the phrase 'one like the similitude of the sons of men' is used (Daniel x. 16; cf. viii. 15). There is here, too, a reminiscence of Ezekiel, but it is the angel, and not God, who is linked with the righteous among men (or the righteous in Israel, since, as already noted, for many writers at this time, there are no righteous men to speak of outside Israel, and 'righteous men' and 'righteous Israelites' were practically synonyms). Here, in a sense, Michael is mediator now, yet for the present he does not altogether prevail. He is to do this, as the twelfth chapter says, at the final crisis of 'trouble', deliverance, and triumph. The idea that even now there is an 'angel' who helps the righteous seems to have been common, for Jesus, making His own original change in the idea, declared that every 'little one' has an angel, not struggling as yet doubtfully in the mid-air, but 'always beholding the face' of God—and the kind of God that He was revealing— 'My Father'.

If now the whole series of ideas about mediation is examined, three things are clear, and there is a groping after a fourth. First, there is a distinction between present and future mediators.

Broadly speaking, the concept of future mediators belongs to the apocalyptic writings and that of present mediators to the other books. Daniel's 'One like unto a son of man' may stand here as type of the first class, and the Prophets as type of the second.

Secondly, to use the old phrases, there are many instances of mediation 'from God to man' and a few 'from man to God'. Under the first kind there come prophets and kings, all such terms as 'glory' and *logos*, and the characteristic apocalyptic figures. Under the second four may be mentioned: there is Moses in a story named earlier (Exodus xxxii. 30 *ff.*), there is the strangely neglected figure of the Servant of the LORD in Deutero-Isaiah, there are the priests in the Temple and especially the High Priest on the Day of Atonement, and there is the symbolic figure of Michael. In the first of these, however, Moses' noble offer is not accepted, and in the other three there is the concept that Jehovah has Himself appointed these mediators. The Servant is what he is because he is 'the Servant *of Jehovah*' and it is Jehovah who has 'pleased' to make him so. The High Priest carries out a ritual that God has appointed, and, as seen above, it was probably on this ground—and not from any sense of effectiveness in the ritual itself—that the pious Jew followed its precepts. Again, if all that is said of Michael in apocalyptic is examined, he is nothing but one of the chief instruments of God's rule.[1] Even in these three instances—to use the modern phrase—the initiative is with God. The root of the Jewish concept of mediation, therefore, is that God helps man. Neither here nor anywhere else in Jewish thought is the initiative with man. As will be seen in the next chapter, all that men can do in order to reach God is to pray and to repent.

Thirdly, the question needs to be asked: What connexion was there between the Jewish doctrine of mediation and sin? Of the earlier human mediators, and particularly of Moses and the Prophets, it may be said that they made the will of Jehovah known and thereby made the nature and scope of sin known. In addition, the Prophets declared that sin would bring disaster. For the rest, they called men to repent, and added that if men would do this, God would save them from the disasters that befell sinners. As already seen, they themselves, by what they *were*, more than by what they *said*, mediated unawares 'from man to God'—an idea that became explicit in the Songs of the Servant. Further, the

[1] For this, see art., 'Michael', in *H.D.B.*

cry of the Psalmist, 'Take not thy holy spirit from me', suggests that it is by the gift of God's 'spirit' that a sinner may be saved, but this idea was not generally pursued. Similarly, Wisdom pleads with men to forsake 'Folly' and choose her—in other words, calls men to repentance. There is just the suggestion that if they repent, she will change their nature, but this idea, too, is not pursued. There is even less of a doctrine of salvation under such concepts as Glory and Name, except in so far as any revelation or manifestation of God may be said to enlighten and succour men. On the Day of Atonement, again, there is no hint that forgiveness for past sins will save men from sinning again. The mediatorial figures in apocalyptic have even less to do with the salvation of sinners. The 'Son of Man', for instance, or the Messiah, appears at the end of the age to punish sinners and to set up a kingdom of righteousness where there will be no more sin, but any idea that bad men will be changed into good men is quite alien to the concept. The Christian concept of a Mediator—a Mediator who *now* saves sinners from their sin and unites them again with the holy God, a Mediator 'from man to God' and between men who are sinners and God—seems to have no place in apocalyptic at all. Outside apocalyptic it has only some adumbrations. The dominant ideas of mediation in Judaism are that God reveals Himself—His glory, His holiness, His righteousness—to men, and that through mediators He has come and will come to the help of righteous men. Before the Return from the Captivity the mediators are predominantly human; after it, predominantly superhuman. Under 'Son of Man', if the history of the phrase from Ezekiel to Enoch is studied, there is some attempt to say, however disjointedly, that a mediator must be both human and superhuman. In all this the Jew was groping after the right idea.

CHAPTER X

SIN AND REPENTANCE

As already noted, there is no reference to sin or to evil of any kind in the first passage in Genesis. In the story of the Garden of Eden, however, which belongs to much earlier documents, there is an account of sin, though the word does not occur. In this myth, God tells Adam and Eve not to do a certain thing, and they disobey Him. In subsequent times, ideas about the things that God commands and forbids widened and deepened and clarified, yet the root idea of sin remained constant. For the Hebrew, from first to last, to sin was to disobey God. The idea that sin did wrong to man was always secondary and indeed derivative, for a Hebrew wronged his neighbour when he did something to his neighbour that Jehovah had forbidden him to do. This was sin, not primarily because it harmed another man, but because God had forbidden it. Here, of course, the emphasis is laid quite otherwise than is common in to-day's thought. A Hebrew of much later days spoke for his whole people when he said, 'Against Thee, Thee only, have I sinned'.[1]

In the story of Eden, Adam and Eve disobey a *known* command, but in the Old Testament sin is not confined to conscious disobedience. When, for instance, Jonathan unknowingly breaks the ban that Saul has laid on food, he is still guilty, even though the people, perhaps by providing an alternative victim, save him from death. Similarly, in the Priestly documents, of much later times, there are offerings for 'unwitting sins'. The Prophets, too, teach that heathen nations will be punished for their sins, without inquiring whether they knew that they were sinners or not. An implied protest against the idea in the Book of Jonah only shows how prevalent it was (Jonah iv. 11). For the Old Testament, to sin is to disobey the will of God, known or unknown.

Again, the Hebrews began, as other peoples did, by defining sin in terms of outward act, not of the motive that lies behind the act. The instances of the sin of Jonathan and of unwitting ritual sins recur here. Under the teaching of the great Prophets a deeper

---

[1] If such a verse as Judges xix. 30 is held to define sin as mere breach of custom, this would be a very plain instance of the 'exception that proves the rule'.

account developed, until, as seen above, Jeremiah and Ezekiel
declared that sin so infected the character that only the gift of a
'new heart' and a 'new spirit' could save men from sinning. None
the less, the Hebrews, again like other peoples, never defined sin
altogether in terms of motive. Indeed, as their final account of
conduct was drawn under the concept of law, it was impossible
that they should do so, for law cannot deal with motive, but only
with outward act. Yet even here it must be remembered that for
the Hebrew 'law' has never been just a criminal code; it has always
involved teaching as well as penalty. Consequently, however
illogically, the Deuteronomist can command motive. He says,
'Thou shalt *fear* Jehovah thy God', and 'Thou shalt *love* the LORD
thy God', and a later lawgiver can add, 'Thou shalt *love* thy
neighbour as thyself, [because] I am the LORD'. Hebrew thought,
taken as a whole, never drew out clearly the relation between the
outward act and the inward motive, either in its account of
righteousness or of sin.

Again, the Hebrews held tenaciously to the belief that there is
a connexion between what we call 'moral' and 'physical' evil.
They believed that suffering is the punishment of sin. As is well
known, the problem, 'Why do the wicked often flourish and the
righteous often suffer?' was the problem that most vexed these
unwavering believers in ethical monotheism. There is no need
to detail the ways in which they tried to meet it, nor their very
partial success in doing so. No believers in ethical monotheism
have ever given a complete answer. The Jews, however, never
reached the conclusion that seems to be prevalent to-day: they
never said 'There is no connexion between sin and suffering'.
They did not even say, 'There is no connexion between *individual*
sin and *individual* suffering'. In spite of all exceptions, they
believed that normally, at least, a man's sufferings are the result
of his sins—and the God-given result. This appears, for instance,
in the assumption that 'those eighteen on whom the tower in
Siloam fell' were especially sinful. There is another example in
Second Maccabees, where the writer declares that every Jew who
had fallen in a certain battle against the Syrians had been guilty
of secret sin (2 Maccabees xii. 38 *ff.*). The writer of Ecclesiastes
may be quoted on the other side (e.g. Ecclesiastes ix. 2), but he
was not a typical Jew. The current opinion in Judaism was that
in spite of seeming exceptions, suffering is the result of sin, and
that in 'the coming age', if not in this one, God will nullify the

exceptions by rewarding the suffering righteous exceedingly and punishing exceedingly the prosperous sinners.

So far we have spoken chiefly of individual sin, but in Judaism there was also a doctrine of societary sin. This had ancient roots, appearing, for instance, in the story of the 'death-devoting' of Achan's family for Achan's sin, and in the Prophetic and Deutero-nomic concept that a nation—whether Israel or another—could sin. The Jewish books of the period before and after the time of Christ, however, show the doctrine in another form. There were three accounts current of the *origin* of sin. Some traced it to the sin of Adam in the Garden of Eden, some to the day when 'the sons of God saw the daughters of men that they were fair', and some to 'the evil imagination of man's heart' (Genesis iii., vi. 1 *ff.*, viii. 21). The last conceived sin as an 'evil impulse' or *cor malignum*, or *yetser hara*, that God had planted in man's nature when He created him.[1] Behind all three accounts there is a common idea. All three attempt to explain the origin of a phenomenon that is taken for granted. All assume that the whole race of mankind is sinful—that is, that there is such a thing as societary sin on the widest scale—and that this fact needs to be accounted for. It is easy to say that this kind of sin comes to men by inheritance, but this is not inherent in the idea. Perhaps here the word 'infection' is better than the word 'inheritance', for even under the third idea—as, for instance, in Second Esdras, whose writer is its chief surviving exponent—the concept that the 'evil impulse' of one man influences other men is found. This racial sin differs from individual, not indeed in being unknown, but in being always involuntary. No man can escape it for no man is merely individual. The Jew was not ignorant of the difficulty here, as is shown by the well-known phrase from the Apocalypse of Baruch, 'Every man is the Adam of his own soul', but he was not able to resolve the antinomy. In the third chapter of Second Esdras the problem is pressed. To use modern terms, the writer says: 'Mankind has gone wrong again and again; several times—with Noah, with Abraham, with Moses, with David—God has tried to counter this by creating a righteous man and so making a kind of fresh beginning; but what is the use of this so long as there is an evil impulse in every man's soul? Men are sure to go wrong again

---

[1] There is a full exposition of this subject in N. P. Williams' *Ideas of the Fall and Original Sin*. The later doctrine of the Fall could find root in the first two accounts, but not, at any rate in the same form, in the third. Now for the first time the serpent in Eden was identified with the Devil (Wisdom ii. 24).

so long as this is so.' Clearly, with change of phrase, the same question could be asked under any account of racial sin. None the less, for Israel involuntary sin, as well as unconscious sin, is still sin. To deny this and to claim that only conscious and voluntary disobedience to God's will ought to be called 'sin', does not mean that the societary phenomenon disappears; it only means that it is to be called by some other name, such as 'moral evil'. The time came when theologians called this racial evil 'original sin'. The phrase was not fortunate, but to-day the phenomenon is one of those that the psychotherapists diagnose. It is there, whatever its origin and name.

To the ideas of individual sin and racial sin the Jew added a third, that of 'cosmic evil'. This phrase, however, is too abstract to correspond exactly to the concepts of the Jew, for he loved to speak in concrete terms. He believed that there were other beings beside men who were sinful; he had a belief in devils, demons, and evil spirits. Here, again, there is no need to examine his ideas exhaustively. They were not fully reduced to system any more than other nations' ideas on the subject have been. All believers in ethical monotheism have to face the question: 'How can there be any kind of evil in the universe of a righteous God?' Some, emphasizing the word 'ethical', tend to say, 'We cannot explain how it came to be there, but we are sure that the *righteous* God did not create it and has now nothing to do with it except to baulk and destroy it'. On the other hand, those who emphasize the word 'monotheism' seem to be bound to say, 'God is almighty and He alone creates; therefore there can be nothing in His universe, not even evil, that He did not create and that He does not control'. The dilemma is well known, and it need hardly be said that no ethical monotheists have been able to give a complete answer. The Jew seems now and then to say that he believed that God *created* evil—as, for instance, in the Deutero-Isaianic phrase (Isaiah xlv. 7), 'I form the light, and create darkness; I make peace, and create evil' (though it might be argued that here the reference is only to physical evil), or in the doctrine of the 'evil impulse' in Second Esdras—but for the most part he leaves this problem alone. It is different with the question, 'Does God *control* evil (now that it is here)?' The Old Testament answer was always, 'Yes'. For instance, 'an evil spirit from the LORD' (distinct from 'the Spirit of the LORD') vexes Saul, or the LORD is said to 'put a lying spirit' in the mouths of the prophets who prophesy before

Ahab and Jehoshaphat, or 'the Satan' (the Adversary) appears in the courts of God, in the Books of Job and Zechariah, as an 'angel' of God whose business is to test men's righteousness by tempting them.

In the period when angelology and demonology developed further in Israel, largely under Persian influence, the common concept of God's control of evil took a rather different form. It becomes less direct. To use a homely metaphor, it is like the control that a dog's master exercises over a dog on a chain. The master leaves the dog a certain limited liberty, but the dog cannot go 'beyond his chain'. In English literature the classic illustration is Milton's picture of the sudden grovelling of Satan and his myrmidons before the power of God. Under this concept, for instance, God, enthroned above the heavens and able at any time to do what He will beneath them, may yet permit the 'angel of Persia' to fight with Michael, or allow the multitudinous demons to vex to some degree the children of men. In other words, the Almighty, for His own purposes, gives rebels some scope for a while. Evil spirits are now no longer His emissaries, but His temporarily tolerated enemies.

While it is possible to describe separately the three kinds of evil —individual sin, racial sin, and cosmic evil—it would be a mistake to think that the Jew separated them. On the contrary, however unsystematically, he held them all together in a single concept, and included with them a fourth phenomenon—that which we call 'physical evil'. With them there went too his concept of death. As has already been seen, under this word he included not only the momentary physical fact, but its sequel, Hades. About this he at last held unswervingly that it ought not to be the final fate of the righteous. The fact that some Jews came to believe that within its bounds there might be a 'Paradise' for the righteous, did not mean that the notion that the righteous ought not to dwell in Sheol or Hades disappeared, for even this lower Paradise is not a perfect state. The Jew knew that ethical monotheism demands that the righteous and almighty God should 'make an end of sin'— and with it of evil in all its horrible complexity. Consequently a part of the burden of all apocalyptic is: 'There shall be no more curse', 'There shall be no more death' ; all apocalyptists 'looked for a new heaven and a new earth wherein dwelleth righteousness'.

Logically this would mean that all evil and all evil beings should be destroyed, in the sense 'become extinct', but this conclusion was not drawn. On the contrary, the ideas of the abyss below the earth, where the evil spirits have their home, and of Gehenna, originally a part of the hollow within the earth called Sheol, tended to coalesce, and to become a realm of suffering 'reserved for the devil and his angels'—and for wicked men. This realm remains after the Apocalyptic Judgement. The concept of Judgement, and with it of punishment, was very strong. It was not confined to the Hereafter—Esdras, for instance, admits that the feeble Israel of his day had long been suffering on earth for the sins of the nation—but it had its climax there. Here it needs to be recalled that for Eastern thought a just judge was properly angry with the wicked, that, indeed, he ought to be angry with them because he was just, that punishment was this 'righteous anger' in action, and that 'vengeance' meant, not something unjust or something that went beyond the proper limits of punishment, but the vindication of justice. Indeed, the Greek word translated 'vengeance' in the English New Testament literally means 'vindication' (*ekdikēsis*).

While Jewish thought drew together cosmic evil (including physical disasters), societary sin, and individual sin in a single whole, this was not so with its answer to the question 'How is this evil to be done away?' The cataclasm would banish cosmic evil from 'the heaven and the earth' by force. Nothing seems clearly to be said of the way in which racial sin would disappear. As to individual sin the dominant idea was that as God is merciful, He will pardon the *penitent*. It is true that there are illustrations of other, or rather of complementary, ideas. In some books there is emphasis on the virtue of almsgiving, in others on prayer, on fasting, and on good works generally. In others the atoning value of the Temple sacrifices, especially on the Day of Atonement, is asserted. There are even passages where the notion occurs that such good works as these are meritorious in themselves. Other such meritorious works are the study of the Law, suffering, and martyrdom. Some added that the righteous men of old, and even of to-day, laid up a kind of store of merit, which may avail for Israel as a whole and even for sinful Israelites. In the twelfth chapter of Second Maccabees there is an instance of prayer and sacrifice for dead Hebrew sinners. In these last examples the societary concept is applied to righteousness, just as it was applied (though in a different way) to sin in the doctrine of racial evil. Yet, when all is said, the chief emphasis was on *repentance*. Most of the other ideas, indeed, if not all, may be brought under the concept that good works are just evidence of true repentance, 'fruits meet for repentance'. The dominant Jewish idea was that God would forgive men their sins if they sincerely repented.[1] The strength of this idea lay in its truth. God does not expect more than the possible from men, and before Jesus came, nothing more than sincere repentance was possible. But it is clear that here there is no adequate answer to the question, 'How are bad men to be turned into good men?' Penitent men unhappily often go on to sin again. Indeed, all men are more or less sinful. Repentance does not eradicate the 'evil impulse' or cure racial sin. About the root problem of salvation neither the sacrificial system nor apocalyptic nor the Jewish doctrine of mediation had anything much to say. In them there is no proper sequel to the Psalmist's cry for a 'a clean heart' or the Prophet's claim that God would 'write his law' in men's hearts. The doctrine of the Suffering Servant yielded no true fruit as yet. When a new Prophet arose, he only spoke with the voice of the better kind of Jew when he called *all* men to repent. Even Pharisees came to John's Baptism. But John did not stop at that point. He went on to say that something more than repentance was needed, and that One was on His way who would bring that something more.

---

[1] For the evidence, see T. Walker, *op. cit.*, chap. v.

I

THE NEW TESTAMENT

CHAPTER XI

THE POSTULATES AND PREACHING OF JOHN THE BAPTIST

The New Testament is a Book of Salvation. It is many other things, too, but this is its primary quality. Consequently, a complete account of its doctrine of salvation would require a complete account of almost everything in it. This, of course, is not possible here. Sometimes, on the other hand, the New Testament doctrine of the Work of Christ has been isolated overmuch. Some books about it almost reduce it to an account of the comparatively few passages that refer directly to the Death of Christ. Here a middle way will be attempted. In this chapter certain presuppositions of the whole of the New Testament will be elucidated, a beginning being made from the records about John the Baptist.

There was a time, not long ago, when it was claimed that such a man as a Philippian jailor would never have said to itinerant evangelists, earthquake or no earthquake, 'Sirs, what shall I do to be *saved*?', but this time seems to be over. No doubt Luke's account of the episode epitomizes what happened rather severely, but the *papyri* show that the term 'save' was current in the eastern half of the Roman Empire. Ever since the time of Alexander mankind had been vexed with 'world wars'. In consequence, men were pessimistic. They submitted ultimately to the veiled despotism of Augustus, but it was only for a moment that it seemed to some that this would end the miseries of mankind. Those who refused to be hopeless turned to religion—that is, they turned from men to God. This accounts for the popularity of the Mystery Cults, for the old religions of Greece and Rome were bankrupt. Men either lost hope altogether or looked for some new 'way of salvation'. Even in the midst of the chaos of to-day many are still so shortsighted as to sniff at the word 'save', but it was not so in the first century.

It was least of all so with the Jew. Alone in the world of that day, he never submitted at heart to Rome. Even those Jews who counselled immediate submission believed that God would some time save His people from the rule of the heathen. How could

they, with the Old Testament behind them, believe anything else?
One of the outcomes of this belief was the apocalyptic literature.
It is the product of a theism that refuses to despair. The Jew
firmly believed in a coming salvation. The Baptist claimed to be
'preparing the way' for One who would 'gather the wheat into
his garner' (Luke iii. 17) and so save some. But from what were
some to be saved? Here it is sufficient to give the Jewish answer,
without inquiring how far some or all of the Gentiles shared it.
The Jewish answer fell into two parts: 'God will save the *righteous*
from everything that is wrong in His world', and 'He will judge,
purify and perfect the *world* itself'. To be rid of heathen domina-
tion was one item in this answer, but it was by no means the only
item. Men who believed that there was one God, living, active,
and righteous, could not but believe that He would abolish every
kind of sin—whether individual or societary—and every kind of
physical evil, too. It is almost impossible to overstretch the scope
of the expected salvation. Only hell itself was excluded. It goes
without saying that here the Baptist agreed with the Jew.

Among all these evils, which did the Jew put first? Once
again, with the Old Testament behind him, he could only give
one answer. In spite of all the difficulties that beset the belief, he
held firmly that the root of all kinds of evil was sin. This was just
the other side of the belief that the righteous would be saved:
they would be saved from all evils because they were not sinners.
There is no need to show that for the Baptist with his cry,
'Repent!', and for the New Testament writers, too, sin was the
root of all evil, and that those who were 'saved' from sin would
thereby sooner or later be saved also from every other evil as well.
Curiously enough, while this is admitted to be true for all the
followers of Jesus, it has been challenged in Jesus' own case. It
has been supposed that here He forsook the beliefs of Israel and
set out to 'save' men from disease and not from sin! The only
ground for this idea is the fact that in the Synoptic Gospels the
term 'save' is generally used of His cures. Something will be said
later on this point, but it seems *prima facie* unlikely that if He
disagreed with the Jews about sin, His disciples should have all
assumed that He agreed with them! Jew and Christian united
in the creed that for a righteous God sin is the worst of evils and
the root of the rest. The difference between Jew and Christian
did not lie here. It lay in the answer to the question: 'How may
the *sinful* be saved?' As has been seen, the Jewish answer, broadly

speaking, was: 'By repenting of their sins and doing their best to be righteous.' The Baptist held that this was an incomplete answer, and all the New Testament agrees with him.

Before turning to the several New Testament writings, it will be an advantage to say something of certain other ideas that all their writers presupposed and that the Baptist anticipated. They are ideas that Jesus Himself also held; where this seems doubtful, more will be said in the next chapter. To describe them will help to show why so much space has been given to Hebrew and Jewish teaching.

The four Gospels all teach that the preaching of the Baptist was the organic prelude of the ministry of Jesus. This is the ground taken also in some of the speeches in the Acts of the Apostles. It is true that probably the followers of Jesus and those of John fell apart and at last even became antagonistic. There is implicit evidence for this, for example, in the Prologue of the Fourth Gospel. It is true too that in many of the New Testament writings there is no mention of the Baptist. Yet it needs to be remembered, here as always, that the stories that found expression in the Synoptic Gospels were current in all the churches to which the Epistles and the Apocalypse were sent. The preaching of John the Baptist is the historical antecedent of the movement that became Christianity, and there are things that John said or took for granted that were also accepted by the Christian Church—and by Jesus Himself.

While John's preaching looked forward to a 'mightier' one, it also looked backward. John is rightly called a Hebrew Prophet. When he wished to say who he was, he quoted the Old Testament. He thought that if he could find foothold there this would suffice for his hearers, and he was right. For the Jew of the time the final appeal was to 'the Law and the Prophets'—not to argument or philosophy or psychology, but to *the* Book. Neither Jesus nor the Apostles rejected this appeal. Nothing is more remarkable throughout the New Testament than the way in which every one accepts the authority of the Old Testament. No writer can let it alone. It is true that it is quoted in different ways, but it is always quoted. Perhaps three different ways may be distinguished. There is the 'proof passage' method, in which texts are torn from their context and applied to Jesus if only their literal meaning admits of this; the leading example of this method is in the first two chapters of Matthew. Then there is a symbolic or allegorical use, such as has a very elaborate example in the writings of Philo. This may be more or less artificial, as when Paul says, 'This Hagar is Mount Sinai in Arabia'. Yet the symbolic use sometimes passes into a third kind of use, for the symbolic may pierce to the principle that underlies an Old Testament passage. As will appear below, this has an example in the way in which the writer to the Hebrews contrasts Jesus with the Jewish High Priest. Thirdly, the spiritual principle that lies behind an Old Testament passage may be elucidated and developed. Here Jesus is the peerless illustration. In a large part of the Sermon on the Mount, for instance, He lays bare the principles that lie behind sayings of 'old time', and then goes on to develop and perfect those principles. While both Jesus and the first Christians appealed to the Old Testament because this was the most likely way of winning a hearing from Jews, they themselves too believed that there was an organic connexion between the religion of Israel and the new truth.

As we have seen, the Old Testament taught the seriousness and the universality of sin. About its seriousness the Baptist hardly did more than repeat the Old Testament teaching—indeed, it was all but impossible to do more. About its universality he put right a current error. As we have seen, in Judaism there was a belief in the universality of sin, and this in two forms: there was a belief that every single man sins, and also a belief that the human race is universally infected by sin. But, at least in some circles, there was also the belief that, since the second phenomenon limits man's freedom to do right and condemns every man willy-nilly to some degree of sinfulness, God, who is not unreasonable, will accept as righteous any man who repents and does his best. There were men who did their best in John's environment. The honest Pharisees fall here, for the Pharisees were not all hypocrites in the modern sense of that term. There is truth in the idea that God will accept every man who does his best, yet, so long as a man's best is not sinlessness, God cannot be content. Even such a man, in Paul's phrase, 'comes short of the glory of God'. It was the denial that something more was needed that was the insidious temptation of sincere Pharisaism. So long as Christ had not revealed the way in which that 'something more' could be achieved, the temptation was very subtle; yet it was still a temptation, and many fell before it. Both the Pharisees and their admirers believed that they needed nothing more than they had.

John taught that they needed something more: Jesus taught that they needed it and that He could give it them. Of course, vast multitudes of 'respectable people' to-day take exactly the Pharisaic attitude—with less excuse, for now the Christ is known. In spite of all that the Old Testament had said, there were men in John's day who did not believe that *they* needed to be 'saved' from sin. John called them a 'brood of vipers'! Jesus ironically said of them that He did not 'come to call the righteous, but sinners to repentance'. Theirs was the sin of those who, having the best there is, do not admit that they need something better, and refuse it when it is offered them. The significant thing about John is not that he baptized, for there seem to be precedents for this, but that he called *all* men, and particularly *all Jews*, to confess in baptism that they were sinners. To respond was to admit both that one had sinned oneself, and that, to use the Jew's own phrase, there is an 'evil impulse' in every human heart that needs to be removed—or, rather, that God must remove before He can say that all is well. Here, too, the New Testament writers, each in his own way—and Jesus, too, as we shall see, in His own way— held with the Baptist. John and the New Testament writers after him, thoroughly believed in 'the wrath of God'. Here, too, they took over without question the Old Testament doctrine, and here, too, their contemporary Jews agreed with them. An attempt has been made to show that Jesus himself did not accept this doctrine, on the ground that (except in Luke xxi. 23) He uses neither of the Greek *words* translated 'wrath' or 'anger', but this is to be a slave of the letter. Without the *concept*, some Parables— such as those of the Wheat and Tares, or of the Man who Built on Sand, or of the Sheep and Goats—mean nothing. Without it, much of the apocalyptic teaching of Jesus would hardly make sense. Without it, such phrases as 'eternal fire', 'the outer darkness', 'Gehenna', and 'where their worm dieth not and the fire is not quenched' would not only be symbolic, but symbolic of nothing. Without it Jesus' use of the word 'perish' would lose its meaning. In the sense described earlier, Jesus believed in 'the wrath of God'.

But, while the idea is universal in the New Testament, its meaning must not be misunderstood. As in the Old Testament, 'the wrath of God' was the sequel and outcome of His justice— not something unjust and undeserved and capricious. Nor do the writers of the New Testament speak often of being 'saved

from wrath'. They usually think and speak of being saved from
sin. It is assumed by them all that if a man were righteous, for
him there will be no wrath. Again, it was assumed by the Jews
and by the Baptist that if a sinner repented, for him there would
be no wrath. By the Christians it was assumed that there was no
'wrath' for believers in Christ. Under all three ideas there lies
another: that if a man does the will of God, wrath dies. There is
no notion anywhere of 'satisfying the wrath of God'. His anger
needs no punishment of guilt in order that it may pass away. It
needs obedience only. The primary New Testament concept is
not 'How can a sinner satisfy the wrath of God?', but 'How can
a man be brought to do the will of God?' If he comes to do this,
there is no place for wrath. For the New Testament writers,
if a man is saved from sin, he is thereby 'saved from wrath',
if the latter phrase is to be used at all. The Atonement deals
directly with sin, and only indirectly and by consequence with
wrath.

The concept of wrath, even when it is regarded as the sequel of
justice, seems to revolt the mind of to-day, but it is doubtful
whether any theist can escape it. When a theist looks at the
world, is he not bound at least to say: 'God has made the world in
such a way that if men and nations sin, misery befalls them'?
He has only two alternatives. Either all the woes of men
must be put down to 'accident' or to the doings of some 'god
of this world' who is evil and who is for the present more efficient
than God Himself. In reality, these two alternatives reduce to
one, for the first only calls this other evil power by the vague name
of 'accident'. At the least this means that the world has more or
less escaped from God's control, and what can a theist make of
that? Where a modern theist says that God has so made the world
that if men sin, they suffer, the Biblical writers speak of 'the wrath
of God'. It is true that, at first sight, there is the difference that
the former attributes indirect action to God and the latter direct
action, but it is very doubtful whether such a distinction exists
for omnipotence, and, in any case, is there any ultimate difference
between the two? Both ascribe a certain responsibility to God.
Of course, other problems arise here, but they lie too far from our
subject for discussion. The believer in a righteous God must
believe that there is truth, by whatever name it is called, behind
the Biblical phrase 'the wrath of God'. And if he believes that the
sinful become worse through sin, and that this, rather than pain,

is the fundamental punishment of sin, the doctrine is clearer still.

But, while the New Testament writers seem to have believed that the 'wrath of God' is already at work in the world, still more clearly they believed in 'the wrath to come'. Here, too, the Jew forestalled them. When the Baptist cried, 'Who hath warned you to flee from the coming wrath?' there were none to reply, 'There is no such thing'. The passages relating to the teaching of Jesus named above show plainly that He shared in the belief. It is found even in writers, such as the Fourth Evangelist, who have little to say in apocalyptic terms. Terrible already, the 'wrath of God' was for these men to be more terrible still.

There is no direct evidence in the brief records about the Baptist to show what he thought about 'death', but no doubt he shared the convictions of his contemporaries and of the New Testament writers, and there is no doubt what these were. As shown above, contemporary Jews meant by 'death' something more than the momentary physical event. They meant also, and primarily, the state that follows this event, existence in Sheol or Hades. Perhaps the best equivalent in modern terms would be to say that while the dead were conceived as less, much less, than 'personal', they still existed. Probably most Jews held that God was not to be found in Sheol or Hades. This, of course, is not consistent with the belief in the omnipresence of God—as some few, notably the writer of the Hundred and Thirty-ninth Psalm, clearly perceived—but popular eschatology is not logical. In any case, the Jew was quite sure that to exist in Hades was not what ought to befall a righteous man, and he rebelled against the idea, as we have seen. The Sadducees are here the exception that proves the rule. To postulate, as some did, a 'Paradise' for the righteous in Hades was not enough. They must return by a 'resurrection' to this upper world when it was re-made in the Day of Jehovah. Only so could there be for them 'fullness of joy' and 'pleasures for evermore'. Death and Hades were a single concept. To say that modern biology teaches that all men will die, and always have died, sin or no sin, does not touch the core of the matter, for biology only deals with the physical event and has nothing to say of the succeeding state. Again, if the Jew had believed that when any man, good or bad, dies, he passes straight to 'heaven', however con-ceived, the physical event would have lost its 'sting'. As a matter of fact, very many people to-day seem to hold just this opinion, and it has ensued that 'the modern man' is not afraid to die.

Christians may decline to define the state of the dead under the concept of a literal 'Hades'—and it is likely that some men of the first century only used the term in a symbolic way—but it is difficult to see how they can hold that every man, whatever his character, passes at death immediately into full and complete fellowship with God, which is the ultimate Christian account of 'heaven'. Whatever may be thought of 'eternal punishment', the idea that *all* men pass *at the moment of death* to heaven is altogether foreign to the New Testament. It knows of a state called 'death' which cannot on any terms be identified with 'eternal life'. And as we shall see, it teaches that when the Lord Jesus Christ saves men from sin, He saves men from 'death', too.

As already more than once implied, there was an apocalyptic element in the preaching of the Baptist. In this, too, he is characteristic of his time. There is no need to examine all the problems that throng here, but some few things must be said. It has already been seen that for the men of that day the line between the symbolic and the literal was not clearly drawn. No reader, for instance, of the Apocalypse of John has ever taken everything in it literally. At most he has chosen a comparatively few things for literal interpretation. It is the same with all other apocalyptic passages in the New Testament. Surely no contemporary took *all* apocalyptic literally! The very variety of Jesus' own apocalyptic phrases about the future of the wicked, some of which have been quoted, seems to suggest that He gave the terms symbolic meaning. At the same time, there are one or two particulars that it seems necessary to take literally. Both John and Jesus accepted the belief in the two ages which has already been described. Both, too, seem to expect the 'end of the (present) Age' soon, though not immediately. Jesus added that He did not know the exact time—'the day or the hour'—when the end would come, but He does seem to have expected it within a generation. The early Christians shared this belief. Yet the nearness of the Judgement that was to close the present age did not prevent the teaching of an ethic. Both Jesus Himself and the Apostles, like the Prophets before them, taught an ethic, however near they thought the end of the age to be. The fact is that none of them held the concept of 'an interim ethic'. They all believed that they were teaching an ethic that would obtain in the coming age. They believed in 'a new heaven and a new earth [that is, a new universe], wherin dwelleth *righteousness*'. This is not invalidated by the fact that in some particulars their ethical teaching presuppose the conditions of the present age, for the faithful were to practise the final ethic at once.

This means that the coming age was not just the sequel of the present age, but that its life was qualitatively different. The best brief expression here is 'eternal life'—that is, literally. 'the life of the age (to come)'. This phrase is ubiquitous in the New Testament and from first to last its literal meaning is transcended. It referred primarily to the *quality* of the coming 'life' and not to its *date*. As has just been implied, the best short account of this quality is 'righteousness', though other ideas, notably happiness, clustered around this. It is for this reason that the belief in 'eternal life' survived all disappointments about the early date of the beginning of the coming age. As has often been shown, the New Testament writers, speaking broadly, grow less and less certain about the date, but they never waver about the quality of the 'life' that is to be. This phenomenon, indeed, had anticipations with the Prophets and their followers. Even though the 'Day of Jehovah', whose nearness they announced, delayed to come, their message of righteousness survived. The phenomenon has continued in Christendom for two millenniums.

While the Baptist expected the 'coming wrath' soon, he expected also that before it came there should arise a successor who would complete and surpass his work. Even when he sent to ask Jesus 'Art thou he that should come or look we for another?', he still believed in 'another'. It may be that in later days, when his disciples and Jesus had fallen apart, the former went further than John and denied outright that Jesus was the 'other', yet there is no evidence that they ever denied that some 'other' was to come. The incompleteness of his own work was a chief element in John's preaching. This means that he rejected the current Jewish belief that repentance was enough. He knew, however vaguely, that something more was wanted. Here he was in line with such writers as Jeremiah and the author of the Fifty-first Psalm.

There is one phrase that shows what his idea of the 'something more' was. He knew that men needed to be 'baptized with the Holy Spirit'. In view of the history of earlier Hebrew and Jewish thought, this phrase carries certain implications. It implies, as indeed the whole Bible does, that men cannot save themselves, but that they need something that comes from God. Everywhere in the Bible the Spirit comes from God and is His gift. The phrase implies also that the outstanding idea about the Spirit was not that it (for at this stage the term 'it' is more nearly what was meant than the term 'he') is omnipresent or eternal or immanent, but that it is 'holy' and that it is given to make men holy. As we have seen, in the Old Testament the phrase 'Holy Spirit' is rare, but in the New Testament it is everywhere. Indeed, 'holy' is now *the* adjective that is found with 'Spirit'. Other adjectives are infrequent and sporadic, but this is ubiquitous. It was an adjective proper to God, and to no one and nothing else except through connexion with God. By this time it had long included the two notions of 'sacred separateness' and a consequent ethical perfecting. As we shall see, it is the commonest word for Christians in the New Testament. The Baptist already saw that the 'something more' than repentance that men needed was to be 'baptized with the Holy Spirit'. Here is a chief reason why he was 'great' among those 'born of women'.

Yet it is more accurate to say that the Baptist expected 'some one more' rather than 'something more'. He does not describe the 'some one' very clearly, but says that he is 'mightier than I, the latchet of whose shoes I am not worthy to stoop down and unloose'. It is a vague phrase but it does imply that the Coming One was to be mighty and righteous. It implies, too, to use later phraseology, that John saw in an elementary way that the 'work' of the Coming One was to depend upon His 'person', or rather that the two went together. 'Mightier' does not suit a mere teacher. The Coming One is vastly greater than John and He will therefore do what John cannot do—He will make men holy. The last phrase is surely the meaning of John's words 'To baptize with the Holy Spirit'.

There can be no doubt that John could have used the phrase 'the Kingdom of God' in either of the two current meanings distinguished above—either of the present rule of God over a confused and rebellious world, or of the perfect rule and realm that was to come. There seems no reason, therefore, to doubt the accuracy of Matthew's statement that John cried, 'Repent ye, for the Kingdom of Heaven is at hand' (Matthew iii. 2). One need only allow that the First Gospel perhaps turned the phrase 'Kingdom of God' into 'Kingdom of Heaven', as is its wont. The phrase only means that John expected the coming age soon. This shows why John so largely succeeded. It is easy to give reasons why crowds went out just to see and hear him. Curiosity would lead many into the desert to see a supposed Prophet, after all the generations without a Prophet, especially when the Prophet was so strangely clad. Again, John's condemnation of the Pharisees and his arraignment of Herod Antipas would be popular with many. But it is one thing to go to see and hear a preacher and another to do what he says. Preachers of repentance do not usually find many whole-hearted followers. Here the contrast between John and Amos, for instance, is complete. But in John's day Israel was seething with discontent, apocalyptic was popular, and the Zealots were abroad. There was a widespread expectation of crisis—indeed, of *the* crisis, the end of the Age. John, unlike Amos, preached not only of doom but of hope. He said that there was a way to be ready to meet the crisis, a way to make sure of sharing in the coming age. Many of the more spiritually minded Jews believed him and submitted to the ordeal of public baptism, and probably the Fourth Gospel is right in saying that Jesus found some of His first disciples among those of the Baptist. Many men, too, who are not particularly spiritually minded will repent for a while in face of an expectation of speedy judgement. It was in an expectant world that Jesus of Nazareth began to preach. It will be shown later that *at one important point* our Lord's teaching differed from John's, but it is impossible that, when Jesus went 'to be baptized of John' or called him 'more than a prophet', He did not mean to endorse John's *main message*. Some expositors forget that the message of the Baptist is one of the keys to the mind of Jesus.

Finally, it needs to be remembered that John was the son of a priest and that, according to Luke's 'special source', his birth was foretold to his father Zechariah in the Holy Place of the Temple, on the day that was *the* day of a priest's life—the day when 'his lot was to enter into the sanctuary of the Lord and burn incense' (Luke i. 9). John believed in ritual, for his baptism was just a fine example of it. Yet baptism was a piece of ritual that had nothing to do with the ritual that his father served. So far as Synoptic records go, John said nothing at all of this. It is unlikely that he denounced it, or that he said that it had no value, or discouraged its use. But it had no great importance for his message, and he did not send men to offer sin-offerings. It is true that, according to the Fourth Gospel, he called the Coming One 'the Lamb of God', but it will be argued later that in this phrase, whether it is John's or not, the reference to the sacrificial system is at most secondary. John's own forerunners were the Prophets, not the priests. An attempt will be made under each chapter below to show that here, too, the attitude of the Baptist is characteristic of the whole New Testament.

CHAPTER XII

SALVATION IN THE SYNOPTIC GOSPELS

It is peculiarly difficult to isolate any particular subject in the Synoptic Gospels. This is partly because, however composite their origin, each is now woven into one piece, and partly because at present there are serious differences of opinion about them and a decision about one involves a decision on others. About some a writer, unless he is to write a book, cannot do more than make the position plain that he is taking for granted all the time. Of such presuppositions, some are mentioned in the next few paragraphs; others will appear later. It will be convenient sometimes to refer to the 'Person' and the 'Work' of Jesus. It need hardly be added that the terms are not used in the later dogmatic sense, but only as brief descriptions of given subjects. It seems impossible to do without labels altogether.

An attempt has been made by some of the exponents of what is called *Form-geschichte* to show that the contents of the Synoptic Gospels, and particularly of the teaching ascribed to Jesus in them, is rather the teaching of the Early Church than His. It is not to be denied that this school has rendered great service to New Testament study, and it seems to have proved that sometimes the form of our Lord's teaching has been moulded to meet the needs of the Christian community in the period that followed Pentecost, but, in the conviction of the present writer, it has failed to prove its main thesis—that the teaching largely originated with the Early Church and does not go back to Jesus Himself. As already stated, it will be assumed here that on the whole the records found in St. Mark's Gospel and in the document known as Q are reliable witnesses of His teaching. In the few cases where there are quotations from the sources peculiar to Luke and Matthew, this will be duly noted.

There is a second presupposition that will seem to some more precarious. The question. 'How far had Jesus a single well-thought-out plan throughout His ministry, and how far did it change as the situation unfolded itself?' has notoriously various answers. Here it is assumed that, at least from His Baptism onwards, He knew His way and, in particular, knew that the

K

course He took would lead to His death. This does not mean that He foreknew every detail of His ministry, but only that He understood the general situation sufficiently to discern the kind of reception that His message and mission would meet. The reasons for this assumption will appear in part from the discussion itself, but there is also a reason of a general kind. It almost reduces to the assumption that Jesus of Nazareth had eyes to see. The combined depth and simplicity of His teaching is sufficient proof of this. Yet it seems to be necessary to add that this was so before the day of His Baptism. St. Luke tells us that He was then about thirty years old. Every young fellow of any intelligence does much thinking by the time he reaches that age. Unless he is a mere recluse, he does much thinking about the political and social situation of his times. The idea that Nazareth was a halcyon village, far removed from the stir of men, is now quite discredited. It was one of a multitude of Galilean villages, in constant touch with each other, and full of political and social unrest. Galilee, for instance, was the breeding-ground of the Zealots. When Jesus was a boy, there was an outbreak a few miles from Nazareth at Sepphoris, which the Romans rigorously crushed, crucifying many. Jesus grew up amid a seething land. Did He alone let it pass Him by unpondered? It seems unlikely and even incredible. We know that He read and re-read the Books of the Prophets until He had pierced to the principles of the writers. They are the books of men with a policy for the world of their time. As Jesus studied them, is it credible that He formed none for His own time, and that until He was thirty, He thought seriously of nothing but the work of a carpenter and the flowers of the fields? It is assumed here that, when He came to John's Baptism, Jesus already knew His own mind. If, however, it were admitted that it was only as time went on that He saw that He must take the Way of the Cross, or even that He did not discern this till He and His disciples withdrew to Caesarea Philippi, it would still only be necessary to rearrange the materials of this chapter. It would then describe, not Jesus' teaching during His whole Ministry, but during the last part of it. There would be considerable change in not unimportant details but the substance of the chapter would remain the same.

There is less difference of opinion about Jesus' attitude to the sacrificial system. He did not denounce it as did some of the Prophets. Still less did He give it the dominant place that the

Jews generally had done since the Exile. It would not be correct to say that He ignored it, though this would not be a great exaggeration. For him the Temple was principally a place, not of sacrifice, but of teaching and prayer. It is to these that He refers in most of the passages where the Temple is mentioned. There are very few instances where He names the sacrifices at all, and in these they are treated as secondary things. Perhaps the story in which He makes most of a sacrificial act is that of the Ten Lepers. Even here it may be debated whether His sending them to 'offer the things which Moses commanded' was not rather a test of their faith that they would be healed on the way than an assertion of the importance of the Temple ritual. At any rate, it is true that He does not relate His teaching either frequently or closely to the sacrificial system. Some claim that in instituting the Lord's Supper He made the one great exception to this rule. Another view is taken below. In general, He seems to have discerned what His contemporaries did not discern, but what, as seen above, was nevertheless the fact, that the sacrificial system had served its turn and was now 'waxing old and nigh unto vanishing away'.

It is far otherwise with His attitude to the Prophets. So far as the teaching of Jesus had any antecedents, they are chiefly to be found in the Prophetical literature. His direct quotations give some evidence of this. It is noticeable, indeed, that He also quoted considerably from the Book of Deuteronomy and the Psalms, but it is from Psalms with the prophetic spirit, and it is not from the ritual parts of Deuteronomy but from those parts where that book chimes with the Prophets. Yet the chief evidence of Jesus' use of the Prophets is not His direct quotations, but His elucidation and perfecting of the principles that those great preachers had taught. Examples will appear below. In relation to the immediate subject, the influence of the later part of our Book of Isaiah (chaps. xl–lxvi), and especially of the passages called 'The Songs of the Servant', is peculiarly clear.

Before the substance of Jesus' teaching is examined, something should be said of its method. As has already been noted, the Eastern, far more than the Western, likes to express principles under concrete terms—that is, he delights in symbol. In this kind of speech Jesus of Nazareth is the greatest of the masters. People who think that the art is easy should try their hands at it. It is in part because of His consummate mastery of this art that the sayings of Jesus, on the one hand, perfectly suit the immediate occasion, and, on the other, perfectly define principles for all time. Both phenomena could be illustrated at length from the Sermon on the Mount. The Parables, again—which are almost always meant to teach a single truth and not a series of truths—at one and the same time meet the needs of the immediate situation (often by way of correcting a current mistake) and expound a timeless truth.

Teaching by symbol lends itself readily to teaching by suggestion. For the present subject, it is peculiarly important to note that Jesus deliberately taught in this way. He was beforehand with the psychologists' assertion that a good teacher will turn his hearers' minds in a given direction and then, as far as possible, leave them to do their own thinking. Jesus knew, too, that until a hearer has learnt a first lesson it is useless to thrust a second upon him. What is still more important, He knew that, particularly when a teacher is teaching about a truth that is not merely theoretical but is to influence the whole of his life, the hearer must *consent* to the first lesson before he can do anything with the second that will help him much. It is of no use to give a book to some one who declines to learn the alphabet. Again, there is a law of atrophy by which a man who sedulously refuses to use opportunities to exercise a given faculty, gradually loses it and a corresponding law by which those who use their opportunities develop their faculties. Jesus put all this, in His symbolic way, in a few words: 'He that hath ears, let him hear.' He expressed the truth more at length when He said: 'To him that hath shall be given and he shall have abundantly, but from him that hath not shall be taken away even that which he hath.'

This means not only that Jesus' method in teaching was symbolic and suggestive, but also that it selected the right kind of hearer. A man who had not 'ears to hear', but steadily refused to listen, shut himself out from further teaching. On the other hand, for a man who was willing to listen, the way was open to deeper and further truth. As already seen, there is a passage in the story of Isaiah's Call that expresses the first half of this truth. Apparently the Prophet had sufficient insight to see that throughout his ministry the majority of his hearers would usually refuse to listen—that they would refuse to see unwelcome truth or to hear an unwelcome message. Yet there would be a 'holy seed' —a godly remnant. Of course, being a Hebrew Prophet and not a modern psychologist, he expressed this as a Law of God and not as the law of atrophy, but for a theist these are fundamentally the same thing. He said: 'Hear ye indeed, but understand not; and see ye indeed, but perceive not.' The passage is quoted both in the Synoptics, in Acts, and in the Fourth Gospel. Some think that Jesus Himself did not make the quotation, and that in the Synoptics it is an insertion of the Early Church, but there seems to be no need to deny to Jesus an insight equal to Isaiah's. In fact the majority of His hearers did refuse to listen. His teaching—and their own way of treating it—did in fact sort them out. This could be illustrated from many passages, but it is obvious in the Parable of the Sower, to which the Synoptists attach the quotation. Our Lord's miracles had drawn vast crowds, as the working of miracles would in any age. Many people, then as now, thought that to gather multitudes was to succeed. Probably the disciples thought so. Jesus says, in effect: 'This is not the harvest, as you suppose, but seed-time. There are four kinds of people here, and three of them will refuse My teaching. I already know that I am to be a leader of a few. I teach by parables because that method is selective. Every parable is a suggestive symbol; those who listen to the suggestion in it will learn more of the truth that I have to preach; the others, refusing to take the first step, cannot take the second.' Here is one of the reasons why Jesus said so little directly to the multitudes about His Person and Work. His teaching was deliberately selective. He was not willing to be called 'Lord' by those who would not do what He said. On the other hand, the disciples' eyes were blessed, for they 'saw', since 'every one that asketh receiveth'. Jesus' method in teaching explains why at first He did not refer to His death at all, and why, when He did begin to speak of its necessity, it was to the disciples that He spoke.

If we now pass from the method of Jesus' teaching to its substance, it is necessary first to remember that, as we have seen, His Ministry presupposes John the Baptist's. Jesus believed in an 'age to come', in 'the coming wrath', and, whether literally or symbolically, in Hades. He also believed in the seriousness, the fundamental seriousness, of sin. It is indeed true that, so far as we have His words, He did not speak of 'sin', but 'sins', but to infer that He did not accept the current account of man's sinful state is again to be the slave of words. The evidence of this is not chiefly that once He said, 'From within, out of the heart of men, evil thoughts proceed, fornications, thefts, murders, adulteries,

covetings, wickedness, deceit, lasciviousness, an evil eye, railing,
pride, foolishness. All these things proceed from within, and
defile the man' (Mark vii. 21-3), though this carries us a long way.
Nor is it that He said to His hearers that unless they repented,
they should all 'perish'. It is not even that, when He taught His
disciples to pray, the prayer dealt expressly with three subjects
and three only—God, bread, and sin. It is that He chose to teach
men what sin is by inference—by teaching then what righteousness is. Here the most convenient illustration is also the greatest:
that body of teaching that Matthew has gathered in the Sermon
on the Mount. There are strange people who say that they 'like'
the Sermon on the Mount. It is the greatest arraignment of
mankind in all literature. It seems to be proved now that there is
very little in it for which precedent cannot be found somewhere in
Hebrew and Rabbinic books, but this only means that Jesus
selected matchlessly, developed perfectly, and epitomized once
for all, the teaching of the race that prepared the way for His
coming. 'Here', He says in effect, 'is all that the Prophets have
taught "fulfilled" (that is, completed). If this does not describe
your character you are "like unto a foolish man, who built his
house upon the sand".' In other words, He already met the error
that has ever since infected the minds of those who 'like' the
Sermon on the Mount: He refused to let his hearers take it as an
account of a beautiful but impracticable ideal. There is no
account of sin to match the Sermon. Yet something more is
implied. So far as we know, no one threw back upon Jesus the
retort that is inevitably made to every other preacher: 'Why don't
you practise this as well as preach it, if you really suppose it to be
practicable?' Nor is there here a mere argument from silence, for
it has been almost unanimously agreed through nineteen centuries
that, judging from all the records about Him, this preacher did
practise what He preached. The words *and life* of Jesus are His
account of righteousness, and, by consequence, of sin. He
proposed to men that they ought to practise a righteousness that
exceeded the righteousness of the best Pharisees. If men allowed
the demand, if they had 'ears to hear', He went on to tell them the
secret of His own righteousness.

So far as His ethic is concerned, then, Jesus seemed to make a
merciless demand. The best that the best men could do fell far
short of it. Yet there is another element in His teaching. He
called all the 'weary and heavy laden' to come to Him that He

might 'refresh' them. He declared that His mission was to 'heal the broken hearted . . . and to preach the acceptable year of the Lord'. He was the friend of 'publicans and sinners'. He claimed to forgive sins. When the Baptist sent to ask Him 'Art Thou He that should come?', He replied in effect that He was, and this means that He knew that it was for Him to baptize with the Holy Spirit'—that is, to make men holy. In brief, He knew that His mission was to 'save' men. It is true that, at least at first, the word seems to be used in the Synoptics in the limited sense of 'healing' diseases of the body. This, however, implies that the writers made the same clear distinction between physical disease and sin that we make to-day, and this is doubtful. The current doctrine of the Jews, in spite of all its difficulties (cf. John ix. 2), was that physical disease was the result of sin. When Jesus, therefore, cast out a demon or even when He healed a blind man, the onlookers would suppose that the man was healed both physically and spiritually. It is true that our Lord seems to have taught, in the passage just noted from the Fourth Gospel, that disease is not *always* the result of sin, but this is far from the doctrine that it is *never* the result of sin. It is very difficult to believe that when Jesus cast out demons, He thought that the cure was merely physical. Besides, in the story of the Palsied Man (Mark ii. 1 *ff.*) Jesus committed Himself to the claim that He could forgive sins and could prove His power to do this by miracle. To-day the psychologists, in this instance at any rate, admit that He rightly treated sin and suffering as a single whole. Yet, in spite of one or two generalizations in the First Gospel, there is no evidence that Jesus healed every sick man. On the contrary, when the crowds seeking healing grew too large, He withdrew to 'preach the Kingdom of God' elsewhere. It was to 'this end' that He 'came forth' (Mark i. 38). In other words, whatever the crowds believed about the connexion of physical and moral evil, they wanted to reduce Jesus in practice to a mere healer of the body—and He refused to be reduced to this. This was not His conception of salvation, however the Synoptists happen to use the term 'save'. Indeed, when they write that a man was 'saved' or 'made whole', it is likely enough that they used the word under the current Jewish idea that a healed body implied deliverance from sin. Further, there are one or two passages where 'save' is not used about miracle. For instance, when the Young Ruler had 'gone away sorrowful', Peter asked 'Who then can be saved?' He cannot possibly have meant 'Who then can be healed?' though, no doubt, he thought that salvation would ultimately include deliverance from every kind of evil. Indeed, this story implies that to 'inherit eternal life', to 'enter into the Kingdom of God', and to 'be saved' are three ways of saying the same thing (Mark x. 17, 23, 26, 30). This identification is everywhere important. It is plain that the disciples followed Jesus, not chiefly because He taught a noble ethic, but because they thought that He could 'save' them, could make them ready for the 'life of the coming age', could lead them 'into the Kingdom of God'. Since the idea is so pervasive, there seems no need to require that the few places where the word 'save' is clearly used in the wider sense, should be suspected of anachronism. The jeer of the priests at the Cross, 'He saved others, Himself He cannot save', implies that the word was current about Jesus.

One of the best tests of character is the way in which a man speaks of himself. Good men, in far the largest part of their conversation, say nothing about their own character. With the 'general public' they make exceptions only when they cannot help it—that is, when other speakers thrust it upon them, or when circumstances demand it. Even with their intimates they say little that commends themselves. The chief and perhaps the only exception is when they are 'men with a message' and cannot do justice to the message without saying something about the messenger. In the Synoptic Gospels, Jesus responds perfectly to this test. For the success of His mission, as we shall see, everything depended upon His Person, yet to the multitudes He hardly said anything about Himself. Almost always the right way with oneself is to let other people draw their own conclusions. This was one reason for Jesus' reticence here. As we have seen, another was that Jesus did not teach a second lesson until men had learnt the first. The first was that God cannot be content with men unless they are everything that men ought to be. This is one message of the Sermon on the Mount.

What conclusions did the Jewish public draw about Jesus? From a well-known passage, we learn that, while they did not fully agree among themselves, they partly did so. If some said that Jesus was John the Baptist (which can only mean 'a second Baptist', for it was common knowledge that Jesus was adult before John was beheaded), others that He was Elijah, and yet others that He was 'one of the prophets', all agreed that He was a prophet. So far, of course, the public was right. Even if they added that He spake 'as one having authority and not as the scribes', this too was a mark of the old Prophets. Yet there was a difference, for where the old Phophets had said, 'Thus saith the Lord', Jesus said, 'I say unto you'. The reason for this will appear later. Meanwhile we must note that the Jews believed that a Prophet spoke 'with authority' because he was a 'man of God'. In their sense of the phrases, a Prophet was 'holy' and 'the Spirit of the Lord' had come upon him. Except at Nazareth, where Jesus 'had been brought up', and where His neighbours had not eyes to see, men *learnt for themselves* that He was a Prophet. This illustrates Jesus' usual indirectness in teaching about Himself.

The story of Caesarea Philippi shows that Jesus used the same method with the disciples. He did not say, 'I am the Messiah', but left them to find this out. It is their great glory that they did find it out, for He had contradicted many of their expectations about the Messiah. This, too, has often been pointed out. When Peter made the great confession, it is as though he had said, 'Though Thou art so different from what we had thought the Messiah would be, yet we know now that Thou art He'. With their knowledge of Him and their willingness to accept all that He had so far taught them, He could now admit it to them, but they must not tell others, for others would be sure to misinterpret what the claim meant. Indeed, as the sequel in the story shows, even the Twelve did not yet fully understand what it meant. But they were right that He was the Davidic King, who was to inaugurate the 'coming age' of deliverance from sin and every other kind of evil.

The word 'king' suggests the word 'kingdom', and it is incredible that when Peter used the word 'Messiah', he was not thinking of the Kingdom of God. About this Jesus had given much direct teaching. What did He mean by the phrase? This, of course, is one of the places where a writer, unless he is to write a whole book on the subject, can only express his own opinion. As has already been seen, the Jews had long believed that God rules over the present rebellious world and will rule in the future perfectly loyal world. In both beliefs the emphasis is upon the fact that God rules. It seems to me that those are right who contend that the primary meaning of the phrase 'Kingdom of God' in the Synoptic Gospel lies here. The phrase means the 'kingship' or 'rule' of God. Yet, since there cannot be any king unless he has subjects, it seems to me that the phrase *implies* a 'realm' or 'kingdom' in the usual meaning of the latter word. There is no doubt that Jesus believed that God is now ruling a rebellious world, and that God will one day rule in an altogether loyal world. But to these two meanings of the phrase Jesus added a third—that with and in Himself the altogether loyal world was beginning to be. 'The Kingdom of God,' He said, 'is in your midst.' This is the 'something more' that He added to John's message. Yet this is not all. He also implied that His disciples would enter—or, rather, were entering—into the Kingdom. As illustration the story of the Young Ruler may again be recalled. The young man, as we saw, was seeking to 'inherit' the life of the coming age—that is, to 'enter into the Kingdom of God', that is, to be 'saved'—but he could not do this because he would not 'leave all and follow' Jesus. Peter claimed, however, that he and his fellow disciples had 'left all,' and the claim was good. Jesus replied that 'now in this time' they were to receive a hundredfold what they had left, 'with persecutions', and 'in the age to come eternal life'. What is this but to say that He is leading those who 'follow' Him into the Kingdom of God? In other words, Jesus' direct teaching about the Kingdom is indirect teaching about Himself. It is the same with some of the Parables—for instance, the Parable of the Sower. Indeed, it is probable that every one of the Parables, rightly interpreted, gives ultimately indirect teaching about Jesus Himself. For the disciples—those who accepted His teaching about the Kingdom and who had begun to assimilate it—Jesus was the Messiah, that is, God's appointed King. While the terms cannot yet be used with the full Christian meaning, it would be correct to say that the disciples were already being 'saved' by 'faith' in their 'Lord', 'faith' being used to mean, not the mere acceptance of teaching as true, but personal trust in another. Nor is this all. Jesus was already training them to be 'fishers of men'— that is, to lead others into a similarly saving faith.

Turning now to the passages where Jesus spoke more directly about Himself, we need to note that here especially it is impossible to keep the subject of His Person separate from that of His Work. As already suggested, He only spoke of Himself when His mission demanded it. Again, it needs to be said that sometimes it is best to take the implications of what He said at their minimum and not at their maximum. This forestalls some disputes.

At His Baptism we are told that Jesus 'saw the heavens rent

asunder, and the Spirit as a dove descending upon him' (Mark i.
10). At the least there is here a symbolic account of a conviction
that came to Jesus Himself. To say that it came suddenly is not
to deny that it had been sub-consciously coming for a long time.
On the contrary, it is probable that no sudden conviction ever
comes to any man without subconscious preparation. Again, the
conviction that He was a 'man of the Spirit' would at least mean
to Jesus that He knew He was a Prophet—that is, a man with a
message from God to other men. If we think that at the time no
one else heard the voice from heaven or 'saw' the dove, Jesus must
later have told of this experience, under symbolic forms, to His
disciples. According to St. Luke, Jesus presently went to preach
at Nazareth and took as His text a passage from the later part of
Isaiah: 'The Spirit of the Lord is upon me, because he hath
anointed me to preach good tidings to the poor; he hath sent me
to proclaim release to the captives, and recovering of sight to the
blind, to set at liberty them that are bruised, to proclaim the
acceptable year of the Lord.' Even if the story is to be placed
later, it still shows Jesus' concept of what the coming of the Spirit
at His Baptism meant. Most of the Old Testament Prophets
had been men of doom, but in the later part of Isaiah there is the
great exception (or, if Isaiah xl–lxvi be by more than one writer,
the great exceptions). Here, as seen above, there is prophesy of a
'righteousness' that *is* 'salvation'. Jesus definitely takes His stand
with this kind of prophet. His principal message is not arraignment, but salvation. To Jewish ears 'the acceptable year of the
Lord' would mean deliverance from sin and therefore from
suffering.

It was at this point that Jesus differed decisively from the
Baptist. This appears in the story of John's message to Jesus from
prison. To John Jesus' method was a 'stumbling-block'. He had
foretold a 'mightier' one who should indeed 'gather the wheat
into his garner', but who should also 'thoroughly cleanse his
threshing-floor' and 'burn up the chaff with unquenchable fire'.
In other words, John foretold a realm won by force. Jesus was
clearly not pursuing such a policy. He was indeed using force
against the demons. He was entering into 'a strong man's house'
and 'seizing' his goods (Matthew xii. 29), but He was not using
this way against evil men. In answer to John's message, He
insisted that His own method of healing the sick and preaching
to the poor was the right policy. To leave it at this, however,

would have misled the people about John. So, when John's messengers had gone, Jesus did justice to John the Baptist. There had been none greater. Yet John had preached the way of violence, and this message had laid hold of the people, who were quite ready to welcome a Messiah of force. 'From the days of John the Baptist' the idea had run that the coming Kingdom was to be 'seized' by violence. But 'now' Jesus insists on taking a different way. He who has but an inkling of that way, he who is 'but little in the Kingdom of Heaven', has passed beyond John's limit. Jesus' prototype, so far as He had one, was not Amos, but Deutero-Isaiah. The Spirit was His that He might save.

There is a third passage that relates Jesus to the Spirit. It is the unique story of the Temptation of Jesus: 'The Spirit driveth him into the wilderness to be tested of the devil'. The juxtaposition of the Spirit and the Devil is true to psychology, for a man's temptations always root in His gifts and opportunities. As has been pointed out, for example, by Dr. Sanday, the highly symbolic story must have reached the disciples from Jesus' own lips. No doubt He told it them to explain something that puzzled them. The thing that puzzled them was His way with miracle. The story assumes that He could work miracles, for otherwise, for instance, He could not have been tempted to turn stones into bread. Men are not tempted to do something that they know they cannot do. In one temptation Jesus refuses to use His power in miracle to serve His own need, in another to advance His cause by mere wonder-working, in a third to take His Kingdom by force. To take it in this way would be like the way of the Roman, who ruled 'all the kingdoms of the world' by force, and He expresses His extreme repugnance of it by saying that it is to worship the Devil. By the nature of the situation, in His use of miracle Jesus would be subject to these three temptations throughout His Ministry. It is likely that His disciples again and again urged them upon Him. 'Why does He not', they would say, 'use His strange powers to supply His own and our needs? Why does He not persuade men by astonishing them? Why does He not use His power to "seize" the Kingdom by force?' Jesus replied that He had thought out all this when He began His Ministry, and that He would take none of these ways. To use the word in its old sense, He used a definite 'economy' in miracle. His consistency in the use of this power is one of the proofs that He had

it. Jesus, like the Prophets, received the Spirit that He might
fulfil a mission. All three references to this, however, show also
that He knew that His mission was to heal and save by love and
not to astonish and overwhelm by power.

This is remarkable in view of another phrase used at His
Baptism, 'Thou art my beloved Son', for it is agreed that there is
here a reference to the Second Psalm, and there the king to
whom Jehovah says, 'Thou art my son', is unmistakably to rule
by force. What, then, did the phrase at the Baptism mean? The
Psalm was held to be Messianic and therefore, at least as early as
His Baptism, Jesus knew that He was Messiah. This is a place
where His own conviction antedated that of His disciples, and
where He kept silence until they had discovered the truth for
themselves. The phrase 'my Son' asks also another question: Did
Jesus just think of Himself as the Son of God in the same way as
the old Hebrew kings had done, at least since the Deuteronomic
times (cf. 2 Samuel vii. 14—a Deuteronomic passage), or had the
name a different content for Him? The answer is to be found in a
passage that appears, with some variations, both in the First and
Third Gospels (Matthew xi. 20–30; Luke x. 1–24). Jesus had been
upbraiding the cities where most of His miracles had been worked,
because on the whole they had rejected the message to which
the 'signs' of the miracles were meant to lead. Yet there were some
who had accepted it, but these were not 'the wise and prudent',
but 'babes'—that is, like children, they trusted even where they
did not understand. For no man understood Him, but only God.
This meant, for this is only the other side of the same truth, that
no man except Jesus understood God. If men had recognized
that Jesus was Son, they would have recognized also that God
was Father, and *vice versa*. This does not require that the Jew
never thought of God as Father, for this is not true to fact, but
that he had not made the belief dominant in his concept of God
and drawn the right inferences. Any one who makes fatherhood
dominant in his concept of God will know that God will seek to
save His erring children, and that this, and not to judge or even
to rule men, will be His master passion. On the other hand, any
one who recognizes Jesus as 'Son' would be well on his way to
recognize that God is primarily 'Father'. It would be out of place
to examine the results of this great saying in Christology. The
important point here lies in the context. Jesus was saving some—
'babes', who were simply trusting themselves to Him. So much

for the preceding verses. The cry that follows, 'Come unto me, all ye that labour and are heavy laden, and I will refresh you', connects the saying about the 'Father' and the 'Son' just as clearly with the Work of Christ. It was for Jesus to 'reveal' the Father and so to save men. He knew that He was Son and therefore Saviour.

Jesus goes on to speak of His 'yoke'. Here He seems to think of Himself as a rabbi, for rabbis laid the yoke of the Law upon their disciples, each according to his own interpretation of it (cf. Matthew xxiii. 4), but He is also speaking out of a carpenter's experience. He had made many yokes and He knew that a good yoke was 'easy'. It was a paradoxical thing, for it eased a burden by adding to it. The ordinary rabbi's yoke gave no ease. Jesus carried a yoke Himself and would fain lay it upon others. His secret was that He 'knew the Father' and lived in continual fellowship with Him. So His 'righteousness' at once exceeded the Righteousness of the scribes and Pharisees and yet was easy to practise.[1] In other words, there is here an anticipation, in untechnical terms, of the Pauline doctrine (e.g. in Romans vii and viii) that it is easier to be a Christian than a sincere Pharisee. An easy yoke may be heavier than one that galls, but it is none the less the helpful kind.

This is perhaps the best place to name the three parables of the fifteenth of St. Luke's Gospel. They are like other parables in telling only part of the truth, but they are all three parables of salvation. They all tell that it is the purpose of God to 'seek and to save' the lost. It is true that in the Parable of the Prodigal nothing is said of the sufferings of the father, but no one can think of his waiting at home unmoved. Two things only are required of the Prodigal: that he should repent and that he should trust himself to his father. When he comes home, to the indignation of the elder brother, he is treated not like a criminal, but as a son. The modern psychologist has discovered at long last that this is the right way to rescue a young criminal. 'The best way to lead a boy to be good', says the expert, 'is to treat him as if he were good. This will encourage, as nothing else will, the seed of good that repentance already presupposes.' Jesus was beforehand with psychology. The Prodigal is not brought into a law court,

---

[1] The text, however, must not be treated as the whole truth. In Gethsemane, for instance, Jesus did not find His way easy. Yet the truth only needs restating, for without His Father He would not then have been able to carry His 'yoke' at all.

but welcomed to a home. It is the way of a true home to treat a penitent child as if he were good. This means, of course, that the Parable of the Prodigal illustrates precisely what St. Paul means by 'justification'.

There is another passage in which the phrase 'My beloved Son' occurs—the story of the Transfiguration—but this is best considered later. We turn now to a third way in which Jesus thought of Himself and His Work. Recent exegesis has shown that he thought of Himself as the 'Servant of the LORD' of the later part of Isaiah. To 'Messiah' and 'Son' he added 'Servant.' There is first the suggestion of the words 'In thee I am well pleased' at the Baptism (cf. Isaiah xlii. 1). The context in Isaiah names the 'Spirit', and the passage is parallel to the one quoted in Jesus' Sermon at Nazareth, which has already been named. According to the First Gospel, there was at this time another reference to the Servant, for when John expostulated with Jesus for coming to his Baptism, Jesus replied, 'Thus it becometh us to fulfil all righteousness', and not only is 'righteousness', as seen above, a synonym in Deutero-Isaiah for 'salvation', but, on one translation, the Servant is called explicitly 'My righteous servant' (Isaiah liii. 11), and, on any translation, the last Song of the Servant teaches at this point that the Servant's sufferings are effective for others in the realm of righteousness. The phrase in Matthew suggests that already at His Baptism Jesus knew that He was sent to save men from their sins and that He knew already that He could only do this if, though sinless Himself, He identified Himself with those that He was sent to save. In other words, there is here the societary concept described above. Even if the passage, being peculiar to Matthew, be counted a later addition, this would still be the best account of it, and it would need to be added to the similar passages found in the early chapters of Acts, which are discussed later.

The chief of the other passages that refer to the Servant occur in relation to the phrase 'Son of Man' and will be taken presently, but it is worth while here to consider some of the things involved merely in Jesus' identification of Himself with the Servant. First, it means that He took the phrase 'the Servant of the Lord' to describe an individual, but also a societary individual—an individual who was to suffer for others, to save them from their sins, and to find his own 'prosperity' or success by so doing. There is no need to dwell further upon these truths, important as they are, for this would only be to repeat the exposition of the Servant Songs. When our Lord thought of Himself as the Servant, He thought of Himself as saving others by suffering for them. Again, if the fifty-third of Isaiah be interpreted, as Jesus interpreted it, of an individual, it teaches that He will die and rise again. It is just in this way that the Servant saves—He 'pours out his soul unto death' and yet 'prolongs his days' and 'the pleasure of the Lord prospers in his hand', and in Deutero-Isaiah 'the pleasure of the Lord' is the salvation of His people. If the Lord's Servant be taken as an individual, He is an individual who saves others by death and resurrection. If Jesus thought of Himself as the Servant, He knew that it was for Him to bear the *sins* of others and so to save them from *sin*. This conclusion cannot be escaped.

This brings us to Jesus' use of the phrase 'Son of Man'. Here, again, it is not possible to lay out the reasons why a particular interpretation of the phrase is adopted, but the interpretation should be made clear. First, in spite of all arguments to the contrary, it seems to me that by the phrase 'Son of Man' Jesus always meant Himself. As will appear below, this seems to give consistency to His use of the phrase, and inconsistency should not be ascribed to a speaker needlessly. Again, as has often been pointed out, the Greek phrase itself is unnatural Greek. It can only have been coined to express an Aramaic phrase. The men who coined it knew both Greek and Aramaic. If the Aramaic phrase literally meant 'a man', as Aramaic scholars assure us, it seems to follow that Jesus gave the phrase a peculiar meaning in Aramaic, for otherwise the disciples would not have turned it by an uncouth Greek phrase, but would have simply translated it by 'a man' or 'man'. In addition, as we have seen, such books as the Book of Enoch show that the phrase was current in distinctive ways. It seems clear that Jesus used the phrase in His own way. The antecedents of that way seem to me to lie rather in the Old Testament than elsewhere. As already seen, in Ezekiel the name 'Son of man' began to combine two ideas: seeming insignificance and Divine mission. Again, in the Eighth Psalm the phrase occurs as a synonym for 'man', and here man's insignificance is set alongside his glory. Here, too, as we have seen, the phrase is both individual and societary. This is also the case in the seventh chapter of Daniel, where the Old Testament most nearly antici-pates the use of the Gospels. Here the final Kingdom is given to

'One like unto a son of man', who stands for 'the saints of the Most High', who have died in the persecution of Antiochus. In other words, they are to prevail over kingdoms of force by suffering. Again, here Daniel escapes from the particularism that marked the normal Judaism of the time. He speaks of a 'son of man', and not of a 'son of Israel'. He foretells a universal Kingdom of the righteous meek. In Daniel, once more, there is the juxtaposition of the ideas of insignificance and greatness. The handful of martyrs in an obscure corner of the Seleucid Empire was to rule the world.

Yet it does not seem to me that Jesus merely took over the ideas of Daniel. In that Apocalypse a group of people, the 'saints', are symbolized in a societary way by 'one *like unto a* son of man'. For Jesus the Son of Man is an individual who is a societary man. This does not mean that Jesus thought of Himself, when He used the phrase, as the 'typical man', though He was this. Nor does it mean that He thought of Himself as the 'representative man', in the sense in which a Member of Parliament represents his constituents, for this is to modernize the phrase. It means that Jesus used about Himself an idea that was old and widespread and that was common among the Jews—the societary idea. Just as a true Eastern King was thought of as 'one with' his people, so much so that in a true sense he *was* his people, so our Lord thought of Himself as 'one with' mankind, so much so that in a true sense He *was* mankind. This is just to bring the ancient societary concept, which recent psychology has brought back upon us, to its climax. To assume, therefore, that the phrase 'Son of Man', when used by Jesus, must either be individual or societary, is to pose a false dilemma. The one text, 'The Sabbath was made for man, and not man for the Sabbath: so that the Son of Man is lord even of the Sabbath', is almost enough to prove this. Or again, in Matthew's Parable of Judgement (xxv. 31 *ff.*), the 'king' and his 'brethren' are one in a societary way because 'the Son of Man' is on the throne.

It is well known that, apart from one passage (Acts vii. 56), the title 'Son of Man' is found only in the four Gospels, and that there it is used only by Jesus Himself. When we remember that the Synoptic Gospels were taking shape at the time when the Epistles were written it seems clear that for some reason the early Christians did not find it natural or easy to use the name for their Lord, and that this makes it incredible that they thrust it upon

Jesus' lips. It is clearly His own name for Himself. This was so well known that, when the Fourth Gospel came to be written, the writer, although he sometimes allowed himself great liberty in using his own terminology to clothe Jesus' ideas, felt that this name must stand. He followed unerringly, too, the Synoptic use and kept the phrase for Jesus' own lips. Here a further point emerges. While Jesus *accepted* another name—'the Christ' or 'the Son of God'—He *claimed* this one. Indeed, when the other title was given Him, He replied by claiming this one, too. When Peter said, 'Thou art the Christ', Jesus accepted the name but He went on to say, not that 'the Christ must suffer', but that 'the Son of Man must suffer'. Again, when the Sons of Zebedee spoke of His 'glory' and of their place in it, He began to speak of His 'cup' and His 'baptism' and of the 'Son of Man' who was to 'give his life a ransom for many'. Once more, when the High Priest asked Him, 'Art thou the Christ, the Son of the Blessed?' He accepted the name, but at once went on to say, 'Ye shall see the Son of Man sitting at the right hand of power'. The reference here is to 'power' and not to suffering, because he was now speaking, not to the disciples, but to the High Priest. Caiaphas did not need to be told that Jesus was about to die. In the crisis of the last few months our Lord turned again and again to this name. This was not only because the name would help others, if they could be brought to understand it, but because it helped Him. As His words to Peter, 'Get thee behind me, Satan', show, He was entering again and finally into a temptation that had beset Him ever since His Ministry began, the temptation to be a Messiah of force. If He were that, however, He would no longer be the meek 'Son of Man' and then He could not save. He would no longer be the Suffering Servant. It is in the passage 'the Son of Man came not to be ministered unto, but to minister, and to give his life a ransom for many' that the identification of the Son of Man with the Servant most clearly appears (the phrase 'for many', in particular, recalling the greatest Servant Song, where 'many' occurs no less than four times), but it is probable that the identification lies behind every passage where the suffering of the Son of Man is mentioned. The 'one like unto a son of man' in Daniel typifies sufferers who are to triumph; the Servant of the LORD in Deutero-Isaiah is also a sufferer who triumphs, but the idea is added that His triumph is to save others from sin by His own death and resurrection.

An examination of the Marcan passages[1] where Jesus speaks of the Son of Man in the few months that divided Caesarea Philippi from the Cross shows plainly that for Him the suffering and the triumph of the Son of Man went together. Our Lord, following His custom of waiting for His disciples to learn one lesson before He taught another, did not speak to them plainly of the coming Cross until they had conquered the presuppositions of their time and were sure that, though He disappointed these, He was yet the Messiah. Then, however, He did speak plainly, for we read: 'And he *began*' to teach them that the Son of Man must suffer many things and be killed and 'after three days rise again' (Matthew xvi. 21; Mark ix. 31). He goes on to say that the Son of Man will 'come in the glory of his Father with the holy angels'. The Parousia is to be the outcome of the Passion. Whether this be a symbolical phrase or not, it denotes triumph. Some of the disciples, whom He had just called to 'take up [their] cross', are yet to 'see the kingdom of God come with power'. While this is not certainly to be identified with the Son of Man's 'coming in glory' (for it might refer to Pentecost, even though the 'coming in glory', too, were expected within a generation), it does denote success. Jesus, like the Servant and the Danielic 'son of man', is to triumph by suffering.

The story of the Transfiguration is the sequel of the first clear foretelling of the Passion. Here, as in the story of the Baptism, it is best to take the story at its minimum of meaning. It is linked with the Baptism by the phrase, 'This is my beloved son'. What had been the God-given conviction of Jesus Himself at the Baptism is now the God-given conviction of the three disciples. Did this mean that the disciples now learnt that 'the Christ must suffer'? It meant that they were being taught this in spite of themselves. From this time onward they were men of divided mind—on the one hand, revolting from the truth that their Lord must be crucified, and, on the other, driven by their faith in their Lord to believe it. To help them, Jesus bade them think of Moses and Elijah. To say, as has often been said, that Moses represented the Law, and Elijah the Prophets, is beside the point. As has been shown earlier, these two men were the outstanding Old Testament examples of success by societary or vicarious suffering.

---

[1] The fact that no passage in Q refers the phrase 'Son of Man' to the Passion perhaps means that Luke and Matthew don't use Q where it repeats Mark. Some sayings in Mark may also have been in Q.

Moses had begun to save Israel at the Exodus by identifying himself with his people, and had gone on completely to save them, in the sense of 'save' that was pertinent at the time, by sharing their lot in the desert. There he had been one with them, yet not one of them. This was the secret of his forty years' agony in the saving of Israel. Similarly Elijah, at the crisis of Ahab's attempt to reduce Israel to polytheism, had saved the Remnant that was the hope of the world. He had seemed to fail, but had in truth succeeded. It is true that neither of the two had died by violence in his enterprise, but to emphasize this is to miss the point. With both there had been an agony of years. Even if either of them had been put to death, physical death would not have been the chief item in what they did. The chief element in the imperfect salvation that they wrought was the fact that they so loved their people that they 'must' identify themselves with them, yet must all the time refuse to sin with them. This means that in their degree they shared both in Jehovah's love for Israel and in His abhorrence of their sins, and that the two passions tore them in two. This is the very tension of salvation. When our Lord was about to 'set his face to go to Jerusalem', it helped Him to think of those who had won a smaller yet similar battle.

Yet there is something more. In the thought of the time 'death had no dominion' over Moses or Elijah—'death' meaning, once more, no mere momentary event, but chiefly existence in Sheol or Hades. The story of Elijah's 'assumption' need only be recalled. But in the thought of the Jews in Jesus' day it seemed incredible that Hades should have swallowed Moses. There is a book called 'The Assumption of Moses', which was probably written in the first century. It is only extant in a Latin version and is incomplete. It does not tell of the 'Assumption' that its name implies, but there are references to this in the Greek Fathers that imply that the book closed with a story of Moses' passing, not to Sheol, but to God. A reference in the Epistle of Jude (verse 9) shows that the early Christians knew the book. Again, its main purpose was not to declare that Moses did not pass to Sheol, but to put certain teaching into his mouth before his Assumption. The book *assumed*, that is, that (starting from Deuteronomy xxxiv. 6) there was a current belief that Moses escaped Sheol and passed into Heaven. Jesus has a saying (Mark xii. 26 *f.*) which suggests that He shared this kind of conviction. It is remarkable too that the 'Assumption of Moses' tells of Jewish victory in the coming days, not by a

Messiah of force, but by the suffering of a martyr. On the Mount of Transfiguration Jesus taught Peter and James and John by the examples of Moses and Elijah that a true saviour saves by uniting himself with those he seeks to save, by being 'afflicted' in 'all their affliction', and that in this way he triumphs over death and Hades.

The second foretelling of the Passion (Mark x. 32–4) repeats the first in substance, showing again, for instance, that this teaching was reserved for the disciples, for only they, and scarcely they, were able 'to receive' it, and that Jesus confidently expected to 'rise again' and so complete His work. Luke adds, however, one significant detail, for he says that now Jesus 'stedfastly set his face to go to Jerusalem' (Luke ix. 51), and that the disciples were 'amazed' and some at least were 'afraid'. They knew that if He went to the city again He would be killed, but they saw that He was determined to die, and He told them that He *must* die because He was 'Son of Man'. Only so could He truly be Son of Man and do what the Son of Man ought to do. It is at this point that Mark places the request of the Sons of Zebedee. In reply to them, Jesus speaks of His 'cup' and His 'baptism'. The 'cup' was an old symbol of a lot ordained by God. In the Old Testament the phrase is commonest in the Prophets, and with them, since their message was usually one of doom, it is a 'cup of vengeance', but this was not the only use of the term. A psalmist, for instance, could speak of 'the cup of salvation' (Psalm cxvi. 13). Jesus used the phrase again in the Garden, asking His Father 'Remove this cup from me'. According to John, He used it also on His arrest (John xviii. 11). It denotes that He knew that it was the Father's will that He should die and that at all costs He would do His Father's will. He spoke also of 'the baptism that I am baptized with'. Was He not here referring back to His Baptism by John? There He was dedicated to a Ministry of Salvation that was only now to be completed. In the companion phrase in Luke (xii. 50) it seems hardly possible to translate the Greek 'I have a baptism with which I *was* baptized, and how am I straitened till it be accomplished', yet it is permissible to ask whether Jesus did not think of His whole ministry as a kind of 'baptism', for this suits so perfectly the word 'accomplish' or 'complete'. In Jesus' mind, all His ministry was a Ministry of Salvation, but only now was it drawing to completeness.

This brings us again to the passage which perhaps more than any other single text reveals Jesus' own conviction about His death—'The Son of Man came not to be ministered unto, but to minister, and to give his life a ransom for many' (Mark x. 45). The fact that the words emerge incidentally, just to point a lesson, shows that they express a truth that Jesus took for granted, and that His disciples ought by now to take for granted. This means that its ideas were integral to Jesus' thought about Himself. It has already been pointed out that here unmistakably the concepts of 'The Son of Man' and the Suffering Servant blend. It is the use of the term 'ransom' that is novel, and this needs some detailed consideration.

In the Greek version of the Old Testament the noun *lutron* (ransom) and its corresponding verb, *lutroun*, are used to translate four different Hebrew words. Of these one (*machir*) need not detain us. The other three of the roots, *kipper*, *padhah*, and *ga'al*, have all been discussed above. The passages where *lutron* translates the first are not here important, except as supporting the contention that this word may refer, not to the appeasement of anger, but to the making of atonement.[1] In the remaining cases, *lutron* translates either the Hebrew term rendered 'ransom' in an earlier chapter or that translated 'redeem' (or rather 'do a kinsman's part'). The verb corresponding to *lutron* does not translate the verb *kipper* anywhere in the Septuagint, but in the vast majority of its many instances it turns either 'ransom' or 'redeem'. The abstract noun *lutrōsis* is not used to render any other terms beside 'ransoming' and 'redemption'. It is to these that we must turn to understand our Lord's use of *lutron*.

But to which of the two must we turn? The answer seems to be 'To both'. It is easy to see how the two might both be used of the same act. Among a kinsman's duties one would be to 'ransom' a kinsman from slavery. By the paying of a price, he would do the kinsman's part. The two words, indeed, are used as synonyms in two significant passages. One occurs in the context of Jeremiah's prophecy of the New Covenant to which our Lord was so soon to refer at the Last Supper. It runs: 'For the LORD hath *ransomed* Jacob and *redeemed* him from the hand of him that was stronger than he' (Jeremiah xxxi. 11). Here, clearly, Jehovah, who is Israel's *Goel*, shows Himself his *Goel* by delivering him from slavery. The other passage (Isaiah li. 9–11) is from the part of Isaiah which, as we have already seen, played so large a part in Jesus'

---

[1] In Exodus xxi. 29 *f.*, for instance, an aggrieved man accepts a *lutron* instead of slaking his anger.

thought. It appeals, in glowing symbolism, to Jehovah's deliverance of Israel under Moses—of which, too, as the story of the Transfiguration shows, Jesus was thinking at this time—and cries out for a second deliverance like it. In the reference to the first deliverance, Israel is called 'the redeemed' and in the confident plea for the second 'the ransomed of the LORD'. Once again it is clear that the two terms are synonymous. It is clear, too, that here under the term 'ransom' the metaphor of purchase has no reference whatever to the price considered as paid to the slave-owner, for the slave-owner is Babylon, but only to the price as setting the captive free. There seems therefore to be good ground for holding that when our Lord used the word *lutron* He thought of Himself as kinsman of 'many', giving His life to set them free. It may be added that Hosea (xiii. 14) uses the two terms together to denote deliverance from Sheol.

Great stress used to be laid on the supposed fact that the Greek term rendered 'for' in this text means 'instead of' (*anti*). This was made an argument for the substitutionary doctrine of the Atonement. But an examination of the New Testament use of this word shows that it does not always denote substitution (e.g. Matthew xvii. 27; Romans xii. 17; Hebrews xii. 2; Ephesians v. 31). Again, it is admitted that the term is not often used of the Death of Christ. In fact it only occurs twice (Mark x. 45, with the parallel in Matthew; 1 Timothy ii. 6, where it occurs with *lutron* in a compound word). A much more frequent word means 'on behalf of' (*hyper*). It occurs, for instance, in the text 'this is my blood of the covenant, which is being poured out *for* many' (Mark xiv. 24), where, as will presently appear, there is also a reference to the Servant Song. It also occurs in the passage named from First Timothy. The idea 'on behalf of', therefore, is more prominent than the idea 'instead of', yet, as shown above, when the former is interpreted in a societary way, it includes the latter in a given sense.

Yet man is inevitably individual as well as societary. This means that Jesus could only be Son of Man, could only be the Suffering Servant, for those who were willing to trust Him, to be 'one with Him'. A man cannot be saved from sin in spite of himself. It has been said that in a sense Jesus *was* mankind. It is better to say that in a sense He *was* a *new* mankind—a new mankind to which only those belong who choose to do so. He is Kinsman of those who do the will of God (Mark iii. 35). This will appear more clearly if other parts of the story of Jesus' last days are remembered. The fact that the Synoptists all give a large place to these few days shows how important they counted them.

From the story of the Sons of Zebedee Mark passes to those of Bartimaeus and the entry into Jerusalem. The crowds with which Jesus and His disciples were now travelling were chiefly Galileans, flocking enthusiastically to the Feast of the Passover. On the whole the Galileans had welcomed Jesus, though in a shallow way, while Jerusalem had on the whole rejected Him. This comes out in a number of the stories of these last days both in the Synoptists and John. It is probable that even without the healing of Bartimaeus the Galileans would have demonstrated on behalf of their own 'prophet', but the miracle in their midst roused them to hot enthusiasm. The name that Bartimaeus used for Jesus is significant, for 'Son of David' could only mean 'Messiah'. As we have seen, Jesus accepted the latter name from the disciples, but He had also bade them keep His acceptance of it secret. The reason was that if this were bruited abroad, the Galileans would have eagerly used it but in their own mistaken sense. Probably, especially if we remember that the Chief Priests challenged Jesus with this name (Mark xiv. 61, xv. 32), many Galileans did call Jesus 'the Christ', meaning by it a Messiah of force. Indeed, on Palm Sunday they as much as said this when they cried, 'Blessed is the kingdom that cometh, the kingdom of our father David'. Jesus, in His own matchless fashion, took the situation into His own hands. One might say that He arranged a pageant, but arranged it in His own way. By His direction, a friend had an ass ready, so that at the critical moment He might indeed admit that He was the Messiah, but might at the same time make it plain that He was no Messiah of force. He selected the one Messianic prophecy that unmistakably said this. It told of the coming of a King of Peace, who was to 'cut off the chariot from Ephraim and the horse from Jerusalem' (Zechariah ix. 9 *f.*). Jesus knew that in a few days, when it became finally clear to the crowds that He would be no political Messiah, but would 'render unto Caesar the things that are Caesar's', the enthusiasm would turn rapidly to resentment and repudiation, as is the way of crowds. As He Himself said, the enthusiastic crowd was like a fig-tree whose leaves deceptively promised figs. Only one question remains: If He foresaw this, why did He consent to take any part in the demonstration at all? The answer seems to be that, in spite of all their errors, the Galileans were not altogether wrong. They were right that He was Messiah, and they were right that He had come to save. Yet there was something deeper still. These 'sons of men' did respond to the 'Son of Man'. They responded in the same imperfect way in which all men of all nations have ever since responded to His story—by the admission that 'This is He', even while they are reluctant to 'do what [He] says'. Few Christians ever consider that their whole missionary enterprise would be foiled if when men learn the story of Jesus, they were just to turn and say, 'Well?' They simply cannot do so. When Jesus fronts men, 'deep calleth unto deep', the sons of men recognize the Son of Man. They know that 'This is He'. This means that they are save-able. The story of Jesus' popularity that culminated on Palm Sunday was the first instance of this. The 'rulers', who still rejected Him, were still committing the unforgivable sin. But the rest could not 'hold their peace'. The crowd on Olivet, with all its imperfections and misunderstandings, did help our Lord to persist to the Cross. Men of this kind were save-able.

There were others who helped Him more, for they were being saved. These were the 'babes' who, though they did not understand His mysterious way—who understood it least of all now—, yet 'believed' in Him. Among them were women, who were still faithful at the Cross. One of them, in particular, expressed her loyalty by anointing Him with precious ointment. She said, in effect, 'Though I see that Thou art set on death, and though I cannot understand this, yet I believe in Thee', and this was for Him an anointing for burial—that is, it helped Him to die. And then there were the Eleven. The remarkable thing about them is not that amid their perplexities they failed Him at one moment, but that they clung to Him at all. When He 'set his face', they 'followed him wondering', but they 'followed'—as a child follows a father whom he trusts even when he does not understand the 'why and wherefore' of what he does. Even in Gethsemane they fled, not because they ceased to trust Him, but because there seemed to be nothing to do for Him. Peter had tried to do what little could be done when he drew his desperate sword, but Jesus Himself had forbidden him to 'do what [he] could'. It was not a coward who drew a solitary sword on a multitude or followed to the place of danger in the High Priest's court, but a bewildered disciple. He denied His Lord for lack of anything else to do, but

He was still his Lord. Again, the group held together after the Crucifixion, for they gathered again in the same Upper Room. It is likely enough that they did expect that in some way that they could not foresee He would 'rise again'. He had not only foretold this more than once, but in the last few days He had told the Sadducees that they 'greatly erred' in doubting the truth of resurrection and had foretold, as He 'sat on the Mount of Olives', that the Son of Man should come 'in clouds with great power and glory'. He had even raised a question about 'The Christ' as He taught publicly in the Temple—a question that would have had little point unless He Himself claimed to be the Messiah—and had quoted a psalm (Psalm cx) that foretold the triumph of the Messiah (Mark xii. 35–7). In effect, as it seems to me, He had here claimed to be both 'Son of David' and 'Son of God'—or, as we say, both human and divine. If we remember all this, it seems likely enough that the disciples expected some mysterious sequel to the Crucifixion. The group that Matthew earlier calls the 'church'—whether the word, as distinct from the idea, be an anachronism or not—held together throughout. Even the two who walked to Emmaus, when they said that they 'were hoping that it was he that should redeem Israel', went on to tell, not of complete despair, but of the women's words. According to Matthew, Jesus had said at Caesarea Philippi that the 'gates of Hades' should not prevail against this group—that is, that it would survive and hold the Keys of the Kingdom of Heaven, even though He Himself was soon to die. Whether the words be an addition of the Early Church or not, they tell the truth. The Son of Man could not save any man against the man's will—but already there were those who were willing.

All this appears again in the story of the Last Supper. Taking the three Synoptic accounts together, we find indeed that Jesus still insists that the Son of Man must suffer—suffer, indeed, through the disloyalty of a disciple—and that the Eleven will 'stumble' in the coming night, but to stumble is not finally to fall. On the contrary, Jesus is expecting triumph, for He 'appoints unto' them (or perhaps 'makes covenant' with them) to 'eat and drink' in His 'kingdom', and this because they have been loyal in His 'temptations'. The faithful are to rejoice with Him in His Kingship. Simon is indeed to be 'sifted' and to fail for a moment, but he will 'turn' and 'stablish [his] brethren'. When next they meet, it will be to renew fellowship, to 'drink of the fruit of the vine', in a kingdom that is at once His Father's kingdom and His own. For Jesus the Last Supper was a prelude rather than a farewell. It was the prelude of a saved mankind. In brief, the Last Supper was a societary act, and it meant that the unity of Jesus with His disciples still held and was still to hold. Its keyword, like the keyword of the Old Testament, is 'Covenant', but the old Covenant was now giving way to the New Covenant of which Jeremiah had spoken, the 'Covenant of the heart', which is societary in the only ultimate way, by the consent of every individual who shares it. The disciples were the beginnings of a saved community.

In considering the Words of Institution, it is best to start from the Marcan account. It rightly omits reference to the 'remission of sins'. This does not mean that the Early Church was mistaken in adding the words, but only that the chief emphasis did not lie here in the Upper Room. As has been seen, neither in the original Mosaic institution of the Passover nor in its celebration in later days was there any reference to sin at all. It is true that in the Feast of Unleavened Bread that had coalesced with the Passover, the leaven was a symbol of sin, but then it follows that the unleavened bread symbolized the absence of sin. It is not impossible, therefore, that when our Lord said of the bread, 'This is my body', there was an implicit reference to His own sinlessness, and that when He called His disciples to share the loaf, He was suggesting that through fellowship and unity with Him they were being delivered from sin, but this is a precarious exposition and, even if it be right, the reference is not to any Temple sacrifice. It was not primarily as sinful, but as faithful, that our Lord thought of the Eleven in the Upper Room (cf. John xiii. 10).

It is necessary to look closely at the several references to the Old Testament in the significant story. We may begin with the Passover. Our Lord had 'desired with desire' to eat it with His disciples before He suffered. He had also carefully arranged for it with the master of the Upper Room. There is unmistakable reference, therefore, to this Feast, but the nature of the reference needs to be examined. As already seen, the immediate reference is not the saving from sin, for the Passover was not in any way like the sin-offering. Again, the strictly sacrificial act at the Passover was the offering of blood in the Temple and not the subsequent feast. Again, if the Last Supper was an anticipation of the Passover, as John suggests, there would be no lamb (or rather, sheep) on the table; if it was a Passover, as the Synoptics seem, at least at first sight, to say, our Lord ignored the lamb, and took instead the unleavened bread, which had no strictly sacrificial significance, as one of His two symbols. Similarly, He chose as His second symbol the wine, which was no part of the Old Testament ritual at all. On the other hand, these two were the chief elements in the common meal, and the common Passover meal, which at this time seems to have taken a larger place in the mind of the Jews than the sacrificing of the sheep in the Temple, symbolized not only fellowship, like all common meals, but the particular fellowship of Israel called the Covenant. It was with the first Passover that the Covenant of Jehovah with Israel as a *people* had begun; with every subsequent Passover every family in Israel claimed its place in the continuing Covenant of the race. It implied faithfulness on their part and promised salvation, not so much from sin as from every kind of evil, on God's part. The New Covenant, symbolized and completed at the Last Supper, gathered all this into itself. In other words, it once again appears that the ruling concept, as in the Hebrew Passover, was the societary one. When He said, 'This is my body' and 'This is my blood', He was speaking in His own highly symbolic way, and He meant, in effect, 'You are still to be one with Me, for I am now to be the bread of your life'. This, of course, is what the sixth chapter of John seems to many also to teach. Christ is the 'spiritual meat and drink' (1 Corinthians x. 3 f.) of the saved community. Whether anything more is meant need not be discussed here.

The phrase, 'This is my blood of the covenant, which is shed for many', is best understood from the repeated Old Testament assertion 'The blood is the life'. It is to be remembered, however, that the 'blood' was not held to be the 'life' because it was offered to Jehovah—on the contrary, it was offered to Jehovah because it was held to be the 'life'. In other words, the identification was presupposed in the sacrificial system and was independent of it. The unique ceremony described in the twenty-fourth chapter of Exodus, which Jesus may have had in mind, has the same presupposition. Half the blood was sprinkled on the altar and half on the people to show that they now shared a common *life* with Jehovah. The ceremony is a symbol of Covenant and is societary. But our Lord said to the Eleven, '*Drink* ye all of it'. This is peculiar to the account in Matthew, yet the other Synoptic accounts imply it, and John repeats it (John vi. 53), as does Paul (1 Corinthians xi. 25). Here there is nothing whatever in the sacrificial system that corresponds. On the contrary, the drinking of blood was expressly forbidden in the Law (Leviticus xvii. 10 *ff.*, etc.), and it is incredible that our Lord was here quoting Jewish ritual. He meant, surely, that His disciples were sharers in His 'life' as Israel had never shared in the life of their sacrifices—or of Jehovah. This is the leading instance of the royal way in which our Lord treated the 'Law and the Prophets', choosing what would suit His purpose, ignoring or changing elsewhere.

Yet He said, 'This is my blood of the covenant, *which is shed for many*'. Here there is a reference to the forgiveness of sins as Matthew makes clear. If, however, Jesus was thinking of the sacrificial system, He now refers, not to the Passover, but to the Day of Atonement, yet the phrase in Mark is not 'which is shed for you', but 'which is shed *for many*', and when the other references at this time to the fifty-third chapter of Isaiah are remembered, together with the use of the word 'many' there, it seems all but certain that here, too, the reference is to that passage. Further, our Lord goes on to speak of His drinking wine 'in the kingdom of God'. This denotes the triumph of the Messianic Banquet of Jewish expectation. There was nothing in the sacrificial system that corresponds to this, but there is in the resurrection and triumph of the Suffering Servant. No doubt the Eleven fell among the 'many', but Jesus' ruling thought here is of the 'many' whom He is to save by His death rather than only of the few that are already in process of being saved.[1] It is significant, too, that both at the table and in Gethsemane He called Himself 'Son of Man' (Mark xiv. 21, 41) when describing what Judas was doing. All unawares, he was helping Jesus to be Son of Man, and so to save man. Again, quoting another Prophet, He calls Himself 'shepherd' (Mark xiv. 27; cf. Zechariah xiii. 7), whose sheep are indeed to be scattered, but not finally, for when the Shepherd has risen again, He will do as shepherds did—'go before' them. Here once more, in the unity of the shepherd and his sheep, there is the societary concept. On the whole, therefore, the manifold and wealthy meaning of the Last Supper has its chief antecedents, so far as it had any, not in the sacrificial system, but in the Prophets—in Jeremiah and Deutero-Isaiah and Deutero-

[1] Again, Otto may be right in finding a reference here to two other passages in Deutero-Isaiah (xlii. 6 *f.*, xlix. 8 *f.*).

Zechariah—and in Daniel. It is the societary idea that is dominant throughout. In Jesus' mind this truth had two chief elements: that the Son of Man is 'one with' a few and is to be one with 'many', and that to be fully 'one with' them He must die for them. At the Supper the first of these is the more prominent, yet the second is also there. Indeed, the first is the very ground of the second. The consciousness of the first, expressed so fully at the Supper, helped Jesus to go on steadfastly to die. Something remained to be done, even for the few. As John puts it, in his symbolic way, they were not yet 'clean every whit' but needed that the Son of God should 'wash their feet'. To save many, or even to save the few, our Lord knew that He must die. When the brief and partial comfort of the Supper was over, this truth passed into the foreground of His mind and overwhelmed Him in Gethsemane.

In the twenty-four hours that began in Gethsemane Jesus did not say much to His disciples. He had said all that they could receive. The time had come to die and not to explain. Yet we can see clearly that our Lord was still set on the same quest. This appears in four ways. First, He accepted from Pilate the name, 'King of the Jews'. It is probable that the Chief Priests used this name in charging Jesus with rebellion, for it was not an Old Testament name, but one that had been used by the later Maccabaean rulers in the recent time of Jewish political autonomy, and Pilate would know this. Yet for Jesus it was a name that He could not refuse with Palm Sunday behind Him. It is likely enough that John is right in adding that He said that He accepted it in His own sense, 'My kingdom is not of this world: if my kingdom were of this world, then would my servants fight' (John xviii. 36), for this is exactly consonant with the whole Synoptic story. In any case, Jesus still held to the conviction that He had a kingdom and that under this claim He would be put to death.

Secondly, there is Luke's story of the Penitent Robber. According to Mark, when the Chief Priests flung the words 'save' and 'the Christ' at Jesus, both robbers reproached Him. Presently, however, one of them made an appeal to Him and used the phrase, 'Thy kingdom'. Probably he had long known of the preaching of Jesus and had been 'kicking against the goads' of conscience. Our Lord's reply spoke of 'Paradise'. We have seen what this meant in current speech. Jesus, no doubt, used it because it told the Robber what He wanted to tell him in a word that he could understand. Yet the use of the word, with whatever qualifications Jesus would interpret it in His own thinking, implies that He did look forward to a happy future and the word 'to-day' shows that He expected this at once.

This takes us back to the agony in Gethsemane, and leads us to the third chief passage. Terrible as the physical sufferings of crucifixion were, we know that many men endured them bravely in those days. We know, too, that many have endured martyrdom unflinchingly because they knew that the God who they served would not forsake them, but would give them a happy and blessed future. Was it, then, from physical suffering only that Jesus flinched—the word does not seem to be too strong—in Geth-semane? Or do the words, 'Abba, Father, all things are possible unto thee; remove this cup from me: howbeit, not what I will, but what thou wilt', refer back to the 'cup' that the Son of Man must drink? There is here the ultimate example of Jesus' complete obedience to His Father, but what was it in His Father's will that He now finally obeyed? In the light of the whole teaching of Jesus about 'the Son of Man'—of the way in which He claimed the name and explained it in terms of suffering, of the way in which He Himself clung to it—is it too much to suggest that this name holds the key to the answer? It had always cost Jesus much to be Son of Man. We do not at all understand what it must have meant for the sinless Son of God to live with sinful men at all. Perhaps if we can imagine how Father Damien must have felt when he was the only healthy man among the loathly lepers, we can come nearest to imagining the repulsion that Jesus must have felt in His sinlessness for the sin in every man whom He met. Yet to save them He must be one with them, though He must also not be one with them. Because of His sinlessness their sins nauseated Him—again, it is not too strong a word—yet He loved them with all His heart and mind and soul and strength. It was this dual experience that made His sufferings, even before the Crucifixion, unique. To use the phrases of the Gospels, He had suffered as no other can ever suffer, because He was at one and the same time 'Son of God' and 'Son of Man'. Yet the dread climax was still to come. In the thought of the time, as we have seen, physical death and Hades went together, and the secret of the concept of Hades was separation from God. However much we criticize the other contents of the concept, here it tells the truth. The final con-sequence of sin is separation from God. If our Lord was to save men 'to the uttermost', He must save them *in that separation*. Yet He could only do so if at one and the same time He was one with them, yet not one with them—separate from God as they were, yet not separate. He was one with them in the utmost result of their sin, for He cried, 'My God, my God, why hast thou forsaken me?' ; He was not one with them in that result for He cried, 'Father, into thy hands I commend my spirit'.[1] It is a mistake to rob either cry of part of its meaning. Logically, of course, they are inconsistent, but logic is never adequate to explain experience, and least of all here. There is no explicit theology, still less metaphysics, in them, but only experience. As was suggested in the first chapter above, there is nothing psychologically impossible here. It is true that the Twenty-second Psalm, from which in the first of the two cries Jesus quoted, goes on to tell of the sufferer's triumph and of a triumph won for others, and it would not be wrong to quote of the Cross its pivotal words, 'From the horns of the wild-ox thou hast answered me', but this must not be used to rob the one verse that our Lord did quote of its meaning. Jesus' sufferings reached their climax on the Cross because, to use John's word, His soul was then 'torn asunder' (John xii. 27) as it had not been until He faced 'death' in its spiritual sense. We shall find that St. Paul says the same thing in his own way. If the earlier teaching of Jesus Himself be remembered, these two cries to His Father express the tension within His own nature by which He 'saved sinners'. It was as though He were being separated from the God from whom He could not be separated.

Fourthly, there are the Synoptic stories of the Resurrection. While the writer is one of those who believe in the physical Resurrection of Jesus, he is also one of those who believe that Jesus' spiritual survival is the crucial truth at this point. Yet Jesus' own survival is not the whole truth. As we shall see in the next chapter, for the disciples the Resurrection meant that He had conquered Hades or Death and had conquered it for others beside Himself. In other words, Stephen, the first of these others, used the right phrase when he cried 'I see the *Son of Man*'. The Synoptists

---

[1] This saying is peculiar to Luke, but in any case it is impossible to believe that the Cry of Dereliction tells the whole truth. If it did so, there would have been no Resurrection. Jesus certainly expected to 'rise again'. On the other hand, all attempts to alter the text of the Cry of Dereliction not only lack evidence in the manuscripts, but make the incredible suggestion that the disciples turned some less difficult saying into this one.

themselves, however, do not say this. Yet there are certain pertinent facts. First, Jesus appeared only to 'His own'—to the women who had been most faithful of all, then to the Eleven, and then, according to Paul, to many other 'brethren'. To appear to any others would have been at last to have yielded to the old temptation to use miracle as mere spectacle. He appeared to a 'prepared people', to those, if the phrase may be allowed, who would know what to do with the Resurrection. In other words, our Lord was still one with His group. The opinion is common now that in the last passage in the First Gospel we have not Jesus' own words, but a summary of the convictions of an early Jewish Church. It is still possible that their convictions were rightly based on the facts.[1] Surely the words 'I am with you always' do go back, in substance at least, to Jesus Himself. He had risen from the dead, not just to go to Heaven, but also to do something on earth. He had now 'all authority' and sent His disciples to 'disciple' the world. Or, as Luke puts it, 'Repentance and remission of sins' were to be 'preached unto all the nations'. The stories of the Resurrection do not tell of a solitary survivor of death, as the story of Elijah's 'assumption' had told, but of a Saviour who is now at last wholly Son of Man, triumphant 'Servant of the Lord' who will 'justify many', the Christ who had 'suffered' and 'entered into (the) glory' (Luke xxiv. 26, 46) of the kingship of the redeemed. 'He hath our salvation wrought.'

[1] The emergence of the Trinitarian Formula in a Church of monotheistic Jewish Christians by *ca.* A.D. 80 is very significant on any showing.

M

CHAPTER XIII

THE GENERAL APOSTOLIC PREACHING

Before the particular teaching of the several New Testament books, apart from the Synoptic Gospels, is considered, something must be said about the common teaching of all Christian preachers in the first century. In some ways this chapter is supplementary to the one on John the Baptist, but its chief purpose is to show that from Pentecost onwards all Christians had much in common, and that, while it is not wrong to distinguish between types of Apostolic teaching, there was still very much that the Christians of the first century all believed. It is necessary to bring out this general agreement even though some of the subjects named in this chapter recur under discussions of the teaching of particular books.

From Pentecost onwards, the first duty of Christians was to witness to certain facts. To-day these would be divided into 'historical facts' and 'psychological phenomena', but this distinction is not made in the New Testament. And are not all 'phenomena' facts? Here the facts of history will be briefly mentioned first and then the facts of 'experience'.

A passage in the tenth chapter of Acts is becoming the *locus classicus* for the contents of the earliest Christian preaching (Acts xi. 36–43). Here we find mention of John the Baptist, the Life of Jesus, His Crucifixion, and His Resurrection. In the second chapter there are some additions, notably the sentence, 'God hath made Jesus both Lord and Messiah' (Acts ii. 36). This phrase describes the meaning that the first Christians gave to 'the Ascension'. They did not believe that Jesus of Nazareth had 'retired' to 'heaven', but that He was now 'Lord' of the universe and its active Saviour. To these facts of the past and present, they added a 'sure and certain' fact of the future: that Jesus was to be 'judge of living and dead'. To-day many scholars have returned to the ancient Christian belief that these facts—including even the Resurrection and Ascension, in *some* sense—are fundamental in Christianity. They are certainly fundamental in the New Testament. It is true that there are not many references to the Life of Jesus outside the Gospels, but it is agreed that the substance of the Synoptic Gospels was all the while being preached in the Church and by the Church. To me such writers as Paul

and the author of Hebrews seem to presuppose that the facts of
the Life of Jesus were well known to Christians. Some illustrations
of this will be given later. At the end of the Apostolic Age, the
writer of the Fourth Gospel, here called 'John', gave much of his
space to the Life of Jesus, and this shows that its story had been
integral to the Christian witness all the time.

Coming now to the facts of experience, we find that the first
Christians 'believed' in Christ. It was Paul who first drew out
the full meaning of this term, and of the correlative term, 'grace'.
Some account of this will be given when his teaching is examined,
but there is no doubt that he was only drawing out the meaning
of an experience which was always universal among Christians,
as the ubiquity of the word 'believe' itself shows. A Christian lived
in conscious fellowship with the Living Christ. Through the
Christ, God 'gave' him 'repentance and the remission of sins'
(Acts v. 31). It is interesting to find that repentance was a gift.
As to 'remission of sins', it is clear that the Christian was aware
that his sins were forgiven through Christ, long before he worked
out any account of how this was. As usual, experience preceded
explanation. In other words, the Christian was quite sure that he
was 'saved' from sin.

But the experience included more than forgiveness for past sins.
It has been seen that in the Synoptic Gospels there were two
convictions about the Spirit of God: that Jesus was the Man of
the Spirit, and that He was to give the Spirit. There are not many
texts to show that the first conviction still prevailed, but there
are enough (Acts x. 38; Romans i. 4; Hebrews ix. 14; Matthew
xii. 18; John i. 32). From Pentecost onwards, the Christian is in
turn 'a man of the Spirit'. There is no need to illustrate this.
Here, too, the first Christians did little more than preach the
experience. It meant primarily a sense of God-given 'power', and
this remained the primary idea, though other concepts were
found to be involved as well. This power was of two kinds: the
Christian had 'power', on the one hand, to witness for Christ, and,
on the other, he had 'power' against sin in his own life. Indeed,
the 'good news' was just the message: 'We can tell you the
way to be rid of sin.' It followed, as matter of course, that the
Christians, being 'men of the Spirit', found at once that they were
a 'society of the Spirit'. The New Testament word here is 'the
Church'. Through the 'one Spirit', the Church was 'the body of
Christ'. Again, the two common uses of the term 'holy' in the

New Testament show the connexion between the Spirit and power against sin. The Spirit is now frequently called 'the Holy Spirit' and the Christians are frequently called 'saints', and this word translates the Greek term for 'holy'. If Christians had not yet given up sinning, they were at least beginning to do so: they were 'being saved', they had begun to live in conscious fellowship with God in Christ, and they could already therefore be called 'holy' since anything and any one is 'holy' through living connexion with God. The Spirit, too, may now be called either 'the Spirit of God' or 'the Spirit of Christ'. In all this realm, also, experience preceded discussion.

In the Apostolic writings, apart from the Synoptic Gospels, the phrase 'the Kingdom of God' or the term 'kingdom' (with the words 'of God' implied) seems to occur twenty-six times. It is found in every kind of book, yet little is said about its meaning. In other words, these writers could take it for granted that their readers had the substance of the Synoptic teaching in their minds and that they already knew the Christian meaning of the phrase. They held all the beliefs about the Kingdom that have already been elucidated. They believed that God is ruling a rebellious world now. The readiest example of this universal postulate is the whole scheme of the Apocalypse. They believed, too, that God is to rule an altogether obedient and therefore a perfect world hereafter. For instance, they expected to 'inherit the Kingdom'. Before the third Christian belief—that with Jesus the Kingdom of God had begun—is examined, a significant fact must be added about the first two.

While the early Christians, like Jesus Himself, borrowed the phrase 'Kingdom of God' from Judaism in these two senses, they made a significant change in them by proclaiming that Jesus of Nazareth shared in the 'rule' of God. From the earliest days of the Church in Jerusalem, Jesus was 'both Lord and Christ'. This means, first, that He shared with God in the control of the present rebellious world. It would be easy to show that this concept is common to all the Apostolic writers. For them all Christ was 'on the throne', in active and effective rule over the universe.[1] Again, the Christians believed that the risen Jesus was to share in the rule of the future perfect Kingdom of God. Here, again, the writer of the Apocalypse may speak for all. When 'the seventh

---

[1] Hebrews x. 12 f. is not an exception, for its reference is to a completed *sacrifice*. Cf. pp. 236 f.

angel sounded'—that is, when the perfect Kingdom had come—a voice cried, 'The kingdom of the world is become the kingdom of our Lord and *of his Christ*, and he shall reign for ever and ever'.[1] The important point here is that after the Resurrection the disciples began at once to put Christ with God, if such a phrase may be allowed. This, of course, involves the problem of the Person of Christ. Since the doctrine of His Work goes organically with that of His Person, the subject necessarily emerges once and again later. It cannot, however, be fully discussed. It must suffice to present results without giving their grounds. Perhaps, therefore, it will be well to say in advance that it seems to me that as the first Christians brooded over their experience of the Christ and put it alongside the records of His life on earth, they were drawn irresistibly to place Him continually in closer and closer relation with God, until at last the writer of the Fourth Gospel said: 'In the beginning was the Word, and the Word was with God, and the Word was God.' It also seems to me that this process of thought was not only irresistible, but justifiable, and that the Fourth Gospel reached the right conclusion.

The first Christians also accepted Jesus' teaching about the Kingdom in the third and novel sense described above. They believed that with Him the 'kingdom of God' had begun in the sense that He had loyally and perfectly obeyed the 'rule' of God. This is why they spoke of His 'obedience' (e.g. Romans v. 19; Philippians ii. 6; Hebrews v. 8), and of His 'patience' (Revelation i. 9). Yet this is not all. They could speak also of the Kingdom, in this third sense, as being *His* Kingdom (Colossians i. 13; Revelation i. 9; cf. John xviii. 36). Indeed, the word 'Christ' itself carries this implication. In all three senses the Christians claimed that Christ shares 'rule' with God.[2]

There are texts that seem to mean that the first Christians transferred the concept of 'kingdom' or 'rule', not only to Christ, but to those who 'believed in' Him, in the first two senses of the word. Of the perfect future 'Kingdom', Paul asks, 'Know ye not that the saints shall judge the world?' as though he were appealing

---

[1] There is, indeed, a solitary passage in Paul that seems, at first sight, to take another view (1 Corinthians xv. 24–8), yet it may be harmonized with the general Apostolic teaching. The passage clearly teaches that for Paul the Christ is reigning over the present confused world and that He will so reign till 'death', the final enemy, is 'abolished', and it does not necessarily deny that in the 'age to come' the Son is to 'reign' in subordination to the Father.

[2] The same three ideas appear if the uses of the term 'Lord' for Jesus in the New Testament are examined.

to a Christian commonplace (1 Corinthians vi. 2; cf. Luke xxii. 30; Hebrews ii. 5–9). Still more daringly, the Apocalyptist can speak of persecuted Christians as sharing now in Christ's rule over a chaotic earth (Revelation i. 9). It is as if we were to say that a Chinese Christian to-day rules the world! But it is in the third sense that the 'kingdom' is most closely related to the present subject. Even here the subject cannot be fully explored, but it is plain that in this third sense the concept was not that Christians ruled, but that they obeyed. Like their Lord when He was on earth, they submitted themselves loyally and obediently to the 'rule' of God (Colossians i. 13; Hebrews xii. 28). This was only another way of saying that they were 'entering into the kingdom'. It may be added that the commonest use of the phrase 'Kingdom of God' in the Apostolic writings is of the future perfect Kingdom, and that, so far as the present writer can see, the concept of the realm that is the complement of the 'rule' takes a more prominent place in these writings than in the teaching of Jesus. It is plain that the third concept of the Kingdom, as in the Synoptists, involves that of salvation.

Why, then, did not the first Christians call the 'society of the Spirit', in which they already lived, 'the Kingdom of God'? Why did they prefer the word 'Church'? The answer is perhaps twofold. First, they did not find it easy to use the word 'Kingdom' of any realm that was not universal already, for in the two other uses of the word universality was a necessary part of the meaning. Still more, however, it was quickly evident that the members of the new society did not always wholly submit themselves to the rule of God. The First Epistle to the Corinthians, for instance, teems with evidence of this. None the less, the society was a society precisely because its members were seeking through the indwelling Spirit to practise a complete loyalty to God in Christ. This was, and has continued to be, its *differentia* among societies. It was possible either to say that its members were 'saved', or were 'being saved', or that they would be 'saved'. There was a Hebrew word (*kahal*) that already expressed this group of ideas, and its Greek equivalent was *Ecclesia*, or 'Church'. It is not inaccurate, therefore, to say that the Church was the 'incipient Kingdom', the last term including the ideas of rule and realm.

It is necessary, perhaps, to recall here what was said earlier about the use of symbolism in the Bible. For the Apostles, as for all Semites, the line between the literal and the symbolic was less clearly drawn than by other men, and, as we have seen, it is not very clearly drawn by the latter. A verse in Paul may be taken as example: 'For our wrestling is not against flesh and blood, but against the principalities, against the powers, against the world-rulers of this darkness, against the spiritual hosts of wickedness in the heavenlies' (Ephesians vi. 12). Some of the Greek words here are abstract terms and seem therefore to be symbols, yet there is little doubt that Paul did believe literally in a cosmogony that placed a number of 'heavenly' spheres between the earth and the highest heaven, and that these were the realms of 'spiritual' beings that had and used great power on the earth. With our modern geography we can only take the verse symbolically. Yet what Paul meant can be put in a symbol that is not altogether unlike his: 'Our wrestling is with an *atmosphere*'. If the Apostle could return to us now, and if modern geography could be explained to him, and if he were then told that all these words could only be taken symbolically, he would reply, 'Well, does it matter?' A twentieth-century version of his saying would be: 'We wrestle with ethical relativity and inevitable evolution and deterministic psycho-analysis and a spurious nationalism and Marxism!' What will the twenty-fifth century's version be? None the less, in all centuries Christians—to quote Paul's clearly symbolic sequel—'take up the whole armour of God' and are able, 'having done all, to stand'. No attempt, therefore, will be made here always to draw a sharp line between the symbolic and the literal. Here the Fourth Gospel is the New Testament term. In one way it is a very symbolic book—in a timeless way. The simplest illustration is its use of such words as 'water' and 'bread' and, most of all, 'light'. It almost escapes, however, the distinctive apocalyptic symbolism of the time. For instance, whether the few references to current apocalyptic ideas be symbolical or not, the writer's fundamental concept of Judgement is: 'This is the condemnation, that men loved darkness rather than light because their deeds were evil' ; and his fundamental definition of 'eternal life' is: 'To know thee, the only true God, and Jesus Christ whom thou hast sent.'

Again, the Apostolic writers shared with their contemporaries the notion of two ages, and of a Judgement that divided them. For these writers the word *aionios* doubtless started with the concept 'belonging to the coming age', but this concept did not stand alone and was not dominant. The dominant thought related to the *quality* of the life to come. As has been shown, this was already so in the Synoptists, and it continued so with every Christian thinker. An examination of its use, for instance, in Paul's writings would clearly show this, even though he does not often use the word. A single quotation will suffice: 'That as sin reigned in death, even so grace might reign through righteousness, unto *eternal* life through Jesus Christ our Lord' (Romans v. 21). In other words, the concept of the two ages is not fundamentally temporal, but ethical. The Fourth Gospel makes this clearer still. For it there is no such thing as 'life' at all unless it has the quality of 'eternal life', and to survive a given point of time, however climacteric, does not in itself connote this quality. For this writer, as fundamentally for all New Testament writers, a confirmed sinner may exist, but he does not live. It follows, of course, that 'eternal life' may begin before physical death. It is the kind of life that believers live.

It follows that for the Apostolic writers, as for Jesus, the work of any saviour, fundamentally, was to turn bad men into good men. Here there falls the concept of the 'wrath' of God. It is common to all the writers, and it has the meaning already described. Ultimately its definition is: 'to leave the sinner to his sins.' There are a few Apostolic texts that, taken alone, seem to say that believers are saved from wrath (e.g. Romans v. 9; 1 Thessalonians i. 10), but on examination it will be found that even here salvation is primarily from sin and by consequence from wrath. As John puts it, a 'believer' *has* 'eternal life' and so 'wrath' does not 'abide' upon him (John iii. 36). When bad men become good men, God thereupon ceases to be 'angry' with them. Indeed, this is almost tautological, for in the New Testament to be a good man is to 'know God' and God is not angry with His intimates. Of course, happiness ensues, for it is the proper sequel of holiness. No Apostolic writer suggests that God will not forgive until His 'wrath' is 'satisfied'. It is enough that the bad man has become a good man.

If some of the facts already mentioned are examined, it is easy to see why it is becoming usual to speak of New Testament teaching as 'realized eschatology'. The believers held that with the coming of Jesus Christ something apocalyptic had happened—indeed, *the* apocalyptic thing had happened. His coming was no mere historical event, but a Divine intrusion. This was not less so, because, after it had occurred, it was possible to trace a long period of preparation for it. In other words, the ideas of discontinuity and continuity are both present. This, indeed, is so with every significant event in history, but here in a unique way. The perfect Rule of God had begun. None the less, it would be more accurate to speak of a *partly* 'realized eschatology', for the disciples knew that the final judgement had not yet occurred. Here, again, the novel point in their teaching was that they gave Christ a dominant place in the concept. The final judgement was to be His Parousia. However near they thought that this was, they thought of it as future. It would be out of place to discuss here the relation between this concept of judgement and the Johannine. For believers, God had acted in a unique way, but the act was not yet complete.

There are certain other terms which are the common property of New Testament writers in speaking of the Death of Christ, and these may be considered at this point. It needs no examples to show that in His Death Christ did something 'on behalf of' men. The Greek preposition (*hyper*) is ubiquitous. Already, of course, this involves a societary idea. Again, there are certain synonyms for 'save'. The English word 'ransom' only occurs once in the Apostolic writings (1 Timothy ii. 6), but words of the same Greek root (*lu*) are fairly common. They are usually translated by 'redeem' or 'redemption' (e.g. Roman iii. 24; Ephesians i. 7; Hebrews ix. 12; 1 Peter i. 18). The root notion is to 'loose' or 'set free' from sin. Two other verbs are used whose meaning is 'purchase' (e.g. 1 Corinthians vi. 20; Galatians iii. 13; Revelation v. 9). The metaphor of the freeing of a slave obviously unites the two sets of words, and there may here be the memory of the custom of the Kinsman. There are two other synonyms for 'save'—'set free' or 'emancipate' (Romans viii. 2; John viii. 36, etc.), and 'acquire' (or rather, 'obtain for one's very own', Acts xx. 28). It is plain that the first Christians thoroughly believed both in the seriousness of sin and in the wonder of their escape from its slavery.

The Apostolic writers also say that it was *by the 'blood' of Christ* that believers were 'loosed' (Revelation i. 5) or 'ransomed' (e.g. Ephesians i. 7; 1 Peter i. 19), or 'purchased' (Revelation v. 9), or 'acquired' (Acts xx. 28). The word 'blood' is also used of Christ's Death without these verbs. In all it occurs in this way about thirty times, and it belongs to all the Apostolic writers. Here three preliminary notes may be made. First, while the physical and the symbolical meanings are here so closely knit together that it is impossible to separate them, yet it is the spiritual truth symbolized that gives value to the word. Secondly, as it is impossible to state the spiritual truth adequately, there is here the greatest example of the way in which men turn to symbols when literal words fail. The symbolic use of the word 'blood' in Christian hymns illustrates this. Thirdly, in seeking to give such a degree of explanation as is possible, it is necessary to remember that the word was also used commonly in the sacrificial system, and that there was certainly some connexion between the Christian use and the use there. The nature of the connexion needs careful examination.

In considering the sacrificial system of the Jews, three meanings attaching to the ritual use of the term *blood* were distinguished, the giving of life, at-one-ment, and cleansing, but it was found that all three could be included under the term 'covenant'. In the preceding chapter, the one instance where the term 'blood' occurs in the Synoptic Gospels in relation to the Death of Christ— the story of the Last Supper—was considered, and it was found that here, too, the dominant concept is covenant. The parallel passage in the sixth of John does not mention covenant, but it expounds its content. There is no doubt that the word 'blood' occurs in relation to covenant also in other parts of the New Testament— for instance, in the Pauline account of the institution of the Eucharist and in such phrases in Hebrews as 'the blood of the eternal covenant'. Other examples are given later. There are passages, particularly in Paul and the Apocalypse, where the word 'blood' is used to denote something that all Christians understood, no exposition being given in the context. Where, however, there is some degree of exposition, it will be found below that the concept of covenant is present, and it may therefore be deduced that this is the dominant concept everywhere.

It was also seen in the discussion of the sacrificial system that the idea of the *sharing* of life' is integral to the idea of covenant— that Jehovah and His people were thought of as sharing a common life. This is expressed under the ritual of blood both when the *making* of covenant is in view (as in the twenty-fourth of Exodus), the *continuance* of covenant (as in the daily sacrifices), and the *renewal* of a broken covenant (as on the Day of Atonement). In the New Testament the idea of the sharing of life also occurs, notably again in the accounts of the Last Supper and the Epistle to the Hebrews. The use of the term 'blood' in relation to covenant has its chief meaning in the societary concept of a shared life—a life shared by Christians with Christ and so with God.

Turning now to the three ideas subsumed under 'covenant' in the old ritual, we find that the concept that the 'blood' of Christ 'cleanses' from sin—that is, that it turns bad men into good men—has four great instances (Hebrews ix. 14; 1 Peter i. 2; 1 John i. 7; Revelation vii. 14). In every instance there are indications in the context that the idea of covenant is in mind—the word 'covenant' itself occurring in the passage in Hebrews, the word 'sprinkling' in the Petrine text, the word 'propitiation' in the Johannine, and the chapter in the Apocalypse beginning with a list of the Tribes of the Covenant People and extending this idea to a 'great multitude . . . out of every nation. . . .'

It will presently be seen that the word 'propitiation', or 'atonement', is rare in the New Testament. The word 'blood' only occurs in close connexion with it once (Romans iii. 25). The term 'propitiation' alone would be sufficient to show that Paul is thinking here of the restoration of a broken covenant, but the context also is an argument about 'law', by which Paul means the Covenant Law of Israel. A similar remark might be made about a Johannine passage where 'blood' and 'propitiation' both occur within a few verses (1 John i. 7, ii. 2).

The third idea, the 'giving of life', needs longer notice, not least because of the great ambiguity of the phrase when it is used about the Death of Christ. At least five meanings may be distinguished: we may say that Christ 'gave His life' (that is, died) for men *simpliciter* (without asking *to whom* He gave it) ; we may say that Christ (or God in Christ) gives life *to men*; we may say that Christ gave a perfect, or sinless, life *to God* for men: we may say that Christ, being the societary Head of a new Israel, by giving His life, gave a redeemed, and so a new, mankind *to God;* or we may say that believers, through their unity with Christ, give their lives *to God*. All these ideas occur in the New Testament, but the immediate question is: Which of them occur in connexion with the term 'blood'? It will be found that they cannot be kept altogether separate.

There is no reference to 'blood' in the immediate context of the phrase 'give His life a ransom for many', where 'give His life' means simply 'die'—or, rather, 'die willingly'—and the same is true of other passages where 'give His life' or 'lay down His life' occurs.

Under the second meaning defined above, to 'give life *to men*', it may be said that the idea is involved in that of covenant, since this meant the 'sharing of life'. For instance, in the story of the Last Supper, our Lord, when He said 'This is my blood', meant that He was giving the Eleven spiritual life and thereby sharing it with them. This idea does not seem to be expressed in the ritual, where the dominant concept is the giving of life, not to men, but to God, unless it be under the text, 'For the life of the flesh is in the blood: and I have *given* it to you upon the altar to make atonement for your lives: for it is the blood that maketh atonement by reason of the life' (Leviticus xvii. 11).

The other three ideas under the 'giving of life' named above all involve the concept of giving *to God*, and it is difficult to keep them separate, just because Jesus is so fundamentally a societary man in the New Testament that He and believers cannot be separated. There is, for instance, a great passage in Hebrews where the two ideas that Christ offered a spotless life to God and that believers are thereby enabled to 'serve the living God'—that is, to give their lives to Him—are expressed, and where the third idea that links these two, the idea that Christ and believers are societarily one and that therefore His gift of His life and their gift of theirs are one and the same gift, is the basis of the whole passage (Hebrews ix. 13 *ff.*). Here the phrase 'the blood of Christ' is the key phrase, and the New Covenant is named in the context. Or, again, there is a passage in First Peter where the phrase 'with precious blood, as of a lamb without blemish and without spot, even the blood of Christ' is the key phrase, and where the same three ideas are present, though the terminology is different (1 Peter i. 17 *ff.*). Or, again, a full exposition of a great Pauline passage where the word 'blood' occurs would be found to involve the same three ideas, though they are not just the ideas that the Apostle is explicitly developing (Romans iii. 21 *ff.*). All these three ideas are adumbrated (to use the metaphor of 'shadow' with the writer to the Hebrews) in the ritual, though they do not occur all together in one piece of ritual. On the Day of Atonement, the High Priest, being a societary man, offered his own and his people's life to God. On that day, however, the idea of spotlessness was to seek, for the High Priest needed to offer for his own sins, and the victims were so closely identified with sin that their bodies were flung outside the camp—points that, as we shall see, the writer to the Hebrews seized. Yet in other parts of the ritual there is the requirement that a sacrifice shall be 'without spot or blemish'. Plainly, therefore, these three ideas might be united under the word 'covenant', for all sacrifices expressed this concept. It follows that all the New Testament references under the term 'blood', when the word is used of the Death of Christ, like all the references in the Old Testament ritual, are references, explicitly or implicitly, to covenant. It is also plain that most of what has been said, and perhaps all, might be gathered under the statement that where the New Testament speaks of the 'blood of Christ' the concept 'life through death' is present.

Yet questions remain: *Why* did Christ need to 'give His life' that 'many' might be ransomed? *How* does the 'blood of Christ' cleanse from sin? *Why* was it necessary for Christ to die that He might share a common life with believers, and so offer their lives with His own to God? It has been suggested that here, too, the ritual gives guidance. It is rightly said that in the ritual the death of the sacrifice is a secondary matter, that a victim was killed in order that there might be 'release of life' or that 'life might be set free'—that the death (and sufferings) of the animal had no value *per se*. It is then argued that such phrases as 'the release of life' give an adequate account also of what the Death of Christ means in the New Testament. This does not seem to be so. The reasons for this assertion may be summarized.

First, it is to be noted that in the New Testament, where the word 'blood' occurs symbolically in passages that do not refer to the Death of Christ, the idea represented is 'death', not 'life' or 'life through death'.[1] This is presumptive evidence that in the passages that do refer to the Death of Christ the term 'blood' emphasizes the concept of death more than the suggested exposition allows. With this there need to be considered the many passages in the New Testament where there is emphasis upon the Death of Christ, without the use of the term 'blood'. These are considered in other chapters. Next, it may be noted that of the verbs named above as used with 'blood' in the New Testament the Greek words rendered 'purchase' or 'buy' and 'acquire' are not used by the Septuagint in the Priestly document

---

[1] E.g. Matthew xxvii. 24; Acts v. 28; Hebrews xii. 4; Revelation xix. 2. The nearest exception is in the phrase 'flesh and blood', meaning 'the merely human'. Even here 'blood' does not stand for 'life'. In Acts xvii. 26 the Revised Version omits 'blood'.

at all, and that the words rendered 'redeem' and 'ransom' are not there used of sin-offerings or in relation to 'blood'. This suggests that the New Testament writers looked beyond the ritual when they wished fully to express what they meant when they spoke of 'the blood of Christ'. Then, of course, the ritual did not express the idea of resurrection at all, and in the New Testament the doctrines of the Death (and sufferings) of Christ and His Resurrection go integrally together. The fact is that *after the Resurrection* the disciples of Jesus found His death had a meaning and value *per se*, and that here there was nothing in the ritual to correspond. It is not too much to say that the emphasis on the Death of Christ in the New Testament is just as clear as the lack of emphasis on the *death* of the sacrifices in the Old. At this central point there was something in the Christian experience that had no ritual anticipation. It was something that is beyond full explanation, but we shall find below that in certain great passages where Paul and John did what they could to explain, they did not use the term 'blood' or refer to the ritual at all. Even the writer to the Hebrews, we shall find, does not merely develop concepts found in the ritual; he also *adds* to them. Meanwhile we may conclude that all that the great, though incomplete, symbol 'blood' means in the New Testament can be gathered under the word 'covenant'.

We now come to the words rendered 'propitiation'. It is legitimate to assume that these words belonged to the common stock of early Christian speech, for, though they do not occur frequently, one or other of them is found in the Pauline Epistles, the Epistle to the Hebrews, and the First Epistle of John, and in every case without detailed exposition (Romans iii. 25; Hebrews ii. 17; 1 John ii. 2, iv. 10; cf. Hebrews ix. 5). They all run back to a Greek root (*hil*) whose *original* meaning was 'propitiate' or 'allay anger'. In the LXX they are used to translate the Hebrew word rendered 'make atonement', which has already been discussed. The leading example is in the ritual of the Day of Atonement (Leviticus xvi), though the terms also occur outside ritual passages. It has been seen that under the Hebrew term the idea in post-Exilic times was not 'to turn away anger', but 'to undo alienation'. Can this be said of the Greek terms, or must we suppose that here the Apostles returned to an earlier and cruder concept?

If the use of the terms in the Septuagint is examined, it will be found that there are passages where it is possible to translate either by 'propitiate' or by 'forgive' (or 'pardon'), but also passages where the first translation seems to be impossible, at least if 'propitiate' be taken to mean 'offer something that will allay wrath and lead to mercy'. For instance, the Greek word is used where Naaman says, 'The Lord *pardon* thy servant in this thing' (2 Kings v. 18). Similarly, the word occurs in a number of psalms—for instance, in the phrases translated in English, 'As for our transgressions, thou shalt *purge* them *away*' (Psalms lxv. 3) ; 'He, being full of compassion, *forgave* their iniquity, and destroyed them not: yea, many a time turned he his anger away, and did not stir up all his wrath' (Psalms lxxviii. 38) ; 'Help us, O God of our salvation, for the glory of thy name: And deliver us, and *purge away* our sins, for thy name's sake' (Psalms lxxix. 9). Finally, the word occurs in a well-known New Testament passage: 'God be *merciful* to me a sinner' (Luke xviii. 13). When the use of the Hebrew term in the ritual of Atonement is remembered and these examples of a similar Greek use are added, it is pertinent to ask whether this meaning does not suit the context in the Apostolic writings where the terms are used of the Death of Christ. There is only one passage where this is even doubtful (Romans iii. 25), and an attempt will be made later to show that even here Paul was thinking of 'reconciliation' and not of the 'allaying of wrath'. It would therefore have been better if the Revised Version had followed the translation of the Hebrew word and had rendered the terms by 'at-one-ment' and not by 'propitiation'. Here, again, the Christian claim was that 'what' the ritual 'could not do', the Death of Christ did: it reconciled men to God.

The relation of the discussion of the Jewish doctrine or doctrines of Mediation, described above, to the New Testament doctrine of Salvation can only be briefly indicated. A full discussion would almost require an account of the New Testament teaching about the Person of Christ. Such a brief account as can here be given may properly be included under 'General Apostolic Preaching', since, while the different Apostolic writers vary from each other in their choice of Jewish mediatorial terms, they yet all use them in the same way, and they all use them about Jesus of Nazareth.

In the Old Testament there were some such terms used of *men*. For instance, the name 'prophet' had been used of men who spoke of God to other men. It was easy and natural for ordinary

Jews, who were contemporaries of Jesus, to use this term about Him. Again, the term 'Messiah' had in ancient times been used of a living king considered as the vicegerent of Jehovah, and though in later writings this name had been kept for a future king, it was possible for Jesus' disciples to use it for Him even while He was on earth. Even the name 'Son of God' had been used for kings in old time and occasionally even for righteous men (e.g. Psalms ii. 7; Wisdom ii. 18), so that it was not impossible for one Evangelist to write, 'Truly this was a righteous man', where another wrote, 'Truly this was a son of God'. Yet, first on the lips of Jesus Himself and then on the lips of Apostolic writers, the phrase is used about Him in a unique way. Here all Hebrew and Jewish uses of the name *for a man* are transcended. If the passages where this unique use occurs were examined one by one, it would be found that it is always related to the new doctrine of salvation. As usual, the Fourth Gospel summarizes perfectly the goal of a prolonged but inevitable process of Christian thought: 'God so loved the world that he gave his only-begotten Son, that whosoever believeth on him should not perish, but have eternal life' (John iii. 16). Of old titles used about men, there remain two. The first is 'High Priest'. This is best discussed under the Epistle to the Hebrews. The other is 'Son of Man'. At first, as has been seen, this was a synonym for 'a man'; then it was used in a societary way in Daniel for 'the saints of the Most High'; and in Enoch for a superhuman being, quite distinct from God. The New Testament use of the phrase has been discussed under the Synoptic Gospels; there are some references below under other books. The important point here is that all these names are used for Jesus in the New Testament under the one concept that He was sent by God to save sinful men.

There is, as was seen, another set of mediatorial terms in Hebrew and Jewish books whose common characteristic is that they describe some activity in God which is inseparable from Him, and yet the terms are used as though the activity were conceived as if it were not just to be identified with Him. The chief are *Shekinah*, 'Glory', 'Wisdom', 'Face', *Logos* (and 'Spirit'). The Apostolic writers borrowed these terms, but they used them in a quite novel way. They related them to a particular historical person, Jesus of Nazareth. As it happens, the Greek word for 'tent' or 'tabernacle' (*skēnē*) has some assonance with the word *shekinah*. The Johannine writer, therefore, in effect uses three of these terms in one sentence about Jesus: 'The *Logos* became flesh and was our *Shekinah* and we beheld His *glory*' (John i. 14). Similarly Paul speaks of the 'light of the knowledge of the *glory* of God in the *face* of Jesus Christ' (2 Corinthians iv. 6), and the writer to the Hebrews describes the 'Son' as the 'effulgence of the *glory* [of God]', clearly echoing a passage about 'wisdom' in the Book of Wisdom (Hebrews i. 3; Wisdom vii. 26). Again, Paul calls 'Christ crucified' 'the *wisdom* of God' (1 Corinthians i. 24). These examples, among many, must suffice. When all the uses of these terms about Christ are taken together, the same point recurs which was noted above under the terms which had previously been used, not of God, but of men. They all refer to a given historical person, Jesus Christ, considered as Saviour. Here, even more clearly than under the former series of terms, mediation is altogether from God to man, and the purpose of mediation is salvation.

There remain two of the terms discussed earlier. The first is 'angel'. In the period after the Exile, as has been seen, this described a being who was neither divine nor human, and the first disciples did not find it natural to use the term for Christ. Indeed, the writer to the Hebrews spends considerable pains, in his first chapter, to show that a true saviour must be more closely related to God than 'angels' are. The use of the other term, 'Spirit', in the New Testament is very different. It will be found later that the Apostolic writers do indeed connect the Holy Spirit closely with Jesus Christ, but in a distinctive way. The important point here, once again, is that the doctrine of the Spirit is a doctrine of salvation. Because He is holy, He makes men holy, and to do that is to save them to the uttermost. The doctrines of the 'personality' of Christ and the Spirit are to-day often studied apart from that of the Work of Christ. The separation of the two subjects may be convenient, but it is artificial. To return to the subject of mediation, the New Testament carries the Old Testament doctrines to an unexpected but adequate climax in the doctrine of the Christ and the Spirit. Here the scattered rays meet and are perfected. On considering this climax, it is hardly too much to say that for the New Testament mediation *is* salvation.

It is clear from all this that the *idea* of a 'mediator' pervades the New Testament. The *word*, however, is rare, but its uses confirm the conclusions reached above. It is used of Moses as mediating from God to men (Galatians iii. 19 *f*.). In Hebrews it is three times used of Christ as mediator of the New Covenant (viii. 6,

N

ix. 15, xii. 24), and, as has been seen, in the Bible it is always God who initiates covenant. A text in First Timothy gathers the principal truths about mediation together: 'There is one God, one mediator also between God and men, himself man, Christ Jesus, who gave himself a ransom for all' (1 Timothy ii. 5 *f.*). Mediation here is from God to man, yet it is through 'man', and its purpose is salvation.

It appears, then, that the Apostolic witness was primarily to certain new facts, and that these included facts both of history and experience. It was only gradually that these came to be related to older ideas—'older ideas' meaning, for the first Christians, chiefly ideas of the Old Testament, for, like contemporary Jews, they accepted this as the authoritative book. This process was never carried out systematically. Such a man as Simon Peter could not and did not retire to seclusion to think out a system. His business was to 'bear witness' to the new facts, and he gave himself so wholly to this that it was only when his witnessing required it that he either asked or answered questions about the results for old ideas. Anything that he said about these was inevitably fragmentary. It was not quite the same with such men as Paul and the writer to the Hebrews. The new facts inevitably raised intellectual problems, as well as problems of practice, or rather, they raised problems that were both intellectual and practical. It is one of the marks of Paul that he solved practical problems by appealing to fundamental principles. Yet no New Testament writer gives us a complete and well-rounded system of doctrine. It is likely that Paul, for instance, had gone far in thinking one out, for the doctrinal parts of his Epistles, when taken together, admit of this or even require it. It is true, again, that, when the teaching of Paul and 'Hebrews' and 'John' is examined, it is found that the account that they give, explicitly or implicitly, of the truths that go with the new facts, passes beyond the limits of Old Testament teaching and begins to form a distinctively Christian theology. Yet for every New Testament writer the facts are always paramount. Explained or unexplained, they are *there*, just as much as light is *there* for the physicist, whether it is explicable or inexplicable or partly one and partly the other.

CHAPTER XIV

THE 'SERVANT', THE 'LAMB', AND THE 'SHEPHERD'

THE first twelve chapters of the Acts of the Apostles give us our only account of the first Christian Church. It is generally agreed that this book was written by St. Luke, the disciple and friend of St. Paul, that he had opportunities of learning the facts about the Church in Jerusalem and its neighbourhood, and that the chapters were written about a generation after the events with which they deal. There is some dispute about their full historicity. There are scholars who maintain that the teaching that they contain does not belong, or does not wholly belong, to the days that immediately followed Pentecost, but to half a century later. Following the method pursued in this volume, we take this teaching at its minimum value—as describing and implying the beliefs of the Jewish Church in and about Jerusalem in the first Christian century. No doubt St. Luke selected events that suited his special purpose, but this does not much affect the particular study now before us.

John the Baptist had been the most popular man in Palestine, and after his death Jesus. The facts about their lives were well known both to Christians and Jews. Paul could assume that even King Agrippa II knew the main facts about Jesus, for His deeds were 'not done in a corner' (Acts xxvi. 26). This helps to explain certain phenomena in the twelve chapters. They presuppose a struggle between the orthodox Jews and the Nazarenes, and the latter needed to emphasize points of difference, not points of agreement. There was no difference of opinion about the fact of the Crucifixion. It was indeed necessary that the Christian account of the death of Jesus should be on record, for after the event the Jews were not at ease with the memory of their share in it, and this accounts, in part, for the altogether disproportionate place that at first sight is given in all four Gospels to the last week of our Lord's life. Yet there is more than this. To the Jews the suggestion that a man, however noble, who had been crucified, could be the Messiah, was anathema. The Christians replied by declaring that the crucified Nazarene had risen again. This was

inevitably the chief point of their emphasis, both for the justification of their own faith and in their perpetual controversy with
the Jews. None the less, they were aware that the Crucifixion
could not be treated as a mere historical event. They remembered, for one thing, what their Master had said about it,
and being, like all Jews, sons of the Old Testament, they could
not but believe that the Messiah had died by 'the determinate
counsel and foreknowledge of God'. As all the Synoptist Gospels
imply—and it needs always to be remembered that these were
taking shape at this time—the Apostles were 'witnesses of the
Resurrection' as organically related to the Death of Christ. It may
easily be that the first Christian document was the Christian
story of the last week of Jesus' life. The dispute with the Jews was
not about His teaching, nor about the facts of His Galilean
Ministry. It centred in the last week of His life. It was obvious
that Jesus could not have risen if He had not died. Since, then,
His Resurrection was God's will, His Death must have been God's
will too. Even if the Apostles had found this part of God's will
altogether inscrutable—and as we shall see, this was not so—they
could not treat it as merely an awkward accident. For them the
Death, Resurrection, Ascension, and the gift of the Spirit, were
an organic whole. This, for instance, is just the substance of a
large part of Peter's speech at Pentecost (Acts ii. 22–36). Whether
it goes back, just as it stands, to that day or not, it represents the
mind of the early Church at Jerusalem.

It is easy to show that St. Luke's record illustrates the previous
chapter in this book. For the disciples, Jesus has been 'exalted to
the right hand of God' and He was on the Throne in power. He
is called 'Prince and Saviour'. In other words, His Person and
Work go together. Through Him God gives 'repentance . . . and
remission of sins' (Acts v. 31). In other words, the new experience
goes with the new fact. There is no denying the implication that
the disciples knew that they were 'saved' in a way that they had
not known before. They knew this because they knew that Christ
had given them the Spirit of God. It is true that little is said about
their hope of their own resurrection and escape from a future Hades,
but this was not pertinent to their immediate task; probably too,
at this time they expected their Lord's Return while they themselves were alive. Yet, when the first martyr died, the story has
significant details. We read that Stephen cried, 'Lord Jesus,
receive my spirit'. Behind this there is something far different

from the old idea of a passage to a miserable Hades. Already Jesus was thought of as 'Prince (or Author) of life'. Already too, the disciples fell back upon a very old phrase for death, for it suited their new experience better than any reference to Hades; for them to die was to 'fall asleep' (Acts vii. 60). Neither here nor anywhere else is there anything like a complete theology, for a complete theology would have been an anachronism. Discoverers proclaim their discoveries, leaving the integration of them with other truths to a later stage. The twelve chapters discuss, for instance, neither the way in which the belief in the Lordship of the Risen Christ could be related to monotheism nor that of 'falling asleep' to Hades. The chapters give materials for a new theology, but they do not integrate them in a new theology. All this suggests that the account that Luke gives is a reliable one.

The appeal to the Old Testament as a final authority is very clear. It takes two forms. First, there is appeal to particular passages—for instance, to a passage in Joel, to the Sixteenth Psalm, and, as in the Synoptists, to the Second and the Hundred-and-tenth Psalms. It may be that the first Christians thought of these passages as directly referring to their Lord (cf. Acts ii. 30 *f.*), yet for modern readers they do not fall within the category of artificial 'proof passages', for in every case there are underlying truths that are fully exemplified in Jesus. As will appear presently, there is another passage that lies closer to the immediate subject. It needs to be noted first that there is a second way in which the first Christians appealed to the Old Testament, for it has a great illustration within these chapters. There are those who think that Stephen's speech is wholly Luke's composition, like the speeches ascribed by Thucydides to Pericles or by Livy to Hannibal. It appears to me unlikely that, if this were so, the speech would break off just where the distinctively Christian conclusions are about to be drawn, but at the least the speech tells us what Luke thought the Palestinian Christians said about the whole Old Testament, and he had good opportunities of knowing what this was. There are passages that imply that some of the early disciples appealed, not only to particular passages, but to the whole Book (e.g. Acts xiii. 16 *ff.*; Hebrews i. 1). The speech is at least a specimen of their method. The first part of it requires that the speaker claimed the concept of Covenant for the Church: that the Christians were the true heirs of Abraham, even though, like the Patriarchal family, they were few and forlorn. When the speech passes to Moses, it speaks of him, in effect, as a saviour indeed, but as a saviour who saved the Israelites in spite of themselves—indeed, after an initial rejection. This lies close to the account of Moses given above, both under the chapters on the Old Testament and in the attempted exposition of the Transfiguration. Finally, the part of the speech that deals with the Temple—and, therefore, for the speaker and his hearers, with the sacrificial system, since in their day sacrifice was confined to the Temple—puts it in a quite subordinate place. There is no hint anywhere in these chapters that the first Christians related the Death of Christ to the sacrificial system. All these things have an indirect bearing on the doctrine of the Work of Christ.

In the last hurried sentences of Stephen's speech he speaks of 'the coming of the *Righteous* One' and of the Jews as 'murdering' Him (Acts vii. 52). In view of what has already been said about the Servant Songs, it is permissible to think that the speech, if it had not been interrupted, would have ended with the claim that Jesus was the Servant of the Lord. This is the more likely since elsewhere (Acts iii. 13–15) Jesus is called alternatively God's 'Servant' and 'The Holy and Righteous One', and this in a passage that unites the Death, Resurrection and Glory of Jesus in exactly the way in which death, resurrection and glory are joined in the fifty-third of Isaiah. It is important to note that here and elsewhere (Acts iii. 26, iv. 27–30) Luke introduces the name 'Servant' for Jesus without explanation, for this implies that it was commonly used for our Lord in the Jerusalem Church. A passage in Matthew (xii. 17 *ff.*) supports this. The story of Philip and the Ethiopian Eunuch indeed tells of the exposition of the passage, but there it needs to be expounded, because the Eunuch is an outsider. It is clear that for the explanation of the Death of Jesus the first Christians turned to the prophecies of the Servant of the Lord. When we remember how these had haunted the mind and words of Jesus Himself, this is easy to understand. It is likely enough that the disciples supposed that these prophecies referred directly to Jesus, but here most of all this does not matter. The fact is that, as millions of Christians have found in the centuries since, the greatest of these oracles can be applied to Jesus without any further exposition than itself. This is because He, and He alone, perfectly realized—to use that word in its proper sense— the principles that underlie the passage in Isaiah. An attempt has been made above to show that this is the climax of the teaching of the Prophets about salvation, and that it drew out clearly ideas that earlier had been immaturely struggling into light. As the exposition of the passage in an earlier chapter shows, this seems to the present writer to mean that the Christian Church began with a societary account of salvation.

For a reason that will presently appear, the Apocalypse of John may be considered next. In the general teaching of this book, certain ideas named in the chapter on the New Testament background are very prominent. Firstly, as already seen, the Kingdom, in all its three senses, is ascribed to Christ. It is agreed that the book belongs to a period when Christians were being persecuted unto death. It was Rome that persecuted and it seemed to most men that for the present, at least, Rome ruled, and not God. It was the faith of the Seer and of those for whom he spoke, on the contrary, that God was ruling in the seeming chaos and welter of the 'great tribulation' in which they were caught. Their characteristic way of saying this appears at once in the first chapter. If it is 'the Lord God' who says, 'I am the Alpha and the Omega', it is the Christ who says, 'I am the first and the last' (Revelation i. 8, 17). Similarly, the Lamb is 'in the midst' of the throne of God. God and the Lamb—or God through the Lamb—is ruling the chaotic world all the time. There is, indeed, another kingdom at present, the kingdom of the Wild Beast (for 'Wild Beast' is the true translation of the Greek term *Therion*), but even this kingdom exists for a while by the mysterious 'mind' of God (Revelation xvii. 17). All the while the Lamb is in control. It is just as plain that there is to come a Kingdom that will be perfect and that it is to be the Kingdom of God and the Lamb, of 'our Lord and his Christ' (Revelation xi. 15). Indeed, this is the presupposition of the whole book, or it would make no sense. Finally, there are intimations that even now the perfect Kingdom has begun to exist in the Church. This is just assumed —for instance, in the text 'Thou wast slain, and didst purchase unto God with thy blood men of every tribe, and tongue, and people, and nation, and madest them unto our God a Kingdom and priests; and they reign upon the earth' (Revelation v. 9 *f.*). Even in the midst of persecution—or, rather, just because they are in the midst of persecution—the Christians *have* kingship, and not only will have it.

It goes without saying that the Lamb—or God through the Lamb—'saves' men. The cry of the redeemed is 'Salvation [belongs] unto our God which sitteth on the throne, and unto the Lamb' (Revelation vii. 10). Again, in this book, the idea that the faithful are saved from Hades is peculiarly clear. In the opening vision the Christ in power says, 'I became dead, and behold, I am alive unto the ages of the ages, and I have the keys of death and of Hades' (Revelation i. 18). There is no need to examine the problem of the general teaching of the Seer about Hades and 'the second death', or to ask whether his eschatology is logically systematized. It is clear that for him and his readers the terrors of Hades had given way to a 'sure and certain hope'. The martyrs had not indeed escaped physical death, but this is no longer the door of a miserable Hereafter but the very 'gate of heaven'. The comparative unimportance of physical death has no clearer illustration. These dead men are not dead, for their names are 'written in the Book of Life'.

But how, according to the Seer of the Apocalypse, are men saved? Here it is best to begin with his references to the Temple and the sacrificial system. In his final account of the realm that is to be, he says, 'I saw no Temple therein' (Revelation xxi. 22). This must not be pressed, however, for 'The Lord God, the Almighty, and the Lamb' are 'the Temple thereof', and the underlying idea here is that, since men are now holy, there is no longer any place for the principle of separation between sinful men and the holy God, which the plan of the Temple in all its many parts exemplified. There are unmistakable references to the sacrificial system, but they need to be exactly noted. For this writer there is an 'altar' in Heaven, but its prototype is not the great open-air altar of animal sacrifice, but the smaller Altar of Incense within the Holy Place. This was indeed cleansed annually by blood on the Day of Atonement, but the 'altar' in Heaven cannot be compared with it at this point. On the contrary, the comparison is with its daily use as an Altar *of Incense*, and incense is taken as symbol of prayer (Revelation viii. 3). It is true that elsewhere (Revelation vi. 9–11) 'the souls of them that had been slain for the word of God' are seen 'underneath the altar'; but here, too, the altar is an altar of prayer and the prayer is not for salvation, but for vindication. The Seer's concept of the 'altar' sheds little or no light on his concept of the way of salvation.

Again, there are two passages where Christians are called 'priests' (Revelation i. 6, v. 10), and one where the martyrs especially are so named (Revelation xx. 4–6). It is remarkable that in all three passages kingship and priesthood go together (as in Psalm cx). There can be no doubt that here the faithful are thought of as sharing with Christ in the reconciliation of man with God, and that they so share because, like Christ, they suffer and die in the service of God. They, too, are mediators, but the use of the term 'priests' for Christians does not in itself certainly say more.

So far, it appears that the Seer's references to the sacrificial system suggest that it was for him occasionally illustrative of his ideas rather than the basis of his thought. Is there a great and decisive exception in his use of such phrases as 'The blood of the Lamb'? Here it is necessary first to point out that he uses the term 'blood' seventeen times and that, apart from the phrases in question, it stands for 'death' and not for 'life through death'. It is only in four great passages (Revelation i. 5, v. 9, vii. 14, xii. 11) that the latter meaning might be found. Here something may first be said of the verbs used in the four texts.

No one pretends that the strange metaphor used in the text 'These are they which come out of the great tribulation, and they washed their robes, and made them white in the blood of the Lamb' has any exact Old Testament antecedent. It is indeed true that to 'wash garments' or 'robes' is a phrase that is found in Leviticus and Numbers, but there the washing is in water, and the ceremony is not strictly sacrificial, but preparatory to the use of ritual (or to entry into the Temple or even into 'the camp'). It is true also, of course, that the symbol of 'washing' is so common that it could be used without any specific reference at all. If one were sought, it might perhaps be found in a passage in Ezekiel which unites the 'sprinkling with clean water' with the gift of the Spirit in a far more nearly Christian way than any passage in the Priestly documents (Ezekiel xxxvi. 25 f.). But the symbol of 'washing in blood' is original with the Seer and derives from his experience that through the Death of Christ bad men become good men. The whole text is just his symbolic way of saying this, and it shows how the new Christian fact and the new Christian experience were regulative for the New Testament writers, and that they were quite able to create their own phraseology.

If three of the four other verbs used in the four passages are examined, it will be found that none of them is used in the Septuagint to translate terms in the Levitical ritual, but that all have some precedent in the Prophets. The first text runs: 'Unto him that loveth us, and *loosed* us from our sins in his blood'. In a passage in Deutero-Isaiah we read of Jerusalem that 'her sin is *loosed*' (Isaiah xl. 2, lxx). The second passage runs: 'Thou wast slain, and didst *purchase* unto God with thy blood men of every tribe, and tongue, and people and nation' (Revelation v. 9). The Septuagint has the Greek word for 'purchase' in the phrase 'Come ye, *buy* and eat' (Isaiah lv. 1). In the text from the Seer's seventh chapter, already quoted, we read: 'They washed their robes, and *made* them *white* in the blood of the Lamb'. The Greek word for 'make white' occurs in the phrase: 'Though your sins be as scarlet, they *shall be* as *white* as snow' (Isaiah i. 18, lxx). For the remaining verb 'overcome' (Revelation xii. 11) no apposite Old Testament quotation can be given, but it is not a notion germane to the ritual system, but to the fifty-third of Isaiah. This argument from terminology should not be pressed, for it is possible, as will presently be argued for a Prophetic passage, that, where terms are absent, the ideas that they convey are present, but so far as it goes, it illustrates the way in which, as commentaries show, the Seer's language reflects that of the Prophets (and Daniel) rather than that of the Priestly documents. It illustrates also the Seer's princely way of using anything in the Old Testament that suits his purpose, and since, as has been shown, the idea of 'life through death' can be found in a certain form in the Levitical system, it is quite likely that this was not absent from his mind. Yet this does not mean that it was the chief source of his ideas. This was the Crucifixion and Resurrection, and after these, as an attempt will now be made to show, a Prophetic passage and not a ritual one. His use of the sacrificial system is still only illustrative.

Is there, however, a clear and dominant reference to it in the figure of 'the Lamb'? Here something ought first to be said about the Greek word *arnion* rendered 'lamb'. It is a rare term, and occurs in the Septuagint neither of the lambs used in sacrifice nor of the word translated 'lamb' in the fifty-third of Isaiah. The nearest Septuagintal approach to the Seer's use is in a passage in Jeremiah, which, as we have seen, both compares and contrasts with the use of Deutero-Isaiah (Jeremiah xi. 19). In the New Testament *arnion* only occurs once (John xxi. 15) outside the Apocalypse, but there it occurs twenty-seven times. It is likely that the Seer used this rare word because of its assonance with *therion*, the Greek term for the Wild Beast. In relation to the

terms used in the seventh verse of the fifty-third of Isaiah, it may
be added that a literal translation of the Hebrew would run: 'He
was led like a sheep [or goat] to the slaughter and as a ewe before
her shearers is dumb'; while the Septuagint means literally:
'He was led like a sheep to slaughter, and as a lamb (*amnos*)
before the shearer is dumb.' So far as the *term* itself goes, therefore, the symbolic figure in the Apocalypse can neither be
referred confidently to the sacrificial system nor to the fifty-third
of Isaiah.

It is otherwise when we look at the *ideas* that the Seer's great
symbol represents. In his fifth chapter—the chapter that gives
the key to the whole of this Apocalypse—the Lamb has three
characteristics. These are expressed in three phrases: 'as it had
been slain' (or, as in xiii. 8, 'that hath been slain'), 'thou didst
purchase unto God with thy blood men of every tribe and tongue
and people and nation', and 'in the midst of the throne' (Revelation v. 6, 9, 12). In other words, the ruling ideas are suffering,
salvation, and glory. There is no example of these three ideas,
taken together, in the ritual system, but they are just the three found
in the last of the Songs of the Servant. Again, as we have seen, these
Songs, like the Seer, teach the salvation of the Gentiles—of men
'of every tribe and tongue and people and nation', and it would
be difficult to discern this idea in the sacrificial system. It seems
clear, therefore, that the Seer's symbol of 'the Lamb' is derived
from a verse in the fifty-third of Isaiah: 'as a lamb that is led to
the slaughter'. The reason for the substitution of *arnion* for another
Greek term has already been indicated. Another question
ensues: Why does the Seer say 'Lamb' and not 'Servant', as the
first Christians had done? The answer is that he needed a symbolic
word that would suit his symbolic scheme. In particular, he
needed a term that could be used in contrast to *therion*, and
'Lamb', unlike 'Servant', moves in the same symbolic sphere as
'Wild Beast'. Further, the proper correlative for 'servant' is
'master', and it was impossible to use the common Greek term
for 'master' (*kurios*) *simpliciter* to describe the ruler of the kingdom
of evil, since it was the commonest Christian word both for God
and Christ. The Seer, who was quite capable of taking his own
way, chose a word suggested by the fifty-third of Isaiah and
applied its group of ideas to Christ. Of course, under the influence
of the new Christian fact and experience, he went further than
the Prophet had done—in particular, he typified the 'prosperity'

or 'success' of the Lamb by the phrase 'in the midst of the throne'
—but this advance is only what one would expect. When it is
remembered that the lamb had no special place in the sacrificial
system, that it was not specifically *the* sin-offering, that it had no
place in the ritual of the Day of Atonement, that the concept
that a sacrifice should be 'in the midst of the throne' has no
ritual antecedent whatever, and that the sacrificial system
nowhere unites the three leading ideas of the fifth chapter of the
Apocalypse, it seems clear that the figure of 'the Lamb' in that
book derives from the Prophet and not from ritual. It is chiefly
through the Seer that the Christian world, from the times of the
Catacombs onwards, has given to the phrase 'the Lamb' a
meaning that has no real parallel in the Levitical code. Indeed,
it has no real parallel in the seventh verse of the fifty-third of
Isaiah *as Jews would read it.* The literal translation of the Hebrew
phrase given above jars on Christian ears just because of the
new use of the word by the Christian Seer.

It ought to be mentioned that the Seer has a text that has often
been taken to teach an 'eternal atonement' (Revelation xiii. 8),
but the Greek here allows that the phrase 'from the foundation
of the world' should be taken, not with 'slain', but with 'written
in the book of life', and the latter connexion is supported by the
parallel text (Revelation xvii. 8). Again, the concept of 'eternity'
involved does not seem consonant with the Seer's general outlook,
but belongs rather to the Epistle to the Hebrews. There is no
need to show in detail that the Seer's concept of salvation is
societary, for this is implied in everything that he says. For
instance, as already seen, the two words 'loose' and 'purchase'
coalesce in the concept of the Kinsman. Again, Christians share
with Christ in the Kingdom in all its three senses, just because
He and they cannot be separated. Again, in the vision of the
first chapter our Lord appears as 'one like unto a Son of Man'
(Revelation i. 13). There is here a direct reference to Daniel,
where also the Kingdom of the Son of Man is contrasted with
that of Wild Beasts. There, however, the figure is in fact societary
and only individual in a symbolic way; with the Seer the phrase
is used of an individual who carries a society with Him.

There is a third document in the New Testament where the
teaching about the Atonement builds chiefly on the fifty-third
of Isaiah. This is the First Epistle of Peter. Two general remarks
may first be made. First, the author assumes that his readers

already thought about the Death of Christ in a given way. This comes out most clearly in the passage where the references are most extensive (1 Peter ii. 18–25). Here the writer is encouraging Christian 'servants', or, more exactly, household servants, to 'suffer wrongfully'. Such suffering would be frequent in large heathen households and its injustice would ordinarily rankle in the mind. Christian servants, however, are not to let it do so, for here, says the writer, they have an opportunity to be like Christ Himself on His Cross. Indeed, it is to this that they have been 'called'. There would have been no use in saying this unless there were already a well-known doctrine that the Christ had been 'called' to suffer. It may be added that here the emphasis is on Christ's suffering, and not on His death, for Christian 'servants' were 'buffeted', not killed. The same appeal underlies a later encouragement to *all* Christians to 'suffer for righteousness' sake' (1 Peter iii. 8–22). Secondly, there is only one way in which the writer says anything distinctive about the doctrine of salvation. All his other references have parallels elsewhere in the New Testament, as will appear below. This is evidence that by the time this Epistle was written, certain ideas belonged to Christians generally.

There is no need to show that the fifty-third of Isaiah lies behind the first passage just named (1 Peter ii. 18–25). It may be noted, however, that no less than six phrases are quoted from it and that they come naturally to the writer's lips here and there in sentences of his own. The Old Testament passage is not so much as named. This means that its ideas were so habitually used to describe the Death of Christ that a Christian writer used them readily without explanation. It may be noted that here our Lord is called neither 'Servant' nor 'Lamb', but 'Shepherd and Overseer'. The word 'shepherd' does not occur in the great oracle, but is derived from the phrase 'All we like sheep have gone astray', for the writer says 'For ye were going astray, but are now returned to the Shepherd and Overseer of your souls'. In the Apocalypse the Lamb is expressly called 'shepherd' (Revelation vii. 17). There are, of course, many Old Testament instances of the use of the symbol of the shepherd and his sheep, and these illustrate, in yet another way, the corporate or societary concept.

While here the writer of the Epistle, in his use of the fifty-third of Isaiah, recalls the Synoptic Gospels, the Acts of the Apostles and the Apocalypse, in the phrase 'the righteous for the unrighteous' (1 Peter iii. 18) he recalls Paul as well as Deutero-Isaiah, and in the phrase 'unto obedience and sprinkling of the blood of Jesus Christ' (1 Peter i. 2) there is a parallel to the Epistle to the Hebrews. It will be noticed that the word 'sprinkling' is undoubtedly of sacrificial origin, whether it refers to the Day of Atonement or to the unique ritual described in the twenty-fourth chapter of Exodus or to both. Similarly, there is an undoubted reference to a frequent phrase in the sacrificial ritual in the following words: 'Knowing that ye were redeemed, not with corruptible things, with silver and gold . . . but with precious blood, as of a lamb *without blemish and without spot*, even the blood of Christ' (1 Peter i. 19). Here the reference to 'silver and gold' as corruptible in comparison with the blood of a sacrifice is very remarkable, for literally the exact opposite was the truth. The Christian writer is not the slave of his quotations. These two passages, however, show that this writer too was quite ready to use selected details in the Jewish ritual to illustrate what he had to say, but he almost asserts that his chief Old Testament authorities were, not the ritual, but the Prophets when he writes: 'Concerning which salvation the *prophets* sought and searched diligently, who prophesied of the grace that should come unto you: searching what time or what manner of time the Spirit of Christ which was in them did point unto, when it testified beforehand the sufferings of Christ and the glories that should follow them' (1 Peter i. 10 *f.*).

It is plain, again, that for this writer, as for the other New Testament writers, the Death of Christ, His Resurrection, His 'Glory', and the gift of the Spirit are an organic whole (e.g. 1 Peter i. 2, iii. 18–22, iv. 13 *f.*). The phrase, 'Who according to his great mercy begat us again unto a living hope by the resurrection of Jesus Christ from the dead, unto an inheritance incorruptible and undefiled and that fadeth not away, reserved in heaven for you, who by the power of God are guarded through faith unto a salvation ready to be revealed in the last time', shows that the writer of First Peter and his readers held the common Christian faith that salvation belongs to believers, that it brings with it a great change of character which may be compared to a new birth, and that for Christians there is no more fear of death but the hope of a future age of glory. The old connexion of physical death with Hades lies behind the phrase, 'put to death in the flesh, but made to live in the spirit' (1 Peter iii. 18), but it lies behind it in the sense that this connexion now has an end.

It is here, if anywhere, that this writer's distinctive piece of teaching emerges. In one passage he says that 'the gospel was preached even to the dead' and in another, as the present Greek text reads, that Christ 'went and preached unto the spirits in prison' (1 Peter iv. 6, iii. 19). These passages need to be discussed here only as they relate to the doctrine of salvation. They are tantalizingly allusive, but this seems to show that the writer was referring to something already well known and believed in the Church (cf. 1 Corinthians xv. 29). The following comments are only pertinent if the two passages refer to the evangelization of the dead, and this is far from certain.

The 'gospel' or 'good tidings' that the first Christians preached was based on two beliefs: that through the Risen Christ they themselves were saved from sin and Hades, and that through Him their hearers, too, could be saved from both. But a certain question was sure to be raised sooner or later. Put in its widest form it would run: 'Has, then, the salvation that Christ works nothing to do with the multitudes who have never heard of Him?' It is plain that the question might be asked about different classes—the Old Testament saints, for instance, or the 'pious heathen'. The Church, led by its Lord (Mark xii. 26), assumed that the former were saved, but there is no evidence that it went on to ask, 'How is their salvation related to Jesus, the only Saviour?' (cf. Acts iv. 12). Similarly, Peter admitted that Cornelius was 'acceptable to God' before he had heard of Christ (Acts x. 34 f.), and surely this implies that a 'devout' Gentile, who had never heard the 'good news', would be saved, yet, here again, the question just named is not asked. Yet it was sure to be asked, and the passages in First Peter show that it may have been asked when the Apostle wrote. If so, it had also been asked about others beside the righteous dead, for one of our texts speaks of the 'spirits in prison which aforetime were disobedient'. On this supposition the answer given would be that the dead Christ preached to them. Even if Dr. Rendel Harris' well-known and attractive emendation of the first text is accepted and we read that '*Enoch* went and preached unto the spirits in prison', and even if the other phrase in the Epistle is referred to this preaching—that is, if it be held that there is no assertion that *Christ* preached to the dead—the same problem recurs in a different form, for it would follow that the dead, who have never heard of Christ, may be saved. There are ultimately only two answers to the question at its widest: that Christ is not the only Saviour, or that He is (and from the beginning of time has been) so closely one with mankind that in all ages any man who sincerely seeks God, and in so seeking turns from his sin, is saved from sin, and from any kind of miserable hereafter, through the Son of Man. This involves the superficially foolish doctrine that a man may be saved by some one of whom he has never heard. When, however, it is remembered that in many ways we all benefit continually and societarily through men of whom we have never heard, the foolishness seems less evident. At any rate, the second alternative is congruous with the Christian doctrine that the Incarnation, while it was an event in time and space, carries consequences that transcend both. It would not follow that the Gospel need not be preached to all men, for on the Christian view of time the historical process is necessary as well as the eternal truth, or rather, because of it.

There is evidence in other New Testament books that the last Servant Song became part and parcel of Christian thought. The writer to the Hebrews, for instance, whose general argument centres elsewhere, yet says that 'Christ' was 'offered to bear the sins of *many*' (ix. 28), and that 'the God of peace' 'brought again from the dead the great shepherd of the sheep' (xiii. 20). Again, the ideas of the greatest of Paul's passages about the Atonement (2 Corinthians v. 18–21), which will be discussed at length later, lie very near those of the Song. Meanwhile, a direct quotation may be noted (Romans iv. 25), in a passage where Paul, for the only time in his writings, connects justification with Resurrection. In this he follows Deutero-Isaiah (Isaiah liii. 11). The references in the Fourth Gospel will be considered under that book.

CHAPTER XV

THE TEACHING OF ST. PAUL

In reading St. Paul, it is necessary always to remember that his writings are letters, and that in letters there are always some things that both writer and reader take for granted, and that these are often at least as important as the contents of the letters themselves. Indeed, they are commonly the basis of what the letters say. Again, the subjects named or discussed may be of varying importance. They may range from the trivial and transitory to the fundamental and permanent. Letters have always, however, one characteristic; they deal with subjects that the immediate situation of writer or reader or both has brought to notice. As has often been pointed out, the Epistles of Paul do not deal at any length with the doctrine of the Atonement. This is because that doctrine was common ground for writer and readers. This does not mean that the Apostle could not and did not state the doctrine sometimes in his own terms, but it does mean that he could assume that all his various readers agreed with him about its substance. We have information about his own way of stating the doctrine in certain passages, but it is nowhere fully drawn out. The passages occur in the midst of discussion of other subjects, and it is assumed that the readers of the letters do not need any extended exposition of the common Christian faith about the Death of Christ. This assumption is made even when the readers belong to Churches that Paul himself had not visited when he wrote them. There is danger in speaking of 'the Pauline doctrine of the Atonement' as if it were peculiar and isolated. It expounded the common faith in a way that Christians generally found no difficulty in accepting.

While it is true that in the Pauline Epistles some things are assumed, some mentioned, and some discussed, it is also true that if all these are taken together, the letters are found to be a great illustration of what has already been said: they build on certain distinctive Christian facts, the Life, Death, Resurrection, and Ascension of Jesus; and on a certain new experience, which is for Paul a fact and organically one with these facts of history. This

o

experience is described in many ways, but it may be summed under the correlative terms, 'grace' and 'faith'. Paul, too, must needs satisfy himself that what he had to say did not contradict the true teaching of the Old Testament. As it happened, the chief controversy of his life centred in the question: 'What is the true nature of the distinctive Christian experience?' With this there was involved a discussion of the true explanation of the Old Testament Scriptures, especially the Law. The so-called Judaizers, as Paul thought, misunderstood the first and made a wrong use of the second. But the Judaizers were Christians, and all Christians believed in salvation through a Crucified Messiah. Consequently, he did not need to do more than refer to this doctrine in the letters that the controversy evoked. As it happened, the topics of his other letters also did not demand a detailed treatment of the doctrine of the Atonement. Modern readers may wish that there had been a controversy about it, since then we should have had a fuller account of the Apostle's teaching on this great doctrine, but we have to be content with what we have, and it seems to the present writer, as will appear later, that there is enough material to furnish a consistent account of St. Paul's thought about the Death of his Lord.

With St. Paul, as with other New Testament writers, the doctrines of the Person and Work of Christ are organically connected. Yet the first cannot here be discussed. It must almost suffice to refer to one of the greatest and most extended of the Christological passages, the first eleven verses of the second chapter of the Epistle to the Philippians. The Apostle here is inculcating 'lowliness', but as is his wont when dealing with a practical subject, he soars into the realm of doctrine. The general teaching of the passage is not in doubt. We may say, if the phrase does not schedule the thought over-much, that Paul thought of four stages in his account of the Son of God: first, there is the stage before the Incarnation; then a first chosen humiliation in the Incarnation, a 'self-emptying' ; then a second stage of chosen humiliation, the 'death of the Cross' ; finally, there is God's exaltation of Jesus as universal Lord. It is plain that, whatever may be said in exegesis of particular phrases in the passage, in the first and last stage Paul, if the phrase may be allowed, puts Jesus with God, and in the second and third with man. It will be found that this is the key to his doctrine of the Atonement. It is plain, too, that for St. Paul the Crucifixion is not merely an

unfortunate though inevitable event in the story of our Lord—
not merely a kind of historical appendix to the Incarnation—
but something that needs to be named, so to speak, 'in its own
right'. If a figure is to be used, one might say that neither the
Incarnation nor the Crucifixion is the *centre* of Paul's thought,
but that each is as independent of the other and yet as dependent
on it as are the two *foci* of an ellipse. A particular phrase, 'being
made' (or perhaps better, 'coming to be') 'in the likeness of man',
will be mentioned again later. Perhaps this is the best place to
refer to the absence of the name 'Son of Man' in Paul's writings.
The reasons for its omission are not yet fully clear and need not
be examined here. It is incredible that Paul, a close friend both
of Mark and Luke, did not know the title, and there is a passage
where it seems likely that he knew of the current Christian
application of the Eight Psalm to Jesus (1 Corinthians xv. 25-7),
and this requires that the phrase 'Son of man' in the Psalm was
applied to Christ. As will appear later, this is clearer still in the
Epistle to the Hebrews. In any case, the passage in Philippians
shows unmistakably that the two ideas of humiliation and glory
that go together in the Synoptic account of the 'Son of Man', are
held together in St. Paul's thought also. Further, we found that
in the Synoptists Jesus *accepted* the name 'Son of God' but *claimed*
the title 'Son of Man' ; Paul correspondingly holds that our Lord
'counted it no prize to be equal with God' but 'humbled Himself,
taking the form of a servant, coming to be in man's likeness'.
Here he but enlarges the scope of the Synoptic witness, applying
to the whole Christian belief about Christ two ideas that in the
Synoptists are confined to the story of His earthly Ministry. The
Philippian passage does not say that 'Christ Jesus' became man
to save men, but this is the presupposition here, as in all Pauline
Christology. For Paul the Son of God chose first to become man,
and then to die, in order to save men. There is no need to add,
that the passage is also typical of Paul's doctrine in teaching that
salvation is not to be won by man, but is the free gift of God—
that in Synoptic phrase, the Son of God 'came' or 'was sent' to
save.

As has already been stated, Paul's chief controversy related to
the nature of the new Christian experience, and this may next be
considered. There is no need to give a protracted exposition on
some points. For Paul the terms 'grace' and 'faith' were
correlative and describe the two sides of one phenomenon, the

fellowship of Christ and Christians. In 'grace' Christ gives Himself to the Christian and in 'faith' the Christian gives himself to Christ. The first is to be interpreted in terms of love and the second in terms of trust, though love involves trust and trust involves love. In the issue Christ and the Christian remain two, yet become one. This is just the culminant example of the paradox that belongs to all true fellowship. For Paul the union is so close that he can speak either of 'Christ in you' or of the believer's being 'in Christ'. Whether this is to be called 'mysticism' or not depends upon the definition of that term. If it is to be used, Pauline 'mysticism' must be called 'dualistic'. It is by this union of persons, who all the time remain distinct, that Christians are saved, for the holiness of Christ, more rapidly or more gradually, drives out the sinfulness of His friend. Another way of saying the same thing is to say that the Christian has received the Holy Spirit. For Paul the indwelling Christ and the indwelling Spirit are one and the same, and the Spirit of Christ is the Spirit of God (e.g. Romans viii. 9–11). At this point the unity of two of the 'Persons' of the Trinity appears—just as distinctions between them appear elsewhere. Paul carries the doctrine of the indwelling of the Spirit in the Christian to the very verge of identifying the 'spirit' of the latter with the Spirit of God, but he does not take this last step. In the eighth chapter of Romans, for instance, he speaks of the 'spirit' of man and the 'Spirit' of God— as Ezekiel and the writer of the Fifty-first Psalm had done (Ezekiel xxxvi. 26 f.; Psalm li. 10–12)—in one breath (Romans viii. 16). Indeed, for Paul the Christian and the Spirit go so closely together that in one passage he thinks of the Spirit's being, so to speak, on the side of the Christian when he prays (Romans viii. 26). It is not too much to say that for the Apostle a man is not fully a man unless he is 'filled with' the Spirit of God and knows that he is. The doctrine of 'grace' and the doctrine of the Spirit are with Paul the same doctrine, expressed in different terms. There is no need to show that in 'Pauline Mysticism' there is a great illustration of one type of the societary concept. Nor is there need to show that for him Christians are 'one with' each other because each of them is 'one with' Christ. In other words, the doctrine of the Spirit carries with it the doctrine of the Church (e.g. 1 Corinthians xii).

In describing the new experience that belongs to Christians and only to Christians, Paul uses certain other phrases and terms. One is 'sanctification'. This is a word of the same root as 'holy' and it implies that there is now through the indwelling Spirit a living link between God and the believer, and that thereby a man who had been bad becomes, or is in process of becoming, a good man. *Being saved.* This may be called an emancipation: 'the Spirit of life in Christ Jesus emancipated me from the law of sin and death' (Romans viii. 2). The metaphor of redemption from slavery recurs here. Again, Paul finds the word 'new' (under two Greek terms) apposite to describe the Christian experience. He speaks of 'a new creation' (e.g. Galatians vi. 15), a 'new man' (Ephesians iv. 24), a 'new covenant' (1 Corinthians xi. 25). For the Christian, indeed, 'all things are become new' (2 Corinthians v. 17 *f.*). For Paul salvation has both a negative and a positive side: God delivers the believer from 'sin and death' on the one hand, and gives him 'eternal life' on the other (Romans vi. 23).

Again, this 'newness of life' or 'of spirit' (Romans vi. 4, vii. 6) depends upon and grows out of a new *relationship* to God 'in Christ'. To describe this new relationship Paul uses two terms that are anathema, at least at first, to 'the modern mind'— adoption and justification. Sometimes to-day they are described as 'legal' or 'forensic' and therewith dismissed. If a reader considers their context in Paul, he will not be satisfied with this. In particular, he will notice that where the Apostle speaks of 'adoption', he goes on to the cry, '*Abba*, Father', and it is not possible to reduce this to the merely forensic. The fact is that Paul was both a Jew and a Roman, and that, for both these, though in different ways, it was as natural to think and speak in terms of law as it is for Englishmen to-day to speak in terms of evolution and psychology. At different periods different intellectual concepts are 'in the air'. It follows that for men of one age the current concepts of another seem 'artificial' and 'unnatural'.

Even to-day, when the practice of adoption seems to be gradually extending in England, most Englishmen think it rather artificial —unless they have themselves adopted a child and heard it for the first time say, '*Abba*'. To the Roman, whose ruling concept even in daily life was law, adoption did not seem unnatural. It was possible under Roman law for the head of a house to adopt any one, and when adopted, the latter *was* 'son'. Emperors followed the custom and no one seems to have thought this artificial. Of course, the particular instance of adoption that was

in Paul's mind—the adoption of a slave—would be very rare, even
if it ever occurred, but then the Apostle wants to say that God
does something astonishing. There was nothing in Roman law
that forbade the adoption of a slave, and we need to picture some
young slave in a large Roman household who is summoned to
the presence of the patrician head of the house. He answers
trembling, for what should the patrician want with *him*? But
when he reaches him, the fearful and wondering lad presently
makes out that the great patrician, who had the power of life and
death over him, is saying, 'You are to be my son; call me
"Father" '. Presently out the word falteringly comes, but here
Paul, abandoning Greek under the stress of his feeling, falls back
upon the first word that a child said to its father in a Jewish
household, '*Abba*'. There is nothing 'merely forensic' here. The
verses throb with feeling. The reason is that Paul had lived for
years in God's household like a slave. His dominant feeling
about God had been fear. Now it was love. Now he was a son.
He was a son because God had 'sent forth the Spirit of His Son'
into his heart. To fall back upon a too colourless word, he was in
a new *relationship* to God. For people who have not thought out
the deep consequences of 'relationship' in life, one may add that
when a young fellow asks a girl to marry him and she says, 'Yes',
it would be quite correct to say that there is only a change of
relationship. True relationship is never a mere matter of arrangement. It is alive.

On this showing, there is no great gulf between the teaching
of Jesus and that of Paul. The 'modern man', indeed, believes
in 'the universal fatherhood of God' in a sense that is alien to the
whole New Testament. Though the phrase 'the universal sonship
of man' is not often used, this, in effect, describes the complement
of this modern doctrine and the idea of adoption is excluded. But
Jesus, at most, taught the potential fatherhood of God and the
potential sonship of every man, and, though the metaphor of
adoption does not include these ideas, they are fundamental
with Paul. Without them he would have had no Gospel. No
metaphor ever covers the whole ground. As we have seen, in
the 'far country' the Prodigal was not a son in the spiritual sense,
but only in the physical, and the physical is not pertinent here.
The root of the matter was just that he was refusing to be son
spiritually. The difference between the teaching of Jesus and
Paul reduces to this: that for our Lord, with His unique sense of

Sonship, the metaphor of adoption would not have been natural, but for Paul, who had served God as if He were a task-master, it was natural enough.

It has already been shown that for the writer the Parable of the Prodigal teaches the substance of St. Paul's doctrine of justification without the word. Something needs to be said summarily about the Apostle's use of the term, though the grounds of the conclusion here stated cannot be laid out. The meaning of 'justify' seems to be 'treat as righteous', and the nearest English word would be 'acquit'.[1] The latter term rightly suggests that the common use of 'justify' in Paul's environment borrowed a metaphor from the law court. A judge 'acquits' a man, or 'treats him as righteous' or 'guiltless', because he believes that he *is* guiltless. In Paul's discussions with Jews the word was sure to occur, for his opponents would ask, in effect, 'Do you mean to say that the Judge of all the earth acquits a man whom He knows to be guilty?' Paul does not decline the word, for he, too, was heir of the Old Testament, but he uses it in what he knows is an artificial way—an artificial way, that is, so long as the ruling concept of God is that He is Judge. But Paul says, in effect: 'For me God is no longer primarily Judge. The Lord Jesus Christ has taught me that God is my Father, and a true father does treat a repentant son as righteous. Indeed, that is just the way in which He saves him from his sin. So long as the sinner gives himself in faith or trust to God, God will treat him as fathers treat prodigals and not as judges treat criminals.' In other words, Paul insists in passing from the law court to the home in his concept of God. It was almost as unnatural to say, 'God justifies the ungodly', as it would be to say, 'A true father acquits a repentant son', but the Apostle said it and made it even a Christian watchword in order to bring out unmistakably the novelty of the Christian teaching. Once more, though in a different way, the question is one of relationship—the relationship of God to believers is that of a Father and not that of a Judge. In other words, as Wesley said, 'justify' is practically a synonym for 'forgive'. Judges do not forgive, but fathers do.

It has already been seen that the concept of 'eternal life' is found in Paul—though he does not use the adjective 'eternal'

[1] Perhaps with the further notions of 'vindicate' and 'deliver'. I owe this suggestion to Professor C. H. Dodd's commentary on Romans. In some other instances I have independently reached the same conclusions as Professor Dodd.

often—and that for him 'belonging to the coming age' does not exhaust the meaning of 'eternal' or even describe the chief element in its meaning. No doubt the Apostle believed that the phrase 'eternal life' describes the kind of life that Christians will live in the coming age, but primarily it denotes 'life' with a given quality—with the quality describable under the terms 'sanctification', 'sonship', and so on, which have already been considered. It is true that 'life' of this quality can only be consummated in the perfect realm of the coming age, for this will at last furnish it with an adequate and perfect environment. Consequently, in Paul's use of the term 'eternal' the immediate reference is to this future perfection—as appears, for instance, in his use of it to describe the body that is to be (2 Corinthians v. 1)—yet it seems to the writer that justice cannot be done to his thought without some reference to the present. This will find support under the brief discussion below of his use of the correlative term, 'death'. The same is true of St. Paul's few references to the Kingdom of God. He undoubtedly believed with the Jew that God is ruling over a rebellious world now, but, like the Acts of the Apostles, he added the Christian belief that He is exercising this sovereignty through Christ. He also undoubtedly believed that God would reign in the coming age over an altogether willing mankind. Both these beliefs, for instance, are required by the one text: 'he [Christ] must reign till he hath put all enemies under his feet' (1 Corinthians xv. 25). But Paul also held the third doctrine of the Kingdom described above. With Christ the reign of God over a willing people has begun. Indeed, the word 'willing' is inadequate. There were now people whose nature, through 'the grace of our Lord Jesus Christ', had begun to be of the kind that the final Rule of God requires. For example, the phrase, 'The Kingdom of God is not meat and drink, but righteousness and peace and joy in the Holy Spirit, for he that herein serveth Christ is well-pleasing to God and approved of men' (Romans xiv. 17 f.), both by the nature of the context and by its own intrinsic meaning, describes a present way of life and not merely a future one. In brief, in Paul's use both of 'eternal life' and 'Kingdom of God' we can see how the non-apocalyptic element is beginning to work itself free from the apocalyptic. This is so even if the Apostle himself was unaware of it. One is tempted to say, 'The kernel is beginning to burst the shell', but it would be more adequate, as the present writer thinks, to say that it is beginning to be clear what is kernel and what is shell in the teaching of Jesus.

'The wages of sin is death, but the grace-gift of God is eternal life in Christ Jesus our Lord' (Romans vi. 23). If the fifteenth chapter of First Corinthians is examined, it is plain that by 'death' Paul does not mean merely or chiefly the physical event. For Christians, he says, the physical event is only 'falling asleep' and fundamentally it does not matter very much whether it befalls them or not. Like their Lord, those of them who die will 'rise again' and escape the grim sequel of the physical event. There is no need to discuss whether St. Paul, who would undoubtedly have called this sequel 'Hades', though the word does not happen to occur in his extant writings, thought of a literal or a symbolic Hades. Probably he would not have counted the distinction of capital importance, for in any case he thought that for sinners the physical event now called 'death' had a very grim sequel. For Christians there is 'sure and certain' escape from this, for they are to be 'for ever with the Lord'. It is important, however, to note that for Paul the state called 'death' may begin before the physical event occurs. For him the sinful are already 'dead in trespasses and sins' (Ephesians ii. 1). Some may argue that, if the Apostle had integrated his whole doctrine more fully than he has, he would have said that a sinner is 'dying' rather than 'dead'. In any case, 'death' begins here and now for the sinful. For the Christian it had begun when he was sinful, but it is now over: 'your life is hid with Christ in God' (Colossians iii. 3). It is clear that for Paul both 'death' and 'eternal life' began before the event of physical death.

It might be said that, if the whole of Paul's doctrine of salvation is included in what has now been said, his doctrine is wholly 'subjective' and not at all 'objective'. This, however, is to use these two terms in an out-of-date way, for psychology teaches that in human life there is nothing entirely 'subjective' and nothing entirely 'objective'. In the particular piece of experience now under examination, it is plain that the fellowship of Christ with the Christian requires that Christ is an 'object', if the word is to be used. It is true that the only guarantee of this 'object' is experience, but this is the only possible evidence of any 'object' in human knowledge. It is true, again, that Christ is not here 'objective' in the same way as a material entity—for instance, a stone—but in the same way as the immaterial entity called 'God'.

That a religious man knows an 'objective' God may be left to Christian philosophy to show.

Again, it might be said that so far we have spoken of what Christ does 'in us' and not of what He does 'for us', but here, too, the phraseology is open to objection. If, by the grace of the indwelling Christ, a bad man begins to be a good man, has not Christ done something 'for' that man as well as 'in' him? Yet there is behind both these unsatisfactory pairs of terms a hitherto unresolved question. So far there has been no answer to the question: Is 'the death of the Cross' essential to St. Paul's doctrine of salvation? It might be suggested, for instance, that all that has so far been said would be true if Jesus of Nazareth had lived a long life, died a 'natural' death, and then risen again. The question, 'Why did Paul so passionately preach a "crucified Messiah"?' has not been answered. Before an attempt is made to answer it, Paul's use of societary concepts needs to be considered.

There is no doubt that this kind of concept played a large part in the thought of St. Paul or that he used it readily in his Christian thinking. For instance, without it his use of the terms 'Jacob', 'Esau', and 'Israel' in the ninth, tenth and eleventh chapters of Romans would hardly mean anything and his whole argument there would collapse. These names stand for nations—that is, societies. Similarly the Parable of the Olive-tree is parallel to the Johannine teaching about the vine, and, like it, demands the societary idea. Again, Paul's use of the comparison of a society with a body in the twelfth chapter of First Corinthians is perhaps the most famous example of the 'corporate' concept in all literature. Writers who have used it to call the Church 'the body of Christ' have not always observed the Pauline limits of the comparison—neglecting, in particular, to note that he does not argue that the Church is physically like a body, but organically so—but they are right that without the societary concept there would be no Pauline doctrine of the Church at all. There is another great illustration of this kind of idea in the Apostle's argument about 'Abraham' in Galatians and Romans. In the fifteenth chapter of First Corinthians, again, when he writes, 'As in Adam all die, so in Christ shall all be made alive', it is not the historical accuracy of the early chapters of Genesis that is fundamental in his thinking, but the concept that all mankind is a unity that may be called 'Adam'. There is involved also, of course, the idea that Christ is 'one with' the new Christian mankind and that it is 'one with' Him. This leads us to another great example of the societary concept and to the one that is the best prelude to the answer to the question, 'What is the place of the Crucifixion in St. Paul's doctrine of salvation?' This passage is the later part of the fifth chapter of Romans (verses 12-21).

No attempt will be made here to discuss every detail of this passage, since its general teaching can hardly be disputed, and it is this that is here important. For instance, nothing is said below about Paul's doctrine of 'law'. Again, it will suffice if a modern paraphrase of the underlying concepts is attempted. This may perhaps serve to convince some modern readers that this passage, which, in Paul's terminology, they seem to find almost repugnant, is quite up-to-date. In the paraphrase there is some enlargement here and there from other parts of the Apostle's teaching, which seem to be implied in the passage. Such a paraphrase might run as follows:

There is a societary or corporate side to human nature which issues in what may be called 'the solidarity of mankind'. This means that what one man does has consequences for other men. It ensued that, when the first sin was committed, it began to infect mankind with a vile disease. We may call this disease 'death'. It is true that when a man has caught this disease, it might be said that he is suffering undeservedly, for he cannot help the infection, but this is not the whole case, for every man adds his own individual sin, for which he *is* responsible, to the sins of mankind, and so deserves to 'die'. His sin, too, still further spreads the vile infection. In consequence of the solidarity of man, 'death' reigns (better, exercises 'kingship') over mankind here and it will complete this kingship in the state that men used to call 'Hades'. It is true that all the time men's good deeds have spread a happy kind of infection, and that this too might be called 'unfair', but on the whole the evil results of the societary nature of mankind were, until Christ came, overwhelming the good results. But then God in His mercy sent His Son into the world. He came as man, for the societary acts from man to man. He lived a sinless life, and this life had societary results. Through God's grace, His undeserved love to men, the individual habit called 'faith' has a corporate result: every 'believer' begins to belong to a new mankind (cf. Colossians iii. 9-11), whose Head is Christ. Through Him not only are the effects of the first sin undone, but the societary effects of all men's later sin, and the degradation due to the believer's own individual sin. Further, the societary results here are not merely negative. They are also positive, for 'believers' not only give up sinning, or begin to do so, but begin to be righteous and grow more and more righteous. In other words, there begins to be a 'reign' or 'kingship' of grace instead of a 'reign' of sin. So the miserable and vile state called 'death' passes away and 'eternal life' begins. This, of course, like 'death', while it begins here, is consummated hereafter. So God vindicates the societary nature of mankind. Its benefits outweigh its banes. 'Where sin abounded, grace doth much more abound.'

It will be seen that, especially under the word 'reign', Paul has here the Synoptic concept of 'the Kingdom of God', and that under his societary account of Christ there lie some of the ideas that the Synoptics include under the phrase 'Son of Man'.

Even this passage, however, does not answer the question, 'Why did Christ need to die in order that this new mankind might begin?' For the Apostle's answer we turn to other passages, and we may begin with the immediate sequel in the Epistle to the Romans (Romans vi. 1–14). Here, as so often, the Apostle's statement of his theology grows out of a practical problem. There were already those who said, 'We may continue [or, better, 'abide'] in sin, for then God will be the more able to display His grace'. Paul replies, 'That is both monstrous and absurd'. It is to the absurdity that he then turns. For a Christian to abide in sin, he says, is a contradiction in terms. There is no need to show in detail that for Paul this is so because 'grace' *per se* drives out sin. Neither is there need to discuss the controversial question of the interpretation of the references to baptism, for all interpretations, though in various ways, found on the societary concept. Two societary phrases may be mentioned. The phrase 'our old man' is plainly a reference to the old mankind which has been described in the fifth chapter, and when Paul says, 'Our old man was crucified with him', he means that through Christ's death believers pass from the old mankind to the new one. Again, in the phrase, 'If we have become united with the likeness of his death' the word translated 'united' is unique in the New Testament and connotes 'organically one'. It may be noted, too, that the phrase, 'He died unto sin once for all', like the reference to 'obedience' in the fifth chapter, links Pauline teaching with that of the Epistle

to the Hebrews. But it is the use of the terms 'die' and 'death'
that bring us to the question named above.

It has been claimed already that when Paul uses the term 'die'
in a theological sense, he usually means 'to pass into the state that
is the outcome of sin' and that he thinks that this state begins here
but is consummated hereafter. It is plain, however, that in the
sixth of Romans he uses the terms in at least one other sense, for
the phrases 'We, who died to sin' and 'Reckon ye yourselves also
to be dead unto sin' (Romans vi. 2, 11), do not admit of the
interpretation just given. On the contrary, 'to die to sin' is just
to escape the state called 'death' under the above definition.
Here Paul's thought might even be summarized under the para-
doxial phrase, 'Christians have died to death'. But it may be
asked whether there is not a third sense of 'die' and 'death' in the
passage—whether, when they are used of Christ Himself, they do
not refer wholly to the physical event called 'death'. If so, we
are left with the doctrine that through Christ's physical death,
and through it only, believers are saved from spiritual 'death'.
It is difficult to give coherence to this concept. It does not
harmonize with the nature of the societary concept which underlies these chapters in Romans. The writer thinks that when Paul
speaks here both of the Death and Resurrection of Jesus he means
more than two physical events: crucifixion and escape from Hades.
He means two spiritual experiences as well, and it is the spiritual
experiences that are the root of the matter. There is little in the
sixth of Romans directly to support this. The phrase, 'Death no
more hath dominion [or, better, 'lordship'] over him', however,
needs mention. Does this merely mean that Christ will not
physically die again? Or does it mean that during His earthly
life, Christ, like other men, submitted to the 'kingship' (Romans
v. 17) or 'lordship' of 'death' considered as the state that is the
outcome of sin—a submission that reached its climax on Calvary?
Is Paul here giving his account of the meaning of the Cry of
Dereliction? Is he here saying, in his own way, that in order to
redeem men from the state called 'death' and to give them, not
mere survival hereafter, but 'eternal life', 'the Son of Man' *must*
Himself know what the spiritual state called 'death' is? To revert
to the kind of phrase used in the first chapter of this book, is Paul
saying that, in order to raise men to His own level, the Son of
God must first come down to their level? When he says in
Philippians that in the Incarnation our Lord 'took the form of a

slave', does he mean that there is a sense in which Christ Himself, when on earth, was in bondage to 'death'? There are other passages in which he seems to say this, though in other terms. Before we turn to them, it may be worth noting that while Paul says that both 'sin' and 'death' have kingship or lordship over sinful men (Romans v. 14, 17, vi. 12, 14), he does not say that 'sin' had lordship over Jesus, but only 'death' (Romans vi. 9). Does this mean that to save men, Christ, Himself sinless, entered into the societary state that ensues from sin, becoming, to revert again to the phraseology of the first chapter, like men, yet remaining unlike? This is just what he says, in an even more extreme way, in the passage to be considered next.

This passage is the latter part of the fifth chapter of Second Corinthians (verses 11–21). Here, too, Paul is dealing with a practical problem: his own apostolate. He says that he 'persuades men' under the contraint of the love of Christ. Using once again the societary concept, he says that 'one died for all, therefore all died'—that is, believers, through their union with Christ, have ceased to belong to the old sin-stricken mankind, and have begun to 'live unto him who for their sakes died and rose again'. The change is so great that it may be called a 'new creating'. Paul claims that this is God's doing, and uses five times in three verses the word that comes nearest to epitomizing his doctrine of salvation, 'reconciliation', making it clear that it is man and not God that needs to be 'reconciled'. The primary change, that is, is in man and not in God, though, no doubt, the change in man makes it possible for God to treat him otherwise than He would have done. Now He 'does not reckon unto them their trespasses'— in other words, He now treats them as a Father and not as a Judge, and they are 'justified'. Finally, Paul gives us his account of the way in which the Death of Christ enables men to 'become the righteousness of God in him'. He says, 'him who knew no sin he made to be sin on our behalf'. The phrase is so brief that we can only believe that the Corinthians did not need a further exposition because they already knew what Paul's teaching about the Atonement was. First, the Apostle declares that Jesus Christ was sinless. In passing, one cannot help asking whether this does not mean that he knew the story of the life of Christ. In any case, Paul uses a phrase that he must have meant to be paradoxical. How could the sinless be 'made to be sin'? Once again the Cry of Dereliction springs to mind. Christ is sinless and therefore one with God; He is one with man, and therefore is passing through the uttermost consequence of sin—and it is this tension that is the agony of salvation. Once again the ideas that gather into the Synoptic phrase, 'Son of Man', recur. Christ is able to 'reconcile' the alienated because, Himself un-alienated, He is yet so closely one with the alienated that He experiences their alienation. Here, too, the nearest human parallel to the unparalleled is to be found in the experience of the human 'saviours' described in the first chapter.[1]

The Epistle to the Galatians says the same things, though the terms used are not all the same. Through their unity with Christ, believers have been 'delivered out of this present evil age', have been 'crucified with Christ', have 'crucified the flesh', and have been 'crucified unto the world' and the world 'unto' them (Galatians i. 4, ii. 20, v. 24, vi. 14). This salvation from sin and death has been wrought because, 'When the fulness of the time was come, God sent forth his Son, born of woman, born under law' (Galatians iv. 4). This is parallel to 'being found in fashion as a man' and 'taking the form of a slave' in the second of Philippians. The parallel phrase to 'he humbled himself, becoming obedient unto death, yea, the death of the cross', however, is neither 'death hath dominion', as in Romans, nor made to be sin' as in Second Corinthians, but 'made a curse'. The context needs to be recalled (Galatians iii. 10–14). No doubt the phrase, 'Cursed is every one that hangeth on a tree', had been quoted against Paul in controversy. Jews were sure to quote it to show that it was an outrage to speak of a 'crucified Messiah'. Paul could not refuse the challenge, for he himself appealed to the Old Testament. He accepted it by quoting another text—'Cursed is every one that continueth not in all things that are written in the book of the law to do them'—and he claimed that Christ bore this curse. In other words, He was 'born under law to redeem them that are under law', and experienced the curse of those that broke

---

[1] The translation, 'he made to be a sin-offering', is not adopted here, even though the Hebrew word for 'sin-offering' also means 'sin' and though a Greek word for 'sin' is used to translate this Hebrew term in Leviticus iv. 24, 29, for (a) it seems to the writer that the true exposition, as given above, does not require or easily admit a reference to the sacrificial system, (b) because the rendering 'sin-offering' requires that the same Greek term be translated first by 'sin' and then by 'sin-offering' in one sentence, and (c) because the usual Greek rendering for 'sin-offering' is another phrase, which Paul uses, as will be seen below, in Romans viii. 3. This other phrase occurs for the sin-offering in the LXX some fifty times. If, however, the translation 'he made to be a sin-offering' be preferred, this phrase would fall under the same kind of exposition as is given below for Romans viii. 3.

law. The terms are different, but there is here just the same logical antinomy but psychological truth as before. Sinful man can only be saved from sinfulness by One who shares the experience of the results of sin, yet is Himself sinless. The sinlessness of Jesus is indeed not asserted here, but it is, of course, implied in such a phrase as 'God sent forth his Son'.

There is another passage where Paul says the same things in yet different words: 'What the law could not do, in that it was weak through the flesh, God, sending his own Son, in the likeness of the flesh of sin and as an offering for sin, condemned sin in the flesh; that the ordinances of the law might be fulfilled in us, who walk not after the flesh, but after the Spirit' (Romans viii. 3 *f.*). The context here too describes the distinctive Christian experience, the word 'Spirit' being dominant. The Spirit, which is part and parcel of the Christian man, is 'holy' and therefore impervious to sin. The 'flesh', on the other hand, is the side of human nature on which sin can and does fasten. The term is wider than its literal meaning and covers anything in man accessible to sin. In the seventh chapter Paul has been showing that, before he knew Christ, he was the miserable slave of 'the flesh'. This was because there was something that 'law' could not do; it could condemn *the sinner* to 'death' (Romans vii. 9–11), but not *sin*. This is just what God does through His Son. It seems to follow that the phrase 'condemned sin in the flesh' requires the meaning 'condemned sin to death', or 'passed the death sentence on sin'. This is likely, both because it gives a clear meaning to an otherwise obscure sentence, and because the word 'condemn' can be used to mean 'condemn to death' when the context requires this (cf. Matthew xxvii. 3; John viii. 10 *f.*; Susanna 41), and it has just been shown that this is so here. What is impossible to law God does by sending His Son, condemns 'sin in the flesh' to death. But how does He do this through His Son? He sent Him 'in the likeness of the flesh of sin'. This is parallel to two Philippian phrases taken together—'in the likeness of men' and 'in the form of a slave'—and refers to the Incarnation. God also sent His Son 'as an offering for sin'. This is parallel to the Philippian 'becoming obedient unto death, yea, the death of the cross' and refers to the Crucifixion. It is reminiscent of the sin-offering, for the same phrase is used in the Septuagint very many times to translate the Hebrew word for 'sin-offering'. Literally the Greek phrase means 'concerning sin', but it is used as a compound noun—'[a thing]

that has to do with sin' or 'that deals with sin'. But while Paul here refers to the sacrificial system, he does so in a very significant way, for the ritual of the sin-offering was part of the 'law', and he is speaking of something that 'the law could not do'. In other words, like the writer to the Hebrews, he is saying that Christ succeeds where the 'law' of the sin-offering failed. He succeeds by taking the place into which man had put himself through his sin— the place of one who, as the sin-offering effectively said by symbol, is separated by sin from the Holy God. Yet, on the other hand, Christ is not so separated, for He is the Son of God. We come back, therefore, to the same antinomy—an antinomy here being as always a statement of two truths, which are not the less both truths because we cannot logically harmonize them.

Two other passages from the Travel Epistles may be added (2 Corinthians viii. 9; Romans viii. 32). Both are passing references, the first to the Incarnation and the second to the Atonement. Neither, taken alone, gives as much light on Paul's doctrine of salvation as the passages just discussed, but both are consonant with their suggested exposition. The first speaks of a poverty that enriches, and is as deliberately paradoxical as the great Corinthian text (2 Corinthians v. 21). The second quotes the Septuagint translation of the words, 'Thou hast not withheld thy son, thine only son' (Genesis xxii. 16), but transfers the phrase daringly from Abraham to God Himself: 'he that spared not his own Son but delivered him up for us all'. Paul finds it hard to express his doctrine of the Death of Christ except by daring phrases. Here God does not accept a sacrifice, as all ritual teaches, but offers one.

Some of the same ideas, though again in a different form, appear in the passages in Paul's later Epistles that speak of 'reconciliation'. In the Epistle to the Ephesians (ii. 11–22) he says that the 'alienation' between Gentile and Jew was caused by the 'law' that the Jew so jealously kept, and he symbolizes this as the 'middle wall or partition' in the Temple, which a Gentile only crossed on pain of death. Here, therefore, he speaks, not of sin in general, but of 'enmity' in particular, and he does not say that Christ 'condemned it to death', but that He 'slew' it. Jew and Gentile are reconciled to each other because they are both reconciled to God. The believers of both races are to form 'one new man'—that is, a new mankind, as in the fifth of Romans. Using the corporate metaphor, Paul says that they are to be 'one

P

body unto God'. This reconciliation Christ effects because He came 'in flesh'—that is, He submitted in the Incarnation to be 'tempted like as we are'. But it was 'through the cross' that His work was perfected. There, Himself slain, He 'slew the enmity'. The same antinomy recurs. So the Christian experience of 'access in one Spirit unto the Father' comes to pass. In the Epistle to the Colossians, two other phrases are added. Paul says that in Christ 'all the fulness [of the Godhead] dwells' (Colossians i. 19). If this is put with the 'emptying' of Philippians, we have the antinomy of the Incarnation. It was 'the Father's good pleasure' both that this should be and that, just because this was so, Christ should 'reconcile all things'—that is, the universe—'unto himself'. Here there are two universal postulates of Scripture: that there is something wrong with the universe as we know it, and that man and the universe go together. Paul claims that it ensues that, when man is altogether reconciled to God, so will the universe be. Their perfecting is ultimately one perfecting (cf. Romans viii. 19 ff.), for Christ, being the Head of a new mankind, is thereby Head of a new universe. A second passage in Colossians (Colossians ii. 8–15) repeats thoughts that have already been examined, perhaps with an even greater emphasis on the Resurrection as the organic sequel of the Death of Christ: 'Having put off from himself (his body) he made a show of the principalities and powers [or, as we might say, of every evil principle that infects the universe], triumphing over them in it.' He triumphs by 'nailing the bond' that declares sinful men's debt to God 'to the cross'—that is, when He was slain on the cross, He was slaying sin. The 'nails' that seemed fatal to Him were really fatal to it. *He* goes on to live; *it* is dead. So He 'blots out' sin.

In this chapter and the last but one we have found three instances of Paul's use of the terminology of the ritual system: 'blood', 'propitiation', and 'sin-offering'. There are a few others. First, there is his use of the term 'sacrifice'. He uses it several times of Christian service, in our modern sense of self-sacrifice. Paul, of course, knew the ritual of the Jews in practice, and he knew well how often the cost of providing a sacrifice in the Temple meant self-sacrifice in a Jewish home. Consequently, he can say that when the Philippians sent him their gifts by Epaphroditus they were offering a 'sacrifice acceptable, well-pleasing to God' and, borrowing another ritual phrase, could say that 'it was an odour of a sweet smell' (Philippians iv. 18). In the same way,

Paul could say that 'we are a sweet savour of Christ unto God' when he is speaking, not of death at all, but of Apostolic preaching (2 Corinthians ii. 15). The term 'sacrifice' is similarly used of Christian service (Romans xii. 1), and of Paul's own approaching death (Philippians ii. 17). We may perhaps expect, therefore, the meaning 'self-sacrifice' when the Apostle uses the phrase 'an offering and a sacrifice to God for an odour of a sweet smell' about Christ's death (Ephesians v. 2). The context requires that this is just the meaning. The Apostle here is not expounding his account of the Death of Christ in full, but encouraging Christians to be like Christ in a way that the Cross illustrated—in self-sacrificing service to men. To import any other ideas from the ritual system into the passage seems to go beyond the Apostle's meaning.

There is another passage where Paul uses the term 'sacrifice' of Christ: 'For our Passover also hath been sacrificed, even Christ; Wherefore let us keep festival [not 'keep the feast'], not with old leaven, neither with the leaven of malice and wickedness, but with the unleavened bread of sincerity and truth' (1 Corinthians v. 7 f.). Paul, of course, knew his ritual, and here he keeps closely to it. He uses 'leaven' as the symbol of sin. This the Corinthians are to 'purge out', just as literal leaven was removed very carefully from a Jewish home *before* Passover. The duty fell to the mother, and Paul would have seen Jewish mothers fulfil this ritual. It is when the leaven of sin is gone that Christians can rightly 'keep festival'. As we have seen, the Passover Sheep was not a sin-offering, and Paul knew this quite well. The Passover was not a fast, but a feast, a festival of Covenant. *Before* it was held, the Sheep 'was sacrificed', and this is the meaning (and not 'is sacrificed') of the Pauline verb. Paul, of course, believed that the Death of Christ on the Cross, unlike the Passover, 'took away sin', but he is not here explaining how Christ did this on the Cross except at *one* point: through the Cross there has come to be a new Covenant, which is the necessary prelude and ground of Christian joy. It does not seem possible to add anything else, except by thrusting upon the Passover ideas that it did not illustrate and by going beyond what the context in the Pauline passage requires. If there is an indirect reference here to the Lord's Supper, as there well may be, it is to a given aspect of it—as a Eucharist or Thanksgiving for something that is past, that has been done 'once for all'. It will be seen that this exposition is consonant with that given above of the Lord's Supper as recorded in Mark. The Festival of Covenant which that anticipated, the Corinthians kept. The Pauline account of the Lord's Supper (1 Corinthians xi. 23 *ff.*) does not add to that of Mark anything relevant to the present subject, and its exposition, therefore, has been anticipated in the chapter on the Synoptic Gospels.

There remains one other passage where Paul uses a sacrificial term: 'All have sinned and fall short of the glory of God; Being justified freely by his grace through the redemption that is in Christ Jesus: Whom God purposed to be a *propitiation*, through faith in his blood, to show his righteousness, because of the passing over of the sins done aforetime, in the forbearance of God; for the shewing, I say, of his righteousness at this present season: that he himself might be righteous and might treat as righteous him that hath faith in Jesus' (Romans iii. 23-6). It has already been argued that the term rendered 'propitiation' would be better translated 'atonement'—that is, reconciliation. The context almost demands this, for the general subject of the passage is God's grace, not His 'wrath'. A writer who was thinking of 'wrath', for instance, would not speak of 'the passing over of the sins done aforetime, in the forbearance of God'. Yet there is one phrase that has been supposed to refer to the demands of justice, if not to the allaying of wrath: 'That he might be righteous and treat as righteous him that hath faith in Jesus.' This, however, seems to rest upon an incorrect exegesis. It will be remembered that in Deutero-Isaiah 'salvation' and 'righteousness' are complementary and not contradictory. It is so here, too. To put Paul's meaning in modern terms, he is saying: 'God pleased to make man so that it was possible for him to sin; He also made man so that every sin should spread its evil infection through the mass of mankind; we have just seen the hideous result (Romans i. 18-iii. 18) ; God, who must have foreseen this, would not even be righteous if He did not find a way to save men from this; He has found such a way by sending His Son.' It is true that in the preceding chapters 'wrath' is named, for while God is responsible for the possibility of the awful situation of mankind, this does not rob man of his primary responsibility, but here, as always, it is taken for granted that, if man repents, the 'wrath' of God dies. There is no demand that man shall bear the punishment of his sin in order to 'satisfy justice', or that Christ shall do so for him. This is not the way with a Father's anger, however just it may be. As Paul himself says, in effect, men who are 'reconciled to God' are *thereby* 'saved from wrath' (Romans v. 9 *f.*). To return to the sacrificial system, the context, here as elsewhere, shows that the reference to ritual is an illustration of the ruling ideas of the passage, not their ground or origin. The Pauline doctrine of Atonement, as laid out above, does not *derive from* Jewish ritual.

To conclude: all the principal Pauline passages, in spite of their variety in language, say the same thing. They all correspond to two of the Words from the Cross: 'Why hast thou forsaken me?' and 'Father, into thy hands', taken together. They all require two ideas that form a fundamental antinomy—the ideas that on the Cross Jesus was so closely one with sinners that He experienced the 'death' that is separation from God, yet so closely one with God that He survived that 'death'. To use Paul's own phrases, on the Cross Jesus was 'made to be sin', yet at the same time 'God was *in Christ* reconciling the world unto himself' (2 Corinthians v. 19–21). Surely Paul was aware of the correspondence between the Words on the Cross and his teaching. Were not the Words the starting-point of his thought? Like all other attempts to explain the Atonement, Paul's is inadequate, but an inadequate attempt may be true as far as it goes. Paul's attempt bases on two things that for him went organically together: the unique facts about Jesus of Nazareth and the distinctive Christian experience. On account of the nature of the questions that arose in the Church of his time, he expounded the latter in his letters more fully than the former, but for him there could not have been any such thing as Christian 'faith' unless Christ had lived, had died, and had risen again. It is as futile to ask which of the three —the Life, the Death, or the Resurrection of the Lord—was the most important for Paul as it would be to ask which angle of a triangle is the most important. None the less, for him the Death of Christ was the one of the three that related most closely to sin: 'He died for our sins.'

CHAPTER XVI

THE EPISTLE TO THE HEBREWS

It seems to the present writer that the unknown author of this Epistle, like the authors of other New Testament letters, wrote in face of a given situation, and that this explains, at least in part, why he includes some things and omits others. He was writing to a church of the second generation (ii. 3), whose members, however, had not gone deeply into the theology of the Christian faith (cf. v. 12–14). They had suffered for Christ's sake, though not yet unto death (x. 32 ff., xii. 4). Now they were passing through a more serious persecution, so much so that some had 'fallen away' (vi. 4 ff., x. 26 ff.). But they were also in *mental* perplexity, through the intrusion of 'strange teachings' (xiii. 9). The perplexity has arisen because for them, as for all early Christians, the Old Testament was 'canonical'. They had not passed through the discipline of the Judaistic Controversy that both vexed and taught some of the Pauline churches. They believed, with the Jews of the time, that the 'law' had been given through 'angels' (i. 4–14; cf. Acts vii. 53). This was their way of saying that it was 'inspired'. In particular, they were in difficulties about the Jewish ritualistic system—not so much because it was practised in the Temple as because it was part of the Book (x. 8). In other words, they had read the rules in the Pentateuch about the Tabernacle and were perplexed because it looked as if these were perpetually binding. The writer of the Epistle faced this situation. He referred, therefore, not to Temple usage, but to Tabernacle law. He knew that a very large subject had been opened for the perplexed Church to which he wrote, and that he could not fully deal with it (cf. ix. 5, xi. 32), so he selected a great example of the Christian way with Old Testament ritual. He chose the rite that could be most closely related to the new Christian truth, and that would show most clearly both the value and the inadequacy of the Old Testament. He mingled warning and encouragement with exposition because he was trying to help those who, under the combined stress of persecution and perplexity of mind, were in danger of following the example of others and 'drifting away' (ii. 1). There is a passage which suggests that the readers addressed were in danger of expulsion from the local synagogues (xiii. 10–15). At this point Paul had anticipated the Jews by himself taking the decisive step of separation at Corinth and Ephesus (Acts xviii. 7, xix. 9), but it does not seem to have been taken at Rome before his arrival there, and there is good evidence that James frequented the Temple till his death. A policy of excluding Nazarenes from synagogues might easily arise in the discussions that must have run through world-wide Judaism in and after the events of A.D. 70. The Epistle, unlike St. Paul's, deals with the subject of the Atonement at length. Large parts of it need, therefore, to be considered.

The writer's method of interpreting the Old Testament needs to be noted. Like Philo, a generation earlier, he believed that the Hebrew records had more than one meaning. In modern terms we might say that he believed that they, or large parts of them, had both a literal and a symbolic sense, and that the second is the important one. Again, it is now agreed that he had come under the influence of a certain concept that derived ultimately from Plato, but which was current in his own times—the concept that 'the things that are seen' are not the 'real' things, but only give hints about them. The 'real' things are, to use a Pauline phrase, 'eternal in the heavens'. Probably we should not wrong the writer if we said that he thought that these were 'eternal' in the sense of 'timeless' or 'transcendent of time'. To use his own words, things on earth are but 'shadows' or 'copies' of the ultimately real things. Like all shadows and copies, they tell us something about the real things, but they do not and cannot tell us all. If, then, we have an opportunity of learning of the real things direct, we may thereby discern what is true in the 'shadows'. The writer does not abandon the current conception of history as a series of 'ages', but combines this with a Platonic account of history as suggesting 'heavenly' truth. In modern phrase, we might say that the actual gives *some* information about the ideal. Of course, the writer makes his own Christian use of this kind of concept. In Jesus the 'ideal' has entered history, and entered it to redeem man. He redeems man by dying for him. There is nothing Platonic here. Again, the writer can say that through Christ 'the heavenly things themselves' are 'cleansed' (ix. 23). In other words, this author believes that within the sphere of the ultimately real man has, or is to have, a place, that this means that man's right relation to God is a kind of fellowship that belongs to the 'eternal' realm, that sin has disordered this relation, and that Christ puts it right again and gives Christian 'boldness' to approach 'the throne of grace'.

It follows that the writer, like all others in the New Testament, held a lofty doctrine of human nature. This is explicit in the second chapter, where he claims, not only that man is to be the head of all creation, and indeed is already its proper head (ii. 6–8), but that 'the world [not 'age' here, but 'inhabited' earth] to come' is to be brought into subjection to man through Christ (ii. 5.) Again, it is plain that for this writer sin is serious indeed. If it were not so, the whole argument of the Epistle would be superfluous. The author, like St. Paul, tends to divide mankind into two classes, 'believers' and the rest, and to call the first class 'saints' and the second 'sinners'. For him believers are at least beginning to be 'sanctified' because they are one with Christ (ii. 11, x. 10, 14). There is one passage where he seems to say that he thinks that the ritual system dealt only with 'sins of ignorance' (ix. 7; cf. v. 2), but if he held this view of the sin-offerings, there would be so great a difference at this point between the Old Covenant and the New that it is hard to understand why he did not develop an idea that was very pertinent to his purpose, for it is plain that he did not confine the Work *of Christ* to the putting away of unknown sins. He knows of no unforgivable sin except apostasy (vi. 4 *ff.*). Again, for a man who thought that his known sins were unforgiven, there could have been no 'boldness at the throne of grace' (iv. 16; cf. x. 2).

There is little need to show that for this writer 'death' covered more than the mere physical event. It was not this, as has already been suggested, that made the men of his day 'all their lifetime subject to bondage' (ii. 15). On the contrary, they believed that 'It is appointed unto men once to die and after that the judgement' (ix. 27), and for sinners there was 'a certain fearful expectation of judgement' at the hands of a God who is 'a consuming fire' (x. 27, xii. 29). On the other hand, for believers the writer expects an 'eternal salvation' or 'redemption' or 'inheritance' (v. 9, ix. 12, 15).

A last introductory word may be added on this author's use of Old Testament quotations. Like the other New Testament writers, he is not at ease unless he can find a basis for his teaching there, though, as we have already seen, he interprets symbolically, without troubling much about the original, literal meaning. At a number of points there are quotations that are basic to his argument as he conceives it. It is noteworthy that none of these comes from the ritual parts of the Old Testament, and that in one instance he quotes a psalm that expressly denies the value of mere ritual (x. 5 *ff*.). Most of his chief quotations are from the Psalms (i. 5–13, ii. 6 *f*., iii. 7 *ff*., x. 5 *ff*.), though there is a crucial one from Jeremiah (viii. 8 *ff*.). In some instances he returns once and again to passages that he has already quoted, in order that he may develop their Christian meaning. It is clear already that even this writer's thoughts do not derive wholly from ritual.

As with other New Testament writers, the true basis of this writer's thought is the new facts of the Life, Death, and Resurrection of Christ, and the experience of 'salvation' that went with them. This is clear if the first two chapters of the Epistle are considered, for these are the foundation of the whole argument. In the first chapter the key-word is 'Son', as it is in every later passage where it occurs. In the famous opening verses, we see first how the writer, like St. Paul and St. John, was thinking out the answer to the question, 'If the things that we believe are true, what is the relation of Jesus Christ to God and to the universe that He made?' Next he goes on to say, as the present writer thinks, that in the life of Jesus of Nazareth the 'effulgence of the glory' of God had shone among men and 'the impress of the essence' of God had been obvious to sincere eyes. In other words, here there is already evidence that the writer both knew the story of the life of our Lord and attached importance to it. Then there is a reference to the Crucifixion, or rather to its results: on the Cross Jesus 'made purification' of sins. Then the writer passes to the Resurrection, which, for him, too, was no isolated event, but carried with it what we call the Ascension, which means, not a retiring from the world, but rule over it. The Son 'sits' with God on the throne of His active power. The quotation from the Second Psalm, which follows, does not refer literally to birth (or to 'eternal generation') at all. This does not suit the context, and, as we have already seen, no one could read the Psalm and think that it referred to a literal birthday. The writer is saying what St. Paul said in the word, 'Declared to be the Son of God with power . . . by the resurrection of the dead' (Romans i. 4). By the Resurrection and the victory won in it God has made it plain that Jesus is His 'Son'. The subject of the whole chapter is 'The Son of God'. Under it the writer is anticipating the idea that only One who is 'one with God' can unite men with God and so save them.

It would not be wrong to say that the subject of the second chapter (verses 5–18) is 'The Son of Man'. It is true that the phrase does not occur except in the quotation from the Eighth Psalm, but it is almost incredible that the writer first quoted this psalm in the way he does and then applied it to 'Jesus' unless he knew the Synoptic use of the phrase. Paul's use of the psalm (1 Corinthians xv. 27; Ephesians i. 22; Philippians iii. 21), indeed, suggests that for early Christians it was just 'The Psalm of the Son of Man'. In the second chapter of Hebrews the word 'Jesus' —as everywhere else where it occurs in the Epistle—is the key-word, and it is chosen precisely because 'Jesus' was our Lord's *human* name. Again, it is very difficult, if not impossible, to read from verse 9 to the end of the chapter and to think that the writer was referring only to the Crucifixion, or even only to Gethsemane and the Cross. The main point is that our Lord lived a *human* life —or, in the author's phrase, 'partook of blood and flesh'—and died a *human* death, and that *thereby* God is 'putting all things in subjection' under man's 'feet'. Again, by the dying of a human death the writer does not refer principally to the event of physical death. He is thinking of 'death' in the common New Testament way—the physical event and its dread sequel. Only so can he call 'the devil' 'him that hath the power of death'. For him Jesus has faced and 'brought to naught' 'death' in this sense. In other words, He has, in obedience to God, put Himself where sin has put man, and so He is able to save man. The whole passage builds upon the societary idea. Jesus is 'Son of Man' and therefore, like the Kinsman of Hebrew thought, one with man. This is what the application of the parallel terms in the Psalm, 'what is *man* . . . and the *son of man*,' involves. Jesus 'has tasted death for every man', or, in Paul's phrase, 'We judge that one died for all, therefore all died' (2 Corinthians v. 14), and so can 'deliver all them that through fear of death are all their lifetime subject to bondage'. 'He that sanctifieth and they that are sanctified belong together.' The parallel with the account of salvation in terms of modern psychology given in the first chapter above is all but complete. There are the ideas that to save others the Saviour must become like them, become indeed 'one with them', and that they, in turn, must so share His life that they become like Him. It is true that the idea that the Saviour must also not be altogether like those He seeks to save, is not explicitly stated in this passage, but this has already been implied in the account of the 'Son', and, as we shall see, it is explicit later in the Epistle. The parallelism in ideas, as distinct from phraseology, between this passage and the teaching about 'The Son of Man' in the Synoptists is unmistakable. Suffering and glory go indissolubly together in both. 'It became Him, for whom are all things, and through whom are all things, in bringing many sons unto glory, to make the author of their salvation perfect through sufferings.' None can be a perfect saviour who is not 'one with' those that he would save, and who has not suffered with them. The inadequacy both of 'author' and 'captain' to translate the Greek word in the text just quoted is notorious. The best rendering is 'Pioneer', and a pioneer is a societary man. There remains the early reading: '*Apart from God* he should taste death for every man' (ii. 9). It seems very unlikely that a scribe would change 'by the grace of God' into so strange a phrase. On the other hand, the phrase would seem ready to the hand of those early 'Adoptionist' heretics who claimed that the Spirit of God, which was given to Jesus at His Baptism, left Him before the Crucifixion, and it may have been changed because of their use of it. In the context (ii. 12) the writer applies a verse of the Twenty-second Psalm to Jesus, and if the rendering 'apart from God' is accepted, it is an exposition of the terrible Cry of Dereliction. It says in another way what Paul said under the phrase, 'Him who knew no sin he made *to be sin*', of which Bengel wrote: 'Who would dare to say it if Paul had not led the way?' If these two chapters are taken together, the writer is found already to be saying that a true mediator between God and men must be one with both. His doctrine of the Atonement, indeed, is here already complete, and it is stated without ritual terms. He goes on to use these because he has set himself to meet the difficulty described above.

To meet this difficulty, he develops the great doctrine of the Priesthood of Jesus and at the end of the second chapter and the beginning of the third the writer gives a first intimation of this, for it is his principal subject (ii. 17, iii. 1). Yet before he develops this there is another preliminary exposition (chaps. iii and iv). This includes an account of Moses, who was for him, as for his contemporaries, the human mediator of the ritual system. Here he shows how Moses is inferior to Christ, and gives a hint of his method by quoting the *whole* of a passage from Numbers about

Moses and *part* of it about Christ (iii. 3, 5 *f*.)—that is, he declares that Moses is in some ways like Christ, but in others unlike Him. The passage about Joshua depends on the same method, but seems to us a digression. As with later digressions, it is inserted because the writer eagerly seizes opportunity after opportunity to encourage and warn the beloved Church to which he is writing. Meanwhile he uses phrases about the Christian High Priest that he will develop later. Here, however, there are two terms to which he does not return. The first is the word rendered 'propitiation', for which, as already shown, the translation 'atonement' is more nearly adequate. The second term is 'Apostle', the meaning being that 'the high priest of our confession', as it were, takes a message on our behalf to God. This idea is repeated and extended later under the term 'Forerunner', and still further extended under the term 'Mediator'.

It is at the end of the fourth chapter that the writer, having laid the foundations of his argument, comes at last to grips with it (iv. 14–x. 18). The chief passage is vii. 1–x. 18, but there is an important preliminary statement in iv. 14–v. 10, and a further example of the writer's method in xiii. 10–16. Before turning to these passages, however, it is necessary to state precisely the questions that the writer sets himself to answer. For instance, he does not really ask, 'In what ways is Jesus like a Jewish High Priest?' but 'In what ways is a Jewish High Priest like (and unlike) Jesus?' To use his own terms, when one is looking both at a man's 'shadow' and the man himself, the question that one asks is not 'In what ways is the man like the shadow?' but 'In what ways is the shadow like (and unlike) the man?' Or again, if one has both an original design and a 'copy' before one, the question one asks is not 'In what ways is the original like the copy?' but 'In what ways is the copy like (and unlike) the design?' In other words, here too the true starting-point of a New Testament writer's thinking are the new Christian facts—'Jesus' and all that in his experience went with Jesus. Like all the other writers, this one feels that he must relate these facts to the Old Testament—or, rather, relate the Old Testament to these facts—but it is the facts themselves that are regulative of his thought. Fundamentally the writer does not say that Jesus is like Melchizedek, but that Jesus is priest after an eternal 'order' of which the two passages about Melchizedek give symbolic glimpses.

We may, then, first ask the question: In what ways does this writer teach that the Jewish High Priest, as he is described in the Book, was like Jesus? As shown above, the Jewish Hish Priest was fundamentally a societary man. When a High Priest entered into the Holy of Holies, he was far more than a 'representative' of others in the modern sense of the term; he *was* Israel. When the writer calls Jesus 'our High Priest', his meaning is that when Jesus entered into the true Holy of Holies in 'heaven', it was as if a new Israel entered. By a 'new Israel' the body of Christians is meant, for the immediate idea is not 'a new mankind', but 'those who are willing to belong to the new mankind that has begun with Jesus'. It is true that they are potentially a new mankind, but it is assumed everywhere, and especially in the writer's warnings, that every man decides for himself whether he will belong to it. It happens that the term 'believe' only occurs twice in the Epistle, and that when the writer comes to expound 'faith' (chap. xi) he does not give the *word* the Pauline sense. But this brings out the more clearly the truth that this writer, who can use even the word 'faith' in an independent way, bases his thinking upon the same *ideas* and *experience* as Paul. The threefold use of the phrase, 'We have a High Priest . . .', is only one illustration of the concept, fundamental throughout, that Jesus and Christians are one because there has been choice on both sides. Paul says the same under the words 'faith' and 'grace'. Without this idea, what use would it have been to plead with the readers of the Epistle against apostasy?

Again, a High Priest was like Jesus in that he had to do with 'the things pertaining to God' (v. 1). Indeed, this was not only a High Priest's primary function, but for this writer his only function. There is no need to show that Jesus, 'our High Priest', deals with God for men. As High Priest, this is His unique function.

Again, a High Priest was like Jesus in dealing with God on behalf of men in respect of *sin* (v. 1). In the ritual of the Day of Atonement, which at this point was the climax of all Jewish ritual, there was the recognition of the 'exceeding sinfulness of sin', of the gulf that sin digs between men and God, and of the impossibility of fellowship between God and men unless this gulf is bridged. This writer has the Pauline belief in the imperative need that man should be 'reconciled' to God, though here again he does not use the *word*. Unlike many moderns, he finds the making of 'atonement' for sin to be *the* purpose of Jesus. So long as sin obtains, it is 'a fearful thing to fall into the hands of the living God'.

Another point of likeness is that 'every High Priest' is 'appointed' by God (v. 1). 'No man taketh this honour unto himself' (v. 4). There is here no mere formal meaning, but the universal New Testament teaching that Christ died for men's sins 'by the determinate counsel of God'. It is God who takes the initiative in salvation. But it is a terrible initiative. It means that the Son of God 'offered up strong crying and tears unto him that was able to save him from death', yet who did not so save Him. The reference to Gethsemane is unmistakable. Yet, by a seemingly bold contradiction of Gethsemane, the writer goes on to say that Christ was 'heard for his godly fear'. The phrase summarizes the Twenty-second Psalm, to which there seems to be a direct reference (Psalm xxii. 21, 24). The contradiction is only apparent, for God did send the 'twelve legions of angels' and Jesus was enabled to persist unto the Resurrection. He 'learned obedience by the things which he suffered', accepting the 'appoint-ment' and will of God. 'Not my will but thine be done.' When all this is considered, may there not be a reference to the Cries from the Cross as well as to Gethsemane, or even to a wider experience still (cf. John xii. 27, xiii. 21)?

Further, 'every High Priest' is 'taken from among *men*' and so 'appointed for *men*'. In other words, a High Priest must be human in order that he may deal with God for the men with whom he is societarily one. Here, too, the writer works out the idea passion-ately. It is not easy to say whether he thought that the Jewish High Priest was like Jesus in 'bearing gently with the ignorant and erring' and that there was some earlier and feebler anticipation of the 'strong crying and tears', the 'godly fear', by which Jesus 'learned obedience'. It would be foolish to ascribe any such anticipation to such a one as Annas, but could the writer have read sympathetically the account of the ritual of the Day of Atonement without feeling that a sincere Jewish High Priest would enter into the Holy of Holies with something of the terror and burden of his own and his people's sin upon him? Whether this be so or not, it is clear that in these poignant verses the writer is saying that the 'perfect' High Priest gained the 'perfection' essential to the 'cause of eternal salvation' by entering on the one hand fully into the experience of those who are 'tempted' to sin, and on the other by obediently submitting to an ordeal from which He was tempted to flee. The chief ways, therefore, in which the

Aaronic High Priest was like Jesus are that he was a societary man, that thereby he had to do with God for other men, that, in particular, he had to do with God in relation to the sin of men, that God appointed him for this, and that in order to do this effectively he ought himself to be consciously 'compassed with weakness' as he drew near to God. *So far* the High Priest was like Christ. It may be noted in passing that in all these ways the Suffering Servant was also like Christ. Again, every one of the assertions could have been made *about Christ* by a believer who had never even heard of the ritual. The latter effectively illustrates them, but they are true in their own right.

When we turn to the subject of the *differences* between the High Priest and Jesus, we find that the writer exhibits some of them under references to 'Melchizedek'. No doubt he had meditated on the passage where Melchizedek is mentioned in the Hundred-and-tenth Psalm because the early Christians, under the leadership of Jesus Himself (Mark xii. 35 *ff.*), referred this Psalm to their Lord. This drew his attention to the other Old Testament passage where Melchizedek is mentioned (Genesis xiv. 18 *ff.*), and, uniting the two, he interpreted them after the method whose best surviving exponent is Philo. None the less, this method of explaining the Old Testament, which is so unnatural to us, is not fundamental to the writer's argument. The latter could be put into words without mentioning Melchizedek at all. It will be found that he is not mentioned much below.

In enumerating the differences between the High Priest and Jesus it will be convenient to begin by taking two passages together (iv. 14–v. 10 and vi. 13–vii. 28), for in these the writer draws out three distinctions between the two that readily go together. He claims first that the Priesthood of Jesus is 'immutable' and, by implication, that the Aaronic Priesthood is mutable, in the sense of transient. This, of course, was an important point for his readers when the Temple fell and its ritual ceased in A.D. 70. In the manner of his own exegesis, he shows this by pointing to two 'oaths': the first to Abraham and the second in the phrase that he applies to Christ, 'The Lord hath sworn and will not repent'. His readers might argue that the first oath meant the perpetuity of the Aaronic Priesthood, but the writer replies that this is not so, for there was no 'oath' about this priesthood, and it was through a priesthood that derived from Abraham through Judah, and not through Levi (and Aaron), that the oath to Abraham had been kept. The writer adds that the High Priest of whom he is speaking is greater than Abraham himself, for Abraham paid tithes to His prototype, Melchizedek. But the writer also states another reason for the transience of the ancient priesthood. It is transient because it is imperfect. He argues that by the very rules of the Book itself it is admittedly imperfect, for the perfect needs no repetition, and generation after generation, priest after priest, year after year, the old ritual of Atonement had been repeated. There was no 'once for all' about it. Here, at first sight, the argument seems to us to limp, for repetition does not always mean failure. A man may repeat his prayers, for instance, just because they do not fail. But there are things whose repetition does imply failure, and one of these is 'covenant', a word that now appears for the first time (vii. 22). A married pair do not repeat the covenant of marriage. The Levitical Priesthood (vii. 11) repeated and repeated the ritual of *covenant*. But, further, as transience roots in imperfection, so imperfection roots in the *character* of the ancient High Priests. Here is the climax of their failure. They were themselves sinful, for they offered sacrifices for their own sins (vii. 27). They were men 'having infirmity' (vii. 28). The true High Priest was indeed 'touched with the feeling of our infirmities' (iv. 15), but He Himself had no infirmity (vii. 28). In other words, He was both like and unlike those whom He set Himself to save. He was 'holy, guileless, undefiled, separated from sinners' (vii. 26). Only He 'who knew no sin' could save the sinful. The culminant point of difference in these passages is that Jesus, 'tempted in all points like as we are', was sinless. It is not only that He was sinless by nature; He maintained His sinlessness through every ordeal; thereby He became a perfect Saviour: He was 'made perfect by suffering', 'learned obedience by the things that he suffered' even though 'he was Son', and so 'having been made perfect became unto all that obey him the cause of real salvation' (ii. 10, v. 8 *f*.). So the writer, returning to the thought of the first chapter, declares that Jesus, having completed His work by 'offering up himself', was thereby made manifest as 'Son, perfected for evermore' (vii. 27 *f*.). The first difference, therefore, between Jesus and the Jewish High Priests is that the former is a sinless and perfect High Priest. It is true that the ritual gave evidence that a High Priest *ought* to be sinless, for on the Day of Atonement it was only when the High Priest had 'made atonement' for his own sins that he was ready to 'make atonement' for those of others, but the writer does not explicitly take this point. It is true also that the ritual speaks of *sacrifices* 'without blemish' and that the writer quotes the phrase, but he could not quote it of the *High Priests*. The first fundamental difference between the two priesthoods lies in the sinless perfection of Jesus. Thereby He is 'able to save [men] completely' (vii. 25).

With the beginning of chap. viii, the writer turns to an exposition of the New Covenant, and with this to the second fundamental difference between the ancient High Priests and Christ. As is his wont, he had already given signs that these subjects were on their way: he had referred to 'a better covenant' (vii. 22) and he had said that Christ 'offered up *himself*' (vii. 27). It is true that the eighth chapter begins with a comparison of the 'two tabernacles', but for this writer the Tabernacle is just the *locus* of Covenant. Our Lord is 'minister . . . of the true tabernacle' because He is 'mediator of a better covenant' (viii. 2, 6). At this point the writer breaks away from the ritual altogether to quote the famous passage in Jeremiah about the Covenant of the Heart. This is again evidence that the true roots of his thought are Christian, for the passage in Jeremiah describes the experience that belonged to every believer because he believed in Christ. Believers in Jesus 'knew the Lord . . . from the least to the greatest of them' (viii. 11). The New Covenant was theirs! The 'time of reformation' to which the old tabernacle had done no more than point, had come (ix. 1–10).

As it is in this part of the Epistle that the writer uses most frequently the symbol of 'blood', it is necessary before proceeding with the main theme to ask: Does he use the word in the three senses described above for the Old Testament? Does he here agree with the other New Testament writers' use of the word, or does he differ from them? It will be found that he agrees with them.

The idea of 'cleansing' from sin has a great example in this Epistle (ix. 14; cf. i. 3, ix. 22 *f.*, x. 22). Are there any of the idea of 'the giving of life', the emphasis being, as in the ritual, on 'life' rather than on 'death'? The writer has the concept that Christ lived a perfect life, but he does not use the term 'blood' in relation to this.[1] Again, he has the idea that our Lord triumphed in the Crucifixion by 'the power of an indissoluble life', but he does not connect this with the term 'blood'. Again, he believes with all

---

[1] Not even in ix. 14, where 'blood' stands for 'death'. See later.

Q

the early Christians, that Christ gives to Christians eternal life, though he prefers the phrase 'eternal salvation', but here again he does not use the word 'blood'. On the other hand, the writer clearly gives the emphasis to the idea 'death'. For instance, when he says that 'the blood of sprinkling speaketh better things than that of Abel' (xii. 24), he is referring to Abel's death and not to his life. Where Abel's death cried to God for vengeance, Christ's death cries to God for pardon. Again, it is this Christian insistence on the Death of Christ and its central position in the doctrine of Atonement that leads the writer, in the passage where the term 'blood' is most frequent (ix. 11–28), to use the Greek term *diathēkē* with alternate translations—'covenant' and 'testament' (or 'will'). He introduces the second rendering in order to say 'a testament is of force *over the dead*, for it doth never avail while he that made it liveth'—that is, he believes that the New Covenant would not have been valid if Christ had not *died*. It is true that in the context he refers to many details of the use of blood in the old ritual, but it is not less true that in referring to them he connects 'blood' with death, and not as the ritual itself had primarily done, with life. The ritual did not emphasize as he does 'the *shedding* of blood' (ix. 22). Again, it is implied that the Jewish High Priest failed in his atonement because he did not offer 'his own blood' (ix. 25), but surely a sincere High Priest did dedicate his own life. So far there seems to be no clear instance where 'blood' stands for 'life' rather than for 'death'.

The ritual use of 'blood' in the Old Testament relates it to covenant, and, since those who were in covenant shared a common life, it is perhaps here that we might expect the clearest examples of the concept that 'the blood is the life'. In relating 'blood' with covenant, the writer, not content to refer only to the Day of Atonement, begins with the story of the twenty-fourth of Exodus and gathers illustrations from various parts of the Levitical ritual, till he can close with the words: 'I may almost say, all things are cleansed with blood, and apart from the shedding of blood there is no remission' (ix. 18–22). Yet, to return to the earlier part of this passage, the writer says expressly about 'the new covenant' 'a *death* having taken place' (ix. 15). It is fair to expound other passages where the phrase 'the blood of the covenant' occurs (x. 29, xiii. 20) in the light of this passage. The text where the writer comes nearest to connecting 'blood' with life (x. 19 *f.*; cf. xi. 28, xiii. 20) speaks in effect, of 'the *death* by which *we* live'.

While, therefore, this Epistle symbolizes both cleansing and covenant by the word 'blood' in the Old Testament way, it cannot be said to illustrate the text 'the blood is the life'. As elsewhere in the New Testament, the Christian emphasis *under the great symbol* is not on life, but on death. None the less, the writer does emphasize life in his own way, as we shall see later. It may be added that it is just possible to find some hint of the idea that the High Priest *ought* to have offered himself as sacrifice in the ritual if it is assumed that when he 'laid his hands' upon the heads of the victims he was identifying them with himself. We have seen above that this is not likely to have been so—that the meaning of the symbol was 'this is mine' and not 'this is I'—but in any case the writer to the Hebrews does not take this point.

If now we return to the third chief difference between the two priesthoods—that the true High Priest 'offered himself'—it will be noticed that the discussion of the use of the term 'blood' has given examples of it. The greatest exposition of this difference occurs in the middle of the ninth chapter (ix. 11–14), which is the doctrinal climax of the Epistle. Its conclusion runs: 'If the blood of goats and bulls, and the ashes of a heifer sprinkling them that have been defiled, sanctify unto the cleanness of the flesh; how much more shall the blood of Christ, who through the eternal Spirit offered himself without blemish unto God, cleanse your conscience from dead works to serve the living God' (ix. 13 *f.*). Perhaps the meaning of 'how much more' is 'How much more shall the blood of Christ *do* . . . *for* it cleanses your conscience . . .'. It is difficult to exhaust the exposition of this passage, especially if its implications are taken into account as well as its statements. The writer, like the Synoptists, thinks of Christ as 'the Man of the Spirit', adding his characteristic word, 'eternal'. He thinks of Him as holy, for He is 'without blemish'. He is therefore able, through the bond that binds Him to believers, to cleanse their consciences, to rid them of sin. Thereby Christ saves them also from death, for now they begin to 'serve the living God'. This means that they are 'reconciled'. Like Paul, the writer says in effect, 'What are our works but sin and death?' The writer goes on to bring out the truth that Christ is 'mediator of a better covenant' because He Himself died. The Epistle to the Hebrews teaches that salvation from sin and death is by the death of a sinless saviour.

In the same two chapters there are the chief instances of the comparison between the two *Tabernacles*. To understand the writer's symbolism here it should be remembered that by its structure the first Tabernacle was a perpetual sermon. It said to every Israelite who approached two contradictory things: 'Here is the place where men draw near to God', and 'Here God dwells for ever separate from men, for He is holy'. In the Holy of Holies the 'Glory' dwelt upon the Mercy-seat. It was hidden by one veil behind another. The writer, therefore, can compare the inner veil to the 'flesh' of Christ, for he believed that in Christ there dwelt the Glory of God (x. 20). As already shown, twice at least in the New Testament the assonance of the Greek word for 'tent' or 'tabernacle', *skēnē*, or its corresponding verb, with *Shekinah* helps to explain a passage (Revelation xxi. 3; John i. 14). This may also be so in the Epistle to the Hebrews. In the first passage where the two tabernacles are mentioned at any length (viii. 2-5) the chief point made is that the true Tabernacle 'which the Lord pitched, not man' is 'in the heavens'. In the second passage (ix. 1-10) the chief point is that until the true High Priest came, 'the way into the Holy Place hath not yet been made manifest', for the 'worshippers' are too sinful to draw near to God. In the third passage (ix. 21-8) the chief ideas are that even the Heavenly Tabernacle needed to be 'cleansed', and that by His sacrifices Christ has cleansed it perfectly 'once' for all. The underlying truth is that Christ has at last made it possible for men, even though they had sinned, to enter into living fellowship with God. Few modern men have any consciousness of the holiness and therefore of the separateness of God, however often they call Him 'holy'. When this sense returns, the symbolism of the tabernacle will no longer seem strange.

In the first part of the tenth chapter (x. 1-18) there is again a good deal of recapitulation, in the writer's manner, the particular point being taken that, while the old *sacrifices* can do no more than call the fact of sin to frequent *remembrance*, under the New Covenant God 'remembers sins no more' (x. 3, 17). Yet, again in the writer's manner, something is brought into the foreground that had not so far been emphasized. This is introduced under a quotation from the Fortieth Psalm. Here 'sacrifice and offering' are repudiated, and the Incarnation takes their place: 'When he cometh into the world, he saith A body didst thou prepare for me. . . . Lo, I am come . . . to do thy will, O God' (x. 5, 7). The context stresses the obedience of Christ. This is partly, again after the writer's manner, to prepare the readers for the next part of the

Epistle (x. 19–xii. 13), where there is a prolonged exhortation to them to 'do the will of God' with 'patience' (x. 36) in their present evil plight. Yet it may also be said that here the writer presents the *life* of Christ as a sacrifice, though he does not say so in set terms. The question now arises, 'What does this writer mean by the term "sacrifice"?'

He most frequently uses it as the current name for the offerings in the Tabernacle, but a first suggestion of the *meaning* that he attaches to the word is given by the use of such compound phrases as '*gifts* and sacrifices' and 'sacrifice and *offering*' (ix. 9, x. 5) The old idea of gift is clearly present. Again, this writer can also use the term in the sense that is predominant in Paul, to describe the self-denial of Christians in almsgiving (xiii. 16), including, too, the 'praise' of God (xiii. 15). Here the idea of gift seems to be the only idea. It seems, therefore, that if we are to say that by implication the writer speaks of the life of Christ in the tenth chapter as a sacrifice, we must add that this means that Christ's human life was a perfect gift to God. Can this be said also of Christ's death? The writer links Christ's death with His life, by his use of the term 'body'. As Christ took a 'body' (corresponding to Paul's 'form of a servant') in the Incarnation, so He 'offered' His 'body' as the one effective sin-offering when He died (x. 5, 10, 12). This use of the word 'body' is the more remarkable because, as we shall note later, on the Day of Atonement the 'bodies' of the sin-offerings were not 'offered' to God. But the word 'offer' suggests gift. It follows that this passage represents the perfect life of Christ, consummated in a perfect death, as the gift to God of the altogether obedient Son. Yet there is a verse that adds something more. It is the will of God that we should be sanctified (that is, saved) through the offering of 'the body of Jesus Christ once for all' (x. 10). It follows that Christ saves us because He 'became man', for this is the meaning of the use of the word 'body'. In other words, Christ is able to save men because He too was man—like other men and yet (through His perfect life) unlike them. The gift of a perfect human life carries with it the gift of a 'sanctified' or perfected mankind (cf. vii. 25, ix. 9, x. 1). Obviously the societary concept of the second chapter is here taken for granted. But in this passage the chief stress is upon something that had no parallel in the old victims—*willingness* to do God's will. In the word of the early chapters of Acts, Christ was the *Servant* of the Lord.

This is perhaps the best place to consider another idea that reverberates throughout the Epistle—the idea that the Christian High Priest has 'sat down on the right hand of God' (x. 12) or 'sat down on the right hand of the throne of the Majesty in the heavens' (viii. 1). To modern readers it may seem that here priests are confused with kings, but it needs to be remembered not only that priesthood and kingship go together in the passages about Melchizedek, but that in the Eastern mind they often went together, and that the Holy of Holies was sometimes called 'The place of [God's] *throne*' (e.g. Ezekiel xliii. 7). Yet how impossible it would have seemed that the High Priest on the Day of Atonement should have 'sat down' upon the 'mercy-seat' where 'The Glory of the Lord' dwelt! On the contrary, he hid himself behind incense lest he should even look upon God. Presently, again, he stole out of the shrine back to the waiting people. For our author this just meant that he had failed. 'Our High Priest', on the contrary, by *taking His seat* on the very throne of God, shows that He has succeeded. He 'intercedes' indeed (vii. 25), but such an One does not need to 'plead'. It is remarkable how little heed has been given sometimes to this bold thought. Even Charles Wesley, usually a very good expositor of the New Testament, wrote:

'Before the throne my Saviour *stands*.'

Something more is added from the Hundred-and-tenth Psalm when this quotation is made in the tenth chapter (x. 10-14) : 'From henceforth expecting till his enemies be made the footstool of his feet' (cf. 1 Corinthians xv. 25). Not only the psalm itself, but the Greek word rendered 'expecting' describes a victory that is sure to come. In other words, we have here what the Gospels call 'the rule of God' in two of the senses of the phrase, with the added concept that Christ shares in the rule: He is on the throne now, sharing with God in the mastery of a rebellious world; He is to share in the final rule of God over an altogether loyal world. At first sight, indeed, the phrase, 'till his enemies be made the footstool of his feet', suggests reluctant submission rather than loyalty, but the writer makes haste to add, 'For by one offering he hath perfected for ever them that are sanctified', and this is his account of the way in which the perfect realm is to come. It is by 'sanctification', not by coercion. This, of course, means that already the Christ is ruling in the third sense of 'kingdom'—ruling over believers now. Here it is enough to refer to the splendid description, in the twelfth chapter, of the Mount Zion unto which believers are already 'come' (xii. 22-4) through 'Jesus, the mediator of a new covenant', and to note the amazing contradiction of the old ritual by which Christians do not silently await the return of their High Priest from the Holy of Holies, but follow in behind Him with 'boldness' (x. 19 *ff*.). There is a sense in which a Christian is not afraid 'before the throne'. Is he not already saved?

With the words, 'Now where remission [of sins and iniquities] is, there is no more offering for sin' (x. 18), the writer concludes what he has to say about the *mental* perplexities that beset his readers because it had seemed to them that the Book required the perpetuity of the old ritual. Thereafter in the main he gives himself to help them, by encouragement and warning, to meet the trials and persecutions that were pressing upon them *from the world without*. Yet it is remarkable that in his doctrinal passages he had not returned to a truth that he had stated in his second chapter: 'Since then the children are sharers in flesh and blood, he also himself in like manner partook of the same; that through death he might bring to naught him that had the power of death, that is, the devil; and might deliver all them who through fear of death were all their lifetime subject to bondage' (ii. 14 *f*.). It is true, of course, that here the ritual had nothing to say. It is true, therefore, that the problem involved was not pressing upon his hearers. This may explain, at least in part, his silence, for he gives more than one hint that he has not exhausted his theme (ix. 5, xiii. 22). The problem referred to is the question: '*Why* was it the will of God that His Son should die? *Why* must He atone by His own blood?' It is plain that the Tabernacle sacrifices did not 'taste death [and Hades] for every man' (ii. 9) or 'bring to naught him that had the power of death [and Hades]'. As has already been shown, in these texts from his second chapter the writer comes nearest to the Pauline paradox: 'him who knew no sin *he made to be sin*'—that is, here he comes nearest to saying *why* Christ Himself must be sin-offering. As it happens, there is something in his last chapter that bears on the subject (xiii. 10-12). Here the writer calls the Cross the Christian 'altar', on which the perfect sacrifice was offered once for all. But he goes on to compare Christ, the Christian sacrifice, with 'the *bodies* of those beasts whose blood is brought into the holy place'. Their bodies

were flung 'without the camp', as Christ was crucified outside
Jerusalem, and they were flung outside just because they were so
closely identified with the sin of the people that they were too
unclean to be offered on the altar or even to be tolerated within
the Tabernacle at all. They *were* sin. In other words, the writer
thought of Jesus as identifying Himself with sinners in the utmost
consequences of their sin. All the thoughts of the fifth chapter of
the Second Epistle to the Corinthians are present in this Epistle
though the terminology is different. Where Paul says 'God was in
Christ', the writer to the Hebrews teaches that Jesus was 'Son' ;
where Paul says 'him who knew no sin', this writer declares that
Christ was 'holy' ; where Paul adds 'he made to be sin', there is
the strange comparison between the sacrifice of the Cross and the
bodies of the outcast animals; where Paul says 'that we might
become the righteousness of God in him', the writer of this Epistle
claims that Jesus has 'perfected for ever them that are sanctified'
(x. 14). In the paradox of the 'altar' on which there is offered
what is cast out from the altar there is once again the Synoptic
antinomy between the cry, 'Father, into thy hands', and the Cry
of Dereliction. In this Epistle, therefore, in spite of all differences
of approach and terminology, there is yet another account of the
one New Testament doctrine of the Atonement.

Again, this Epistle has more to say of the ritual system than the
whole of the rest of the New Testament and it is sometimes called
the Epistle of Sacrifice. If this means that it teaches that without
the Death and Ascension of a High Priest who is both Son of God
and Son of Man there is 'no remission', the name is justified. But
while the writer declares that the ritual system taught the two
truths that remission of sins can only come by 'death' and that
the 'real' mediator must 'sum up' mankind, he adds that it did
this with the ineluctable inadequacy of a 'shadow', and that it did
not even so much as fore-shadow two other truths—that the 'real'
mediator must be the Son of God, and that He must Himself die
and rise again.

CHAPTER XVII

THE GOSPEL AND EPISTLES OF JOHN

IN discussing the Gospel and Epistles of John it is once again necessary that the writer should make clear his general attitude to the books in question, even though he cannot find room to give the reasons. As already stated, it is assumed here that the Epistles were written either by the same author as the Gospel or by some one so closely related to him that all these books may be treated together and quoted under the name 'John'. Again, it is assumed that, while the writer knew the substance of the Synoptic documents, he was also the heir of an independent tradition that went back to the days of Jesus Himself. Again, if the word 'original' is to be used about him, it should be clearly defined. It might be maintained that there are no original *ideas* in the Fourth Gospel. What we find in it is a new set of *words* to describe ideas that are already present in the Synoptic Gospels. Yet there is more than mere repetition under new terms. The ideas are further developed and their meaning more fully brought out. Illustrations will be given below. Further, it seems to the present writer that this further exposition of the ideas is a true exposition, that John does bring out, after half a century of thought, truths that were either altogether implicit or only partly developed in the teaching of Jesus as recorded in the Synoptic Gospels. In other words, he illustrates the continued use of the method of learning that, as we have seen, Jesus Himself deliberately followed; He turned the disciples' thoughts in the right direction, and then left them to do much of the consequent thinking for themselves. In the words of John himself, the Holy Spirit 'guided' him into further 'truth', yet he did this by 'taking' of Christ's teaching. To give a simple instance: if Jesus said to His disciples, on the ground that they were *His* disciples, '*Ye* are the light of the world', their own minds would lead them to the conviction that Jesus Himself was 'the light of the world' (John viii. 12) in a higher way. Again, there is fair agreement now that the writer of the Fourth Gospel himself knew, and assumed that his readers already knew, the contents of the first three Gospels. This does not necessarily mean that the

Synoptic Gospels were already read and authoritative in the Church, but only that their substance was generally known. It is also fairly well agreed that, pre-supposing this, John sometimes silently corrected some detail of the current tradition, sometimes added to it, and sometimes just took it for granted. For instance, the fact that he does not mention the Transfiguration, the Agony in Gethsemane, and the Cry of Dereliction, does not mean that he thought them unimportant, but that he assumed that they were already integral parts of the Gospel tradition. In particular, if his accounts of the events from Gethsemane to the Resurrection be read alongside Mark's, it will be found that he either omits what Mark says altogether, or summarizes it in a few necessary words to maintain the continuity of the story, *except* where he has some detail (or even incident) to add. This is true also of the same story in Luke and, in a rather less degree, in Matthew. Accordingly John does not repeat any of the four 'Words from the Cross' that were already well-known, but adds three that were derived from his own independent line of evidence. Similarly, his quotation from the Twenty-second Psalm (John xix. 24) assumed that his readers knew of the Christian associations of the psalm. Again, he is not only 'original' in some of the terms that he uses and in developing the ideas of his predecessors, but in introducing the received teaching (under different terminology) in new stories about Jesus. Instances of this kind of 'originality' will also be given below. Again, it is probable that John knew some, at least, of the Epistles of Paul, but here, too, he was not bound at all to his great predecessor's terminology. He was so sure about the independent tradition of which he was heir that he could stand clear even of Paul himself. It is impossible to say whether he had read the Epistle to the Hebrews. It is true that if one were to seek a summary either of the Pauline teaching or of the teaching of Hebrews, it is likely that the best would be found in this writer (John iii. 16; 1 John ii. 1 *f*.), but this need mean no more than that the teaching of the first Church was fundamentally one. One or two links between the Fourth Evangelist and the remaining New Testament books will be pointed out later. Finally, the Fourth Gospel will be quoted with its minimum of meaning, not as a record of the things that Jesus taught, but as a record of the teaching of a great Christian of two generations later. This does not mean that the present writer believes that nothing in the Fourth Gospel goes back to Jesus

Himself, for he thinks far otherwise, but only that it seems best to assume no more than some students are prepared to grant.

The writer has left us his own account of his purpose in writing his Gospel: 'These [things] are written that ye may believe that Jesus is the Christ, the Son of God, and that believing ye may have life in his name' (John xx. 31). This means that John, like all the other New Testament writers, knows nothing of the modern distinction, as artificial as it is convenient, between the Person and the Work of Christ. For him they are organically one. It is true that under 'the Person of Christ' there is a point where this writer clearly differs from the Synoptics. As was shown above, in the Synoptics our Lord says little about His Person, but leaves His hearers, for the most part, to discover the truth about it. In the first three Gospels He only speaks of His Person where He must do so in order to teach the truth about His Work. Under the minimum method just described, there is no need to ask how far John is right in making Christ say much more about Himself than the Synoptics do. The important point is that there is nothing in John's own doctrine about the Person of Christ that does not bear upon His Work. For instance, if any of the following statements is considered, it will be found to involve both the Person and Work of Jesus: 'I am the light of the world' ; 'I am the way, the truth and the life' ; 'The Word became flesh'. It follows that the whole of the Fourth Gospel is a Book of Salvation, and that, strictly speaking, the whole of it should be expounded at this point. It must suffice to mention some of the ways in which its writer teaches, in his own words, the truths that were common to all Christians about the *Work* of Christ in the broad sense, and then to examine more closely the teaching of this Gospel about the *Death* of Christ.

John only uses the term 'faith' (as distinct from the verb 'believe') in one passage (1 John v. 4), and the term 'grace' in two (John i. 14–17; 2 John 3), yet a great part of his writings is just an exposition of these two things. They describe the two sides of one phenomenon—the way in which Christ and the believer become one. Of this unity, for instance, the discourses in the sixth chapter of the Gospel and in the chapters from the fourteenth to the seventeenth are just expositions. They teach what ought to be called 'Christian mysticism', not 'Pauline mysticism'. The first might be summed in the text, 'He that eateth my flesh and drinketh my blood hath eternal life', and the second in the text, 'And the glory that thou hast given me I have given unto them; that they may be one, even as we are one; I in them and thou in me that they may be perfected into one' (vi. 54, xvii. 22). In other words, salvation is by fellowship with God, a fellowship that Christ makes possible. The corporate or societary concept here reaches its culmination.

Again, this writer completes the New Testament teaching about the Holy Spirit. For him, as for the Synoptists, Jesus is 'the man of the Spirit', though, while he says this at the same point as the Synoptists, he characteristically adds a story to say it (John i. 32 ff.). Similarly, where the Synoptists tell that the Baptist said, 'I baptized you with *water*, but he shall baptize you with the Holy Spirit', John writes, 'Except a man be born of *water* and the Spirit, he cannot enter into the Kingdom of God' (iii. 5) The Fourth Gospel, however, states explicitly that the gift of the Spirit (in the New Testament sense of a *conscious* 'receiving' of the Spirit of power) waited until Jesus had been 'glorified' (John vii. 39). Under this subject John introduces his own term 'Paraclete', but it is best to take this at a later point. Once more, however, the societary concept is clear; God and Jesus and Christians are 'one' because they share, each in a distinctive way, in 'one Spirit'. The Christian doctrine that the Holy Spirit is Himself God only brings this truth to an almost incredible climax.

John only uses the word 'salvation' once (John iv. 22), and he does not use 'justification' or 'adoption' or 'redemption' at all. Here his favourite metaphor is regeneration, or the 'new birth'. There is no need to catalogue the places where he speaks of being 'begotten of God' or of being 'born from above' or of 'becoming children of God'. It is clear that here the chief idea in salvation is that through believing in Christ bad men become good men. With other New Testament writers, John uses the word 'sanctify', and this, as already seen, implies 'holiness'. Again, where Hebrews says that Jesus was 'made perfect through suffering', John says that the Father 'sanctified' the Son and that the Son 'sanctified' Himself (John x. 36, xvii. 19). Again, John never calls Christians 'saints', but he does say that a true Christian 'cannot sin' (1 John iii. 9). He is paradoxical here, for he also says, 'If we say that we have no sin we deceive ourselves' (1 John 1. 8). So long as a Christian is not perfect, there is something paradoxical about him; he is both saint and sinner. He is not yet altogether healthy, but he has passed the crisis of his disease. If one may carry the metaphor a little farther, the microbes of sin are not all gone, but they are going. 'There is a sin not unto death' (1 John v. 17).

There is no need to show again that John has the same concepts of 'sin' and 'death' and 'wrath' as other New Testament writers. Under each of these terms, however, there is a kind of culmination in his writings. From the Gospel of Mark onwards, the sin of sins is to reject Jesus. This is the 'sin against the Holy Spirit' which, when it is persistent and resolute, 'hath never forgiveness'. Of course there is here no reference to 'honest doubt', but to what is far more common, dishonest motive. In John's terminology, there are those who see the 'light' and know that it *is* 'light', but prefer 'darkness'. In John Jesus says outright, 'If I had not come and spoken unto them, they had not had sin, but now they have no excuse for their sin' (John xv. 22; cf. iii. 19, ix. 41, xvi. 9). When men 'behold' or 'see' Christ, they come to the decisive watershed of life.

The concept of 'death' is best understood in contrast with that of 'life' or 'eternal life'. While the Synoptists and John all use the two phrases, 'the Kingdom of God' and 'eternal life', as synonyms, the former prefer the first phrase and John the second. For John, 'This is life eternal, that they should know thee, the only true God, and him whom thou didst send, Jesus Christ' (John xvii. 3). In other words, 'life' is primarily qualitative, and 'eternal life' has the quality that comes from fellowship with God. Clearly the concept here is not chiefly that there is a happy heaven in the Hereafter, but that God offers the sinner the true kind of life—which may begin now. This may be called 'realised eschatology' in the sense that the Christian has already begun to live for ever. None the less, John teaches that there is a Parousia, which will carry with it a state when 'we shall be like him; for we shall see him even as he is' (1 John iii. 2). In such a concept, however, a believer's physical death plays no decisive part. At most it furthers a process that has already begun. John, indeed, leaves apocalyptic in the background, and this perhaps is its right place. Similarly, while John can say that 'all that are in the tombs shall hear the voice (of the Son of Man), and shall come forth, they that . . . have done ill unto the resurrection of judgement' (John v. 28 *f.*), it is quite wrong to infer that physical death plays a large part in his concept of 'death'. On the contrary, for him 'death' is the state of the sinner *now*, whether he be happy or miserable or just comfortable. The believer, on the other hand, 'has passed out of death into life' (v. 24; cf. viii. 51 *f*. 1 John iii. 14) For John, in other words, the qualitative concept of 'life' and 'death' is altogether dominant, and the culmination of New Testament thought here, too, is reached. Similarly, while one of the two Greek terms for 'anger' or 'wrath' does not occur at all in John and the other only once, the single text shows that for him the 'wrath of God' already 'abides' upon men who commit the sin of sins (iii. 36). There is nothing either apocalyptic or hedonistic here; the man who refuses to 'obey' or 'believe' the Son thereby loses 'life', and to lose it *is* the 'wrath of God'. 'Wrath' and 'death' are practically synonymous. None the less, the repeated use of the phrase, 'I will raise him up at the last day', in a passage where the paramount concept of 'life' falls in with what has just been said (John vi. 39–54), shows that here, too, apocalyptic ideas are not denied.

It is well known that the phrase 'the Kingdom of God' is only used by John in one passage (John iii. 3–5), but we need to ask whether he has any or all the *ideas* underlying the three concepts of God's rule distinguished above. Here it is necessary to note that, apart from one passage (John ix. 32) which does not bear upon the subject, John does not use the phrase 'this age' at all. He has the phrase 'unto the age' (rendered 'for ever') several times, but for him the dominant concept here, too, as under the term *aionios*, or 'eternal', is qualitative and not temporal. For the present world he does not use 'age', but 'cosmos'. While he can use this term for the present world considered as save-able (e.g. John iii. 16), usually he means by it the system of evil that confronts and opposes God. While it may be said that all the while he takes it for granted that God is in ultimate control of the rebellious world now, his chief idea is that God has set Himself to deal with the rebellion, and to deal with it by sending His Son to meet it. Again, while it is true that John takes it for granted that there will be a perfect rule and realm of God hereafter, his chief interest is not in this. His dominant idea, usually without the phrase, is that the Rule of God has already begun in Christ and in those that believe in Christ. It may indeed be claimed that the mere use of the phrase 'The Christ', which is fairly frequent in John, implies that the Kingdom of God has begun. Further, when challenged by Pilate with a claim to kingship, Jesus replies, 'My kingdom does not belong to this world'

(John xviii. 33–7). This means that in some sense He identifies the Kingdom of God with His own kingship. He claims too that He already has 'servants'. Of them He says that, though they are 'in the world', and, like Himself, are 'sent into the world' that 'the world may believe', yet 'they do not belong to the world' (John xvii, *passim*). The idea of a present Rule of God is plainly present. Here, again, we might speak of a 'realized eschatology'. For this writer the final Rule of God has begun. Here too he develops under other terms ideas that are only beginning to be explicit in the Synoptic Gospels.

There is no need to show in detail that for John salvation is altogether the act of God. It would be enough to quote his most famous text (John iii. 16) or to pursue the term 'sent' as used of Jesus. If 'the whole world lieth in the evil one' (1 John v. 19), it cannot do any one little thing to save itself.

It would be possible to sum up what has been said about the agreement between John's general doctrine of salvation and that of the rest of the New Testament under correlative terms, whose use John brings to a climax. On the Godward side, the Son of God is 'manifested', on the manward side, there are those who 'behold' Him. Similarly, the Son of God is 'the light of the world', and believers 'walk in the light' ; on the other hand, there are those who have the opportunity to 'behold' the light and prefer to walk in the darkness. In brief, these commit the sin of sins. Again, there is a text that suggests that 'the world' has 'beheld' the Son of God, but, refusing all the while truly to 'behold' Him, will cease to be able to do so (John xiv. 17–19). This only develops the Synoptic saying, 'Seeing they see not' (Matthew xiii. 13; cf. Mark viii. 18).

Perhaps this is the best place to give some details about John's use of the term 'Behold'. It may have originated from the opening words of the Servant Song, '*Behold*, my servant' (Isaiah lii. 13; cf. John i. 29). It is true, however, that in the Septuagint the Greek word is not the one that John favours most (*theōrein*), but a commoner word. Yet it is also true that John uses three Greek words to express his symbolic sense of 'behold' and that the word in the Septuagint rendering of the Servant Song is one of them. It occurs, for instance, in the phrase, 'Ye have *seen* me and yet believe not' (John vi. 36). Here to 'see' is to have the opportunity of 'believing'; elsewhere to 'see' is to 'believe', in the New Testament sense of living union—as, for instance, in the text, 'He that hath *seen* me, hath *seen* the Father' (John xiv. 9). There is a second Greek term in the First Epistle—for instance, in the text, 'We have *beheld* and bear witness that the Father hath sent the Son to be the Saviour of the world' (1 John iv. 14). It is this word that comes nearest to the literal sense of 'see' (cf. 1 John i. 1), but it occurs also in the Prologue to the Gospel, and there the literal and symbolical meanings seem to be clearly blent (John i. 14). The third and favourite word only occurs in the Gospel in sayings ascribed to Jesus, and hovers between literal and symbolic meanings, and between 'believing' and the opportunity of 'believing' (John vi. 40, 62, xii. 45, xiv. 17, 19, xvi. 10, 19, xvii. 24; cf. 1 John i. 1). The metaphor suits also the passage referring to the Brazen Serpent, discussed below, though the word itself does not occur. It was by 'looking' at the Serpent that a stricken Israelite lived. Here, too, there is just an exposition of Matthew's saying, 'Blessed are your eyes, for they see' (Matthew xiii. 16), and indeed of the passage in Isaiah on which it builds (cf. John xii. 40). John's use of 'behold' is a study in faith and unbelief—that is, in salvation.

What is the attitude of the Fourth Evangelist to the Temple and its ritual? A summary of his references, with comments, may be made. He does speak of the 'lamb of God', but it is of a 'lamb' that 'bears away', or 'bears the burden of', 'the sins of the world' (John i. 29, 36). Perhaps both ideas are present (cf. 1 John iii. 5). There is no such lamb in the sacrificial system, as we have already seen. Indeed, there is no sacrificial animal in the whole system except the 'goat for Azazel' on the Day of Atonement to which this saying can be exactly applied. Not even the sin-offerings, when they were killed, could rightly be said either to 'carry away' sin or to 'bear the burden' of sins. The phrase, like the other New Testament passages about 'The Lamb of God', suits the last Servant Song and not the Temple sacrifices. In descriptions of the latter, the sufferings of the sacrifices are nowhere named. Where the phrase 'to bear iniquity' does occur, it is used of the sinner, not of the sacrifices.

On the other hand, John uses the symbolic word 'blood' (1 John i. 7) with the meaning of 'cleansing', and he has the word for 'propitiation', or rather 'at-one-ment', twice (1 John ii. 1, iv. 10), the context of the second passage in particular excluding the idea of the 'assuaging of wrath'. Like the writer of the Hebrews, he thinks of the 'glory' of God or the *Shekinah* as dwelling in Jesus,

and therefore, just as the former compares the 'flesh' of His Lord
to the Temple 'veil', John compares the 'body' of his Lord to the
Temple itself (John ii. 21). He tells the story of the cleansing of
the Court of the Gentiles, and he has many discourses in the
Temple, though it is for him a place of teaching rather than of
sacrifice. At the Feast of Tabernacles Jesus seems to borrow two
symbols from its ritual, but these are not from the sacrifices, but
from the Pouring Out of the Water from Siloam and the Temple
Illumination that closed the Feast (John vii. 37, viii. 12).

Again, there is the Discourse about the Bread of Life, when the
Passover 'was at hand' (John vi. 4). With this the comparison
between Jesus and the Passover victim under the phrase, 'A bone
of him shall not be broken', should be noted (John xix. 36). An
attempt was made above to interpret the Synoptic teaching about
the Last Supper, taken by itself. It anticipated, however, John's
exposition in his sixth chapter, for he says in effect, that he was
thinking about the Passover when he wrote the chapter. What
was said under the Synoptic Gospels might be repeated here.[1]
There is no need to suppose that the discourse has somehow got
out of place in the manuscripts, for this is only the greatest instance
of the curious way in which John expounds teaching already
adumbrated in the Synoptics at a different point in the story. It
is true that here, and here only, he attaches the teaching to a
story that the Synoptists had already told, but he adds a good
many details, and it is more than credible that after the Miracle
of the Loaves Jesus, according to John's independent authority,
gave some such teaching as could be expanded, and rightly
expounded, in the Discourse. If Jesus fed a crowd by miracle,
would not the crowd follow Him and ask for the miracle to be
repeated? And would not a Jewish crowd recall the Miracle of
the Manna, and urge that this should again be repeated? And
would not Jesus, as in the story of His Temptation in the Synoptists,
refuse to be a mere miracle-worker? Further, as in the accounts
of the Last Supper, Jesus here compares His 'flesh' to 'bread' and
not to the flesh of the Passover victim (John vi. 51).

Again, it is possible that the phrase, 'I sanctify myself' (John
xvii. 19) derives from the ritual of the Day of Atonement, the
same contrast being implicit as is explicit in Hebrews—namely,
that while the Jewish High Priest 'sanctified himself' for his own

---

[1] For further exposition perhaps the writer may refer to his book entitled *The
Sacramental Society*, pp. 162 *ff.*

R

sake as well as for the sake of others, Jesus did so only for the sake of others. It has already been shown that the phrase 'to drink the blood [of the Son of Man]' does not derive from the sacrificial system (John vi. 52–9). If now all this writer's references to the Temple and its ritual be taken together—and if it be noted that he selects just what will illustrate his theme and leaves the rest, and that he sometimes illustrates by likeness and sometimes by contrast—it seems to follow that the whole ritual system only furnished illustrations of ideas derived from other sources. In the larger part of the Johannine teaching, indeed, there are no references to ritual at all.

To turn now from the general subject of Salvation to the place of the Death—or, rather, of the Death and Resurrection—of Christ in the Johannine books, it is clear, first, that John believed that the *fact* that Jesus died and rose again was vital to Christianity. This is true, whatever *explanation* of the fact he offers. It is plain, first, from the large place that John, like the Synoptists, gives to the story of the Death and Resurrection of Jesus. It is plain also in another way. It is agreed that when John wrote, the Docetic heresy was rife, or rather that Docetic ideas were afloat, for it is unlikely that an integrated Docetic account of Jesus had already been formulated. The general idea was that it was incredible that the Son of God could have been really human. To-day there are many who are so sure that Jesus was human that they wonder whether He could also have been divine. It is remarkable that some who lived within two generations of His life on earth were so sure that He was divine that they doubted whether He could have been fully human. They suggested that He only *seemed* to be a man, and the suggestion took different forms. One suggestion appears to have been that from first to last this was so, and John therefore states very emphatically 'The Word became flesh' (John i. 14;cf. 1 John i. 1–3, iv. 2f.; 2 John 7). Another suggestion appears to have been that Jesus received the Holy Spirit for His work at His Baptism but that the Spirit left Him before the Crucifixion, the mind of the time finding the idea that the Son of God suffered on the Cross almost intolerable. In consequence, John asserts (1 John v. 5–9) almost vehemently that Jesus 'came . . . not with the water [of baptism] only, but with the water and with the blood [of crucifixion]'. Again, some appear to have said that Jesus' body, at least the body that hung upon the Cross, was the body of a phantom. But the perennial belief about a phantom is that, even if its body could be pierced, nothing like 'water and blood' could issue from it. In particular, the 'bodies' of phantoms are bloodless. John, therefore, includes in his story of the Crucifixion a solemn asseveration that at first seems strange in modern ears: 'There came out blood and water. And he that hath seen hath borne witness, and his witness is true: and he knoweth that he saith true, that ye also may believe' (John xix. 34 f.). If the Fourth Gospel is the Gospel of the Incarnation, it is also the Gospel of an Incarnation that was consummated in the Crucifixion and Resurrection. Its writer, whatever his explanation of the necessity of the Crucifixion may be, did believe that the truth that Jesus died is fundamental in Christianity. Just as the Synoptists say that 'the Son of Man *must* die', so the Fourth Gospel says that 'the Son of Man *must* be lifted up'.

There is no doubt, again, that John thought of the Cross as the decisive moment of Christ's victory over 'the world, the flesh and the devil'. For him these three went together, though the symbolic use of the term 'flesh' is not common with him. It would not be wrong to say that for John the Son of God came to save the 'world' from the 'flesh' and the 'devil'. In order to do this, as will appear below under an attempted exposition of other phrases, this writer held that He must 'come in the flesh' and 'come into the world'. These are the arena of a war with the Devil: 'For this was the Son of God manifested that he might destroy the works of the devil' (1 John iii. 8). This recalls the cry of the demons in the Synoptists: 'Art thou come to destroy us?' The three uses of the phrase 'the prince of this world', taken together, show that Calvary was the decisive moment in this war (John xii. 31, xiv. 30, xvi. 11). It is likely enough that under the terms 'devil' and 'prince', as under the terms 'flesh' and 'world', John's ideas lie on both sides of the line that we draw between the literal and the symbolic. Here there falls John's use of the term 'hour'. Sometimes it means 'time' (e.g. xvi. 2) and sometimes 'appointed time' (e.g. iv. 23), but John uses it in a special sense to describe the crisis of the Cross (John ii. 4, vii. 30, viii. 20, xii. 23, 27, xiii. 1, xvi. 32, xvii. 1). Mark, indeed, had already pointed the way to this (Mark xiv. 35). Here it is likely that Jesus Himself has given us the clue in a phrase that He uses in another connexion—the phrase in which He speaks of a woman's travail, with its strange mingling of agony and joy, as her 'hour' (John xvi. 21). Our Lord's Cross and Resurrection were 'the travail of His soul'. There is nothing so utterly vicarious, in the true sense, as travail. Without it the race would perish.

This is borne out if a particular passage where the word 'hour' occurs, the story of the Coming of the Greeks (John xii. 20–36), is considered. No doubt the story was dear to John's readers because they too were 'Greeks', yet it is remarkable that here, under a different story and in different phraseology, this writer should say what the Synoptists had said under the story of Gethsemane. As usual, however, he adds while he repeats. He depicts Jesus as expecting victory—the victory being the salvation of such men as these Greeks, who have somehow been 'drawn unto' Him. 'Now is the Son of Man glorified'; 'Now shall the prince of this world be cast out'. It is not just His own victory but God's: 'God is glorified in Him.' Yet the victory is to be won by ordeal. Here Jesus applies to Himself the word that, in the Synoptic account, He had spoken to others when first He said that 'the Son of Man must suffer' : 'He that loseth his life shall save it', and save others too (John xii. 24 *f.*). Here, as in Gethsemane, His soul is 'torn in pieces' as He faces the ordeal, but here, too, He cries in effect 'Not my will but thine be done' (cf. John xii. 27). Here, again, He is aware that all the time His Father is helping Him, though the phrase is not of the help of 'twelve legions of angels', but the conviction which the 'voice from heaven' passes on to others, 'I have both glorified [my name] and will glorify it again'. In other words, the Crucifixion is to manifest the nature of God by what it does for men. Finally, there are the words, 'now is the crisis of this world; now shall the prince of this world be cast out. And I, if I be lifted up from the earth, will draw all men unto myself'. For this writer, the Death and Resurrection of Jesus were an 'hour' of agony and victory— an agony and a victory, not just over physical death, but over all that the New Testament means by 'sin' and 'death', for the phrase 'the prince of this world' epitomizes the power of both (cf. Luke xxii. 53).

Yet the question remains: *How* did the Fourth Evangelist think that the Death and Resurrection of Christ won this victory? *Why* was it necessary that He should die? To come closer to John's answer, it may be noted that already more than once the concepts of suffering and victory have occurred together. As we have seen, these two concepts are the ruling ideas of the last of the Servant Songs, and other New Testament documents show that this passage greatly influenced early Christian thought about the Death of Christ. Does this influence appear in the Fourth Gospel? Since its writer quotes the Isaianic passage (John xii. 38), it is hardly likely that he was ignorant of its Christian use. Did he here, too, repeat and develop, under other stories, the ideas that begin to appear in the Synoptists, and that recur in the Book of the Acts, the First Epistle of Peter, and the Apocalypse?

First, there are two passages where it seems to be clear that he did. One of these has already been mentioned. It is the Baptist's word: 'Behold the lamb of God that taketh away the sins of the world' (John i. 29, 36). The remarkable thing here is that the phrase should be ascribed to the Baptist. This falls in with the Synoptic account, though characteristically under a new incident, for we have already seen how many references there are to Deutero-Isaiah in the Synoptic stories of the Baptism of Jesus and the events that immediately followed. Here the added idea falls under the words, 'of the world', yet, on one exegesis, the last Servant Song tells of the salvation of the Gentiles.

The other passage is the one in which Jesus says, 'I am the good shepherd' (John x. 1–18). For the present purpose the chief sentence is, 'The good shepherd layeth down his life for the sheep'. There is no such idea in any of the many Old Testament passages that use the word 'shepherd' symbolically, and the reason is plain. If a shepherd on the Judean hills 'laid down his life for the sheep', he died a heroic death, but he did not save the sheep. When the wolves had dragged him down, they would go on to tear the sheep. To save his sheep, a shepherd must risk his life, but not lose it. Yet, as has already appeared, especially under First Peter, it was easy to call the Suffering Servant the 'Shepherd', for in the great Song the Servant saves the 'sheep' by dying for them. Also, we have seen that, if the Song is interpreted of an individual, it teaches that he is to die and to rise again. The Fourth Gospel has in this passage the words, 'I lay down my life of myself; I have the right to lay it down, and I have the right to take it again. This commandment received I from my Father' (John x. 18). *In this way* this Shepherd, unlike other shepherds, is to succeed: 'There shall be one flock, one shepherd.' Yet John adds something that is not in the Song—there the sufferer is indeed submissive, but he does not choose his fate; our Lord, as the Synoptists put it, 'set his face to go to Jerusalem', deliberately to die. Here again John draws out the teaching of which they were perhaps not fully aware: 'I lay down my life of myself' (cf. John xv. 13; 1 John iii. 16.)

Turning now to two of John's favourite terms, 'glorify' and 'lifted up', we may note first his use of each. When *he himself*, as distinct from Jesus, uses the word 'glorify', he uses it twice of the Resurrection and Ascension (John vii. 39, xii. 16) and once of the martyrdom of Peter (John xxi. 19). There is nothing singular here. When *Jesus* uses the word, He does so most commonly to describe what we may perhaps call 'the interior life of the Trinity'; the Father is said to glorify the Son, the Son to glorify the Father, the Father to glorify His 'name' in the Son, and the Spirit to glorify the Son (John viii. 54, xii. 28, xiii. 31 *f*., xiv. 13, xvi. 14, xvii. 1, 4*f*.); once, however, the disciples are said to glorify God and once to glorify the Son (John xv. 8, xvii. 10) ; again, the Raising of Lazarus is both for 'the glory of God' and that 'the Son of God may be glorified' (John xi. 4). Three passages remain that bear more closely on the present subject. In two of them the word 'glorify' occurs with the word 'hour' : 'The hour is come that the Son of Man should be glorified' (John xii. 23) ; 'Father, the hour is come; glorify thy Son, that the Son may glorify thee' (John xvii. 1). In the first of these and in the third passage, 'Now is the Son of Man glorified, and God is glorified in him; and God shall glorify in himself, and straightway shall he glorify him' (John xiii. 31 *f*.)—the word 'glorify' occurs with the phrase, 'the Son of Man'. It has been suggested above that under the term 'hour' the two ideas of suffering and triumph occur together; in these three passages the term 'glorify' unites the same two ideas, the emphasis being on triumph. The concepts expressed by 'Son of Man', 'hour', and 'glorify' (in three passages) go closely together.

There are three passages where the phrase 'lifted up' occurs (John iii. 14, viii. 28, xii. 32, 34). The nearest New Testament parallel is in the Acts of the Apostles, where the word is used, under the rendering 'exalt', of the Ascension (Acts ii. 33, v. 31). The three Johannine passages, however, require the union of the two ideas of suffering and triumph—here, in contrast to 'glorify', the emphasis being placed on suffering. Again, while God is said to 'glorify' the Son in the Crucifixion and Resurrection, God's part in the Atonement being thereby affirmed, the Father is not said to 'lift up' the Son. He 'must' be 'lifted up' because He is the Son of Man. This point will recur later. Here it is enough

to note that in two of the three passages the name 'Son of Man'
appears with the term 'lifted up' (John iii. 14, viii. 28), and that
in the third the writer thinks that he has written, 'If the Son of
Man be lifted up from the earth', when he has not done so
(John xii. 32, 34). This surely shows how closely the two ideas
went together in his mind. One passage suggests that the 'lifting
up' of the Son of Man is the act of men (John viii. 28). God
'glorifies' His Son—this is God's part in the Death of Christ; men
'lift up' the Son of Man—this is man's part. It follows that, as
under the term 'hour', so under the terms 'glorify' (in the three
passages named) and 'lifted up', the same two ideas combine as
in the last Servant Song. There the Servant suffers and so
triumphs. There His triumph issues in the kind of joy that
follows a woman's 'hour' of 'travail'. There His triumph is to
'justify many'—to save others. It can hardly be an accident,
therefore, that the Septuagint translation of the Song begins with
the words, 'Behold, my servant shall understand; he shall be
lifted up and *glorified* exceedingly' (Isaiah lii. 13). It seems plain
that John had long pondered the Song, and it may confidently
be deduced that he identified the Son of Man with the Servant.
In another of the Servant Songs, we read: 'Thou art my servant;
Israel, in whom I will be glorified' (Isaiah xlix. 3; cf. xliv. 23).
For John, as for the other New Testament writers, Jesus is the
Head of the new Israel (John i. 49–51). Very significantly,
however, he calls the Head of the new Israel, not the 'Son of
Jacob', as the passage just named seems to require, but the
'Son of Man'.

With these passages in mind, it is perhaps not too hazardous to
find a reference to the 'righteous Servant' in the phrase, 'Jesus
Christ the righteous' (1 John ii. 1). Here the word 'at-one-ment'
also occurs, and, if this passage alone were in question, it might
be said that John owes as much to the Temple ritual as to
the Prophet. The most striking thing here, however, is the use of
the term 'Paraclete' for the Ascended Christ. Undoubtedly the
nearest English translation for this Greek term is 'advocate', yet
this is inadequate. In the city life of 'Graeco-Roman times' the
paracletos was the active representative of a resident community
whose members were not citizens and had no right to speak for
themselves. He was 'no mere professional pleader engaged for
the occasion and linked to his client, like a modern barrister, by
his brief and his fee; he was the standing counsel of those he

represented, the established patron and champion of his humble dependants. Originally this relationship was hereditary, and the Advocate was the head of the clan, bound by sacred family ties to those whom he served, who might expect his aid whenever public speech and influence were necessary to them or advice in difficult affairs. He was . . . the man whose word weighed in the state . . . who was sure to stand by his clients and to see them through in their wrongs and quarrels with the world'.[1] In other words, the idea underlying the word was societary. It might be said to be the nearest Graeco-Roman equivalent for the Hebrew *Goel*. As it occurs without interpretation in the Talmud and Targums, in Philo, in two Greek translations of the Old Testament (Aquila and Theodotion), and in John,[2] it is plain that it was commonly used by Jews in the first century, and it is quite possible that the Jewish community in a Gentile city had a 'Paraclete' to represent it in the city's affairs. So, where the writer to the Hebrews says 'High Priest' John says 'Paraclete'. In Philo the High Priest himself needs a 'paraclete', that author using the term of the breast-plate, which he compares to the *Logus* under the term 'son', but in John's Epistle the true High Priest is Himself the Paraclete. Himself 'righteous', He stands for and atones for the sinful men who have believed in Him. The text approximates to the Pauline saying, 'Him who knew no sin, he made to be sin on our behalf'. There is another approximation in a text that seems to recall the Servant Song: 'He was manifested to take away [or bear] sins; and in him is no sin' (1 John iii. 5). We are again on the edge of the same antinomy.[3]

This leads to the consideration of the passages where John uses the phrase 'Son of Man'. It occurs twelve times (always on Jesus' own lips, as in the Synoptists, except in xii. 34, an exception that proves the rule) and it is always the key to the passage. It has been seen that in the Synoptists, after Caesarea Philippi, Jesus uses the phrase 'Son of Man' when *others* have used the phrase 'Son of God'. On the other hand, John makes Jesus frequently call

---

[1] G. G. Findlay, *The Expository Times*, vol. xx., p. 448.

[2] Hastings' *Bible Dictionary, sub voce.*

[3] It is possible that John used the word 'paraclete' because of his pondering of Deutero-Isaiah, for there the corresponding verb is used frequently in the Septuagint of God (Isaiah xl. 1, 2, 11, xli. 27, xlix. 10, 13, li. 3, 12, 18 *f.*, liv. 11, lvii. 5, 18, lxvi. 12 *f.*), and once of a prophet (Isaiah lxi. 2). It is true, however, that the term here expresses the idea, 'to call another to one's side to *give* him help', whereas the term 'paraclete' goes back to another meaning of the verb, 'to call another to one's side to *ask* his help'. The New Testament uses the verb with both meanings.

Himself 'the Son' or the 'Son of God', a use that is rare in the Synoptists. The difference, however, must not be misunderstood. In the first place, it may be maintained that, here as elsewhere, John only makes explicit what was implicit before, for the Synoptic stories require that Jesus thought of Himself as the Son of God. In the second place—and this lies more closely to the present subject—in John, as in the Synoptists, the name 'Son of Man' occurs where the name 'Son of God' is either used or implied. In other words, in John, as in the other Gospels, in Paul, and in Hebrews, the two ideas go together. In three passages, all in the earlier part of the book, where 'Son of Man' occurs, 'Son of God' occurs too (John i. 49–51, iii. 13–18, v. 25–7). In four other passages the concept 'Son of God' is implied by the use of 'the Father' in the context (John vi. 27, 53–7, viii. 28, xii. 23–8). There remain four passages: one that implies the idea of 'Son of God' under the phrase 'ascending where He was before'(vi. 62); a passage where the reading is uncertain (ix. 35) ; a passage where 'the multitude' use the term in a way that suggests either that they were not used to the term or that Jesus' use of it puzzled them (xii. 34); and the passage, 'Now is the Son of Man glorified and God is glorified in him' (xiii. 31). It seems to follow that for the thought of John the truths that underlie the names 'Son of God' and 'Son of Man' are complementary. For John's creed the two truths were not only both essential, but were organically connected in his doctrine of salvation.

There is no need to show that for John the name 'Son of God' denotes that Jesus was 'one with' God. The doctrine of the Trinity includes, while it transcends, the societary idea. But the name 'Son of Man' requires, as in the Synoptists, that Jesus was 'one with' man. It is for this reason that 'the Son of Man' is the proper judge of men (John v. 27). But in most of the passages where the name 'Son of Man' occurs, the context requires that it is because Jesus was 'Son of Man' that He is able to *save* men. The passages are quoted elsewhere in this chapter and there is no need to quote them again here. But John makes an addition to the content of the concept: he teaches that our Lord was in some sense 'Son of Man' *before* the Incarnation. 'What then if ye should behold the Son of Man ascending *where he was before?*' 'No man hath ascended into heaven, but he that *descended out of heaven, the Son of Man*' (John vi. 62, iii. 13). To find John's own exposition here, we must turn to a passage in the Prologue, where the phrase 'Son of

Man' is not used, since this is kept for Jesus' own lips, but where the idea that underlies it is clear. If a Scotticism may be used, the best translation here (John i. 11 *f.*) would perhaps be: 'He came home, but His ain folk received Him not, but as many as received Him, to them He gave the right to become children of God'.[1] In the Incarnation He who was by His eternal nature Son of Man was coming home. The societary concept is unmistakable. Some committed the sin of sins: they refused to 'receive' Him. Yet there were those who 'received him', 'believed on his name', took Him home to their hearts. In other words, they were willing to be 'one with' the Lord who was already 'one with' them, and in consequence He gave them the 'right' to share His other home—to 'become children of God'. The concept of the Kinsman, whether the writer was thinking of the Hebrew *Goel* or not, is here dominant (cf. the word 'orphans' in John xiv. 18).

But, if our Lord was in some sense eternally 'Son of Man', why must He become incarnate in order to save men from sin? To use the language of the first chapter of this book, He could only save sinful men by, at one and the same time, becoming one with them and remaining different from them. In John's phrases, He must 'become flesh' to save those who are 'in the flesh'—come 'into the world' to save those who are 'in the world'—yet remain 'Son of God' and so sinless all the while (cf. 1 John iii. 5). He must live the life that sinners live, yet without sinning. Must he also die the death that sinners die (in the New Testament sense of 'death'), yet without sinning? John says this in the text, 'As Moses lifted up the serpent in the wilderness, even so *must* the Son of Man be lifted up, that whosoever believeth may in him have eternal life' (John iii. 14). To show this, both the passage in Numbers (Numbers xxi. 8 *f.*) and the whole passage in John need to be carefully considered.

Under the term 'serpent', the minds of Christians turn naturally to the story of the Fall, for there the serpent has long been identified with the Devil. This identification goes back at least as far as the days of Jesus (Wisdom ii. 24), and it is found in the New Testament (2 Corinthians xi. 3; Revelation x. 9, xx. 2) and probably in the Fourth Gospel itself (John viii. 44). Under the symbolic interpretation here implied, the 'serpent' of the Garden of Eden stands *both* for *sin* and *death*. In the story in

---

[1] The references to 'the world' in verse 10 and the phrase 'them that *believe*' in verse 12 seem to show that in verse 11 the writer is not speaking only of the Jews.

Numbers, however, the serpents do not stand for *sin*, for they do not fall upon the Israelites until *after* they have sinned. The serpents stand for *death*, considered as the result and punishment of sin.[1] They stand for the 'wrath' of God. There is a passage in the Book of Wisdom (xvi. 5–14), however, which speaks of the Brazen Serpent as 'the symbol of *salvation*'! It is likely that John was thinking of this passage, for presently the one text occurs where he speaks of 'the wrath of God' and his phrase there, 'The wrath of God abideth upon him', is practically a quotation from the passage in Wisdom. He had to hand, therefore, an account of the story in Numbers that combined under the serpent symbol the ideas of 'wrath' or 'death' and 'salvation'. It may be added that the passage in the Book of Wisdom refers to 'the word' of God, and expressly includes Hades with death (Wisdom xvi. 12–14).

In the story of Nicodemus (John iii) John sets Jesus over against Judaism at its best. Our Lord begins by an uncompromising claim that all men are so bad that they 'must be born again'. Nicodemus does not deny this. How could he with the current doctrine of racial sin in mind? In other words, he admits the impotence of Judaism, described in an earlier chapter, to 'save' men in the sense of turning bad men into good men. What he asks is: '*How* can these things be?' Jesus says that to be saved in this way a man must 'be born of water and the Spirit'. Here, as already suggested, John is just repeating, under his own terminology, what the Synoptists had said. Jesus next goes on to say, in effect that 'no man knoweth the Father save the Son', but John expounds this under the phrase, 'No man hath ascended into heaven, but he that descendeth out of heaven, the Son of Man'. The Son of Man, therefore, has news of 'heavenly things'. Then there comes the phrase that declares that the Son of Man must be 'lifted up' like the brazen serpent. Here John says that what was symbolic in Wisdom is actual in Jesus. In Him 'death' *is* 'salvation'. The serpent was symbol of both, and therefore of Him. So John transfigures Judaism into Christianity. The Son of Man saves the mankind with which He is one, by enduring the 'death' that comes to sinners. His death is the key to the 'eternal life' that 'whosoever believeth in him' receives. In other words, the phrase that compares Christ with the serpent in Numbers says

---

[1] It is in such passages that the doctrine of vicarious punishment found foothold. As argued in the first chapter above, however, the true punishment of the sinners is to remain sinful, and this idea cannot be applied to Christ.

just what Paul says in the phrase, 'Being made a curse for us'. It would be quite possible to paraphrase the thought of the Johannine sentence in words that follow the form of Paul's phrases in the fifth chapter of Second Corinthians: 'Him who was life God made to be death on our behalf that we might have eternal life in him'. It is plain, too, that John's phrases are parallel to those in the second chapter of Hebrews. Where Hebrews has, 'Since then the children are sharers in flesh and blood, he also himself in like manner partook of the same', John writes 'Son of Man' ; where Hebrews has, 'that through death he might bring to nought him that had the power of death, that is, the devil', John writes 'must be lifted up' ; where Hebrews has, 'and might deliver all them who through fear of death were all their lifetime subject to bondage', John writes 'that whosoever believeth may in Him have eternal life'. The three New Testament thinkers all have the same societary teaching and all end with the same antinomy. Through the Christian centuries, the 'babes' in Christ have known the truth by experience without arguing about it:

> There is life for a look at the Crucified One,
> There is life at this moment for thee;
> Then look, sinner, look unto Him and be saved,
> Unto Him who was nailed to the Tree.
> Look, look, look, and live!

The best summary of the teaching of the Fourth Gospel about salvation is John's own. As is his custom, he gives it at an unexpected place—in the first part of the third chapter in his Gospel (John iii. 1–21). His greatest text occurs in the midst of it: 'God so loved the world that he gave his only begotten Son, that whosoever believeth on him should not perish, but have eternal life'. This text, however, should not be isolated. It immediately follows the text about the brazen serpent, which goes organically with it, as, for instance, the occurrence of the phrase 'should not perish' shows. Again, the great text is followed by an account of salvation that emphasizes man's duty of 'believing'. The chief points in John's third chapter are: that men can only be saved if they are made over again; that this could only be if the Son of God were also Son of Man and died the death that sinful men die; that God in His love sent His Son to save men in this way; and that every man decides for himself whether he will be 'one with' the Son of God, and share 'eternal life' with Him. This account of salvation is both societary and individual throughout.

CONCLUSION

It has often been said that there is no one doctrine of the Atonement in the Bible. In this book some attempt is made to show that this is a mistake, especially when the Atonement is taken as part of the larger doctrine of Salvation. The beginnings and growth of this larger doctrine may be traced, 'in divers manners', in the Old Testament, the climax being found in the last of the Servant Songs. Next, the New Testament doctrine has its chief source in the Life, Death and Resurrection of our Lord Jesus Christ, and in the distinctive Christian experience that ensued. So far, however, as Jesus Himself, and the New Testament writers after Him, give any explanation other than these facts themselves, its roots are to be found in the Old Testament, and, broadly speaking, the New Testament explanations begin where the Old Testament left off—with the great Servant Song. It is further maintained that, while Christian doctrine has one of its sources in the sacrificial system, this is quite secondary, the main source, apart from the Christian facts, being the teaching of the Prophets and of the Psalmists of prophetic spirit.

Some of the chief concepts in the Bible doctrine of Salvation may be recalled. The root idea throughout is that God has made man to live in fellowship with Himself. In other words, the societary idea is fundamental. At first this fellowship is conceived as outward, God promising to give prosperity to Israel if Israel will obey Him. Yet, from the story of Abraham onwards, an inward fellowship is implied, even where it is not yet described or even conceived. Ultimately, it can only be expressed as 'eternal life', and 'eternal life' is to 'know'—to be intimate with—God. All other boons wait upon this one and will at last inevitably accompany it. There is only one thing that can mar this fellowship. This one thing is sin. This too is at first defined in outward terms, but, at least by finer minds, it is conceived in spiritual terms in the later part of the Old Testament. The teaching of Jesus, for instance in the Sermon on the Mount, brings this development to its climax. Just as all benefits accompany fellowship with God, so all evils accompany sin. At first these evils, too, are thought of in outward terms, such as defeat in war or the failure of harvest, but ultimately they, too, centre in an inward state—a state that is called 'death'. The ultimate concept is that God is holy, and so the unholy cannot hold fellowship with Him.

Yet the truth that God is love, always implicit, also becomes at last explicit. This means that He cannot leave a sinner to his sin. The Father still craves fellowship with His children. He therefore, if the phrase may be allowed, sets Himself to save them. Here, as everywhere else, it is God who 'takes the initiative', for a sinner can do nothing whatever to save himself from sin. A man might more easily reach the sun!

Af first this truth does not clearly appear, for, through the long centuries of Israel's earlier history, it is assumed that man can repent of himself, and of himself begin to do all that is right, but, just in proportion as the concept of the dire results of sin for character developed, the hopelessness of human effort grew evident. The Fifty-first Psalm is here the Old Testament climax, and, here as elsewhere, the climax of Old Testament thought is the postulate of the New. It has sometimes been said that 'man's part' in salvation is to 'repent and believe', but an exact theology teaches that the power to do even this comes from God. In the deeper parts of the Old Testament and throughout the New salvation is wholly 'of God'. This truth, of course, leads to the amazing Christian conviction that God sent His Son into the world to save men. Man had nothing to do with the Incarnation!

Yet the Incarnation, by itself, is not enough. To save man from sin, the Saviour must, at one and the same time, be sinless and experience what is meant by sin. This is what fellowship demands of a Saviour. Here is the core of the truth. It has so often been stated above that it need not again be described at length here. One or two objections, however, may be anticipated.

It is true that this doctrine is nowhere fully expounded in the New Testament. All that can be said is that in the New Testament there are the 'materials' or 'data' for it. This is so, however, with other doctrines, notably the doctrines of the Person of Christ and the Trinity, for the New Testament is not a system of theology.

Again, it is true that the doctrine involves an antinomy—that is to say, it requires that two statements are both true even though to the human mind they seem contradictory. It will, no doubt, be admitted that human knowledge, on every subject, ends in mystery, that there comes a point where man has to say, 'I cannot explain'. The theist will admit, further, that this is peculiarly evident when we speak of any truth that involves *God*. Indeed, it may be said that any doctrine of God that explains everything is *thereby* proved untrue. Yet there is special difficulty with the kind of mystery called 'antinomy', for here we not only say that we cannot understand, but assert a seeming contradiction in terms. But how frequently Christian thinkers are thrust upon antinomy! After centuries of controversy, Christendom came to say about God: 'He is both One and Three.' Similarly, the doctrine of the Person of Christ is found to involve a fundamental antinomy that carries with it a number of derivative ones: If Christ is both 'God and Man' or 'God-Man', is He not both finite and infinite in knowledge, in power, and in yet other ways? Again, the controversy about the relation between the Sovereignty of God and the Freedom of Man seems to-day to have ended with an antinomy. Like Paul in his letters, we say silently, if not in so many words: 'We believe in both, though we cannot harmonize them.' It is quite likely that the controversy about the Future of the Wicked will end in a similar way, for there is clear New Testament evidence for Eternal Punishment, yet will not God at last be 'all in all'? A doctrine cannot be rejected merely because it is an antinomy. It is enough if the materials for this one, as for others, are found in the New Testament, and if it verifies itself in the experience of Christians.

It has long been common to divide doctrines of the Atonement into two classes. These used to be called 'objective' and 'subjective', but now many repudiate this terminology, partly, as already stated, because the psychologist teaches that there is nothing in experience that is wholly 'objective' and nothing that is wholly 'subjective', and partly because the theological use of the two terms is not without ambiguity. Sometimes, again, the distinction has been put under the phrases, 'What Christ does for us' and 'What Christ does in us'. The 'societary theory' here advocated, if that name may be used, clearly claims that Christ, by His Incarnation, Death, and Resurrection, does everything for us in the realm of Salvation, and, through His indwelling Spirit, does everything good in us. Finally, the difference is sometimes put under a question: 'Does this theory of the Atonement require that the Death of Christ makes any difference to *God*, or does it merely mean that *man* is changed?' Here the phrase 'the wrath of God' used to be introduced. It has been seen that the separation between man and God that sin brings may be called either 'death' or the 'wrath of God', the fundamental truth being that there cannot be fellowship between the holy God and sinful man. Through Christ, this fellowship becomes both possible and actual for the believer. Surely, to speak after the manner of men, it does 'make a difference' to God that He is now in fellowship with His child. The fact that there *is* fellowship is itself a difference on *both* sides. May we not go on reverently to say, further, that the renewal of fellowship gives God joy, as the Prodigal's return gave joy to his father? Is there not 'joy in the presence of the angels of God over one sinner that repenteth'? Further, there is this difference to God that He can now do for His child—with whom, since he is now 'child', there is fellowship—what He could not do when there was no fellowship. In other words, there is a difference, if we are to use human words, not only in the feelings of the Father, but in His actions. The societary doctrine, being in terms of fellowship, knows nothing of a God who waits in anger, or even waits aloof, for some one else to do something. He 'sends' the Son, and He welcomes the sinner. This, of course, involves another antinomy: it means that we ascribe to God both what is of value in changelessness and what is of value in change. For this antinomy there is, however, an obvious analogy, for the nature of every *living* thing is just that it changes while it remains the same—a phenomenon of which science has at present no logically harmonious explanation. To return to the two kinds of doctrine, it may be claimed that they are not contradictory, but complementary.

It is no part of the purpose of this book to give an account of the historic theories of the Atonement. It may again be recalled, however, that, while their advocates tried to frame a theory that did justice to the New Testament evidence, each used the 'thought forms' of his own day. It is agreed that Anselm, for instance, used, at least to some degree, the thought forms of the feudal system, and Duns Scotus the thought forms of absolute monarchy. Yet, inasmuch as the subject of all theories involves the question of the relationship between two *persons*, God and man, no theory has been able to exclude altogether the phenomena that we now call 'psychological'. Since the thought forms of to-day are dominantly psychological, modern theories seek to express themselves in psychological terms. Schleiermacher led the way here, and the theory independently developed in this volume from the study of the Bible is much like the doctrine that he reached through psychological and philosophical study. Perhaps, since human psychology is fundamentally the same in all periods, it might be claimed that the final doctrine will be psychological, and that it will emerge more clearly as the psychologist attains more assured results, particularly in the realm of the corporate or societary. While, therefore, it may be freely admitted that modern theories —and not least the societary theory advocated in this book—are inadequate, as earlier theories have been, yet they do look in the right direction. To the present writer they seem also to return to the New Testament way of approach to the doctrine of salvation.

INDEX

INDEX OF SCRIPTURE REFERENCES

1 When a passage occurs in more than one of the Synoptic Gospels, it is usually quoted under Mark if it occurs in the Second Gospel; in other cases, usually under Luke.

1 When a passage occurs in more than one of the Synoptic Gospels, it is usually quoted under Mark if it occurs in the Second Gospel; in other cases, usually under Luke.